Web Server Constuction Kit for the Macintosh

Stewart Buskirk

Hayden Books

Publisher
Lyn Blake

Publishing Manager
Laurie Petrycki

Acquisitions Editor
Stacy Kaplan

Development Editor
Kezia Endsley

Technical Editors
Tim Webster
Bill Doerrfeld

Copy Editor
Bront Davis

Cover Designer
Karen Ruggles

Book Designer
Sandra Schroeder

Production Team Supervisor
Laurie Casey

Production Team
Steve Adams
Heather Butler
Angela Calvert
Dan Caparo
Kim Cofer
George Hanlin
Glenn Larsen
Joe Millay
Erika Millen
Erich J. Richter
Karen Walsh
Suzanne Whitmer

Indexers
Tim Griffin
Bront Davis

Web Server Construction Kit for the Macintosh

Library of Congress Catalog Number: 96-75193

ISBN: 1-56830-271-1

Printed in the United States of America

1 2 3 4 5 6 7 8 9 0

Warning and Disclaimer

This book is sold as is, without warranty of any kind, either express or implied. While every precaution has been taken in the preparation of this book, the authors and Hayden Books assume no responsibility for errors or omissions. Neither is any liability assumed for damages resulting from the use of the information or instructions contained herein. It is further stated that the publisher and authors are not responsible for any damage or loss to your data or your equipment that results directly or indirectly from your use of this book.

Dedication

To my wife, Kathy Ann Baker, whose amazing skills at life and love created this writer and enabled this book.

Acknowledgments

Very special thanks are due to Uwe Willenbacher and Rad Proctor, who gave so freely of their encouragement, time, and resources that I could not help but finish this book, if only to please them.

Michael Martin provided both the Mac on which this book was written and an insight into technology and life that influenced each and every page.

Bill Doerrfeld and Tim Webster, both accomplished Mac developers in their own rights, are due kudos for managing to correct my mistakes and omissions with such good grace, humor, and expertise. Much of this book grew directly out of their suggestions.

Stacey Kaplan took a gamble on an untested writer, while Kezia Endsley had the courage and skill to guide a new author through the book writing process and offer the discipline, encouragement, and patience he needed in exactly the correct amounts.

And a lifetime of belly rubs are due to Moon Goddess, Boy, and Cissy for knowing how to purr just when I needed to hear it.

About the Author

Stewart Buskirk lives in Pittsburgh, Pennsylvania, about two miles from the birthplace of the Lycos Web catalog, with his wife, three cats, two Macs, and a terribly abused coffee machine. Stewart has been developing database applications on the Mac for both the commercial and academic communities since 1987, picking up a B.S. in Molecular Biology along the way, and managing Macintosh-based Web servers for a variety of clients across North America since 1994.

Today, Stewart develops Web projects for Proctor-Willenbacher, a San Francisco Internet services consulting firm, while assisting with ongoing research at Carnegie Mellon University into the effects of Internet usage on social behavior.

Trademark Acknowledgments

The staff of Hayden Books is committed to bringing you the best computer books. What our readers think of Hayden is important to our ability to serve our customers. If you have any comments, no matter how great or how small, we'd appreciate your taking the time to send us a note.

You can reach Hayden Books at the following:

Hayden Books
201 West 103rd Street
Indianapolis, IN 46290
(800) 428-5331 voice
(800) 448-3804 fax

Email addresses:
America Online: Hayden Bks
Internet: hayden@hayden.com

Visit the Hayden Books Web site at http://www.hayden.com

Contents at a Glance

Table of Contents

Part III: Site Administration

Part IV: Appendixes

INTRODUCTION

This book is written for anyone with an interest in creating a professional World Wide Web server on a Macintosh. It provides the tools, information, and background necessary to establish a Web site and master its administration and development. Inside, you'll find:

- Descriptions and demonstration versions of all the major Web server applications available for the Mac, allowing you to choose the software that best fits your needs.
- The answers to the most commonly asked questions about Mac-based Web serving from both new and experienced developers.
- Hundreds of invaluable URLs (on the accompanying CD and in the text) that will put the resources of the entire Internet immediately at your fingertips.
- Dozens of demos, shareware, and freeware applications that you can try out immediately without searching across the Internet and downloading files for hours.

With this book and a Macintosh, you can start testing Web servers within minutes and continue developing Web sites indefinitely!

NOTE

Unlike similar books, the *Web Server Construction Kit for the Macintosh* is designed for use with any Web server software, even new applications released in the future. After you decide on the software that will form the basis of your site, an application-specific book can be a valuable investment to help you use your software effectively. This book, however, is intended to be your overall reference to Web serving and provide a comprehensive guide to the issues and concerns you face as your site evolves.

Most importantly, I am committed to keeping this book and you up to date on the very latest information, software, and resources. I accomplish this by providing a Web site for keeping you informed of the current state of the art in applications and solutions, and by including many links to recommended online resources within the HTML pages on the accompanying CD-ROM.

As part of this effort to provide a dynamic resource in addition to the static materials you are holding in your hand, I strongly encourage you to send your criticisms, comments, and insights about this book to Hayden Books or me so that we can make corrections, additions, and other information available to everyone in a timely manner. Please see the front matter of this book for information on contacting Hayden Books—you can reach me directly via email at stewart@prowillen.com.

Assumptions about the Readers

Every writer needs to make a few assumptions about the readers and their backgrounds. Fortunately, the prerequisites for this book are fairly minimal, as I've tried to explain Web-related terminology and concepts as they appear, with additional definitions in the glossary (Appendix B). However, you will find this book most valuable if you have the following background:

- ☐ You are comfortable with standard Macintosh terminology and procedures.

  This book is intended for intermediate and advanced MacOS users who are familiar with installing new software and understand the basic organization and usage of the MacOS. You should reach this level of expertise after just a few weeks of regular Mac usage.

- ☐ You have already spent some time exploring the Internet.

  In particular, you should already feel comfortable using a Web browser application such as Netscape Navigator or NCSA Mosaic and be able to send and receive email across the Internet.

- ☐ You have a connection to the Internet.

  You don't need Internet access to try out the Web servers included on your CD (see Chapter 5 for instructions on testing servers without an Internet connection), but you do need access to email and the Web to utilize Mac-related resources on the Internet, find current information on new versions of the software mentioned in this book, and generally make best use of the information presented here.

- ☐ You have access to a CD-ROM drive.

  The CD that accompanies this book is an integral part of the entire "publication," and you will need at least periodic access to a CD-ROM to take advantage of the resources, links, and software on the CD. Please see the section titled "About the CD" later in this Introduction for more information about using your CD effectively.

And, of course, you should have an interest in creating or managing a Web site, either for yourself or an employer.

Accuracy

Some portion of this book will be out of date by the time you read this—that's an inevitable consequence of the speed at which the Web is evolving and the time required to publish a book after the writing is done. Web sites used as illustrations will change or even disappear, new applications and new versions of old applications will appear, and information about methods and recommendations will become outdated.

Nevertheless, this book is as much about learning the basic concepts and issues faced by all Web site managers, today and in the future, as it is about specific software recommendations and site management methods. The illustrations of sites highlighted within this book may be out of date by the time you visit them yourself, but the concepts those illustrations were meant to illuminate will long outlive the sites themselves.

You have two resources to turn to for updates on the printed information in this book:

- **On the CD**—The HTML pages for each chapter (see the section entitled "About the CD") contain links to Internet resources relevant to that chapter's contents, including sites for locating current versions of software on the CD and announcements of new applications. I included as many links to other compilations of resources as possible, so that you have a variety of sites to choose from when searching for current information.

- **On the Internet**—The Web site for this book (`http://www.mcp.com/hayden/webserver`) provides updates and corrections specific to this book and the CD, as well as new information that I would like to bring to your attention. Please add that site to your bookmarks or hotlist of important Web sites and stop by regularly—the resources there will add immeasurably to the value of this publication.

Conventions

The following typographic and graphical conventions help to clearly identify various elements in the text so you can more easily follow the text and differentiate between elements:

- URLs addresses within the text appear in `monospace` typeface.

- HTML tags within the text appear in all caps and with brackets, such as the <ISINDEX> tag.

- Code that shows scripting commands or other programming languages appears in `monospace typeface` as well:

```
(scnm)script_name
(refr)referer
Server: <server name><CRLF>
(Agnt)user_agent
(Kcip)client_ip
```

```
Server: <server name><CRLF>
(Kact)action
```

- **Bold text** denotes folders on the CD.

The following graphical elements also denote special text.

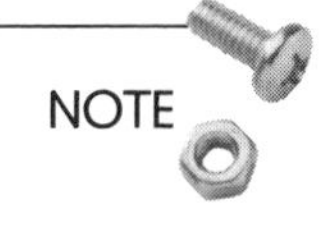

Notes provide you with extra information on the topic at hand or provide definitions and background information for new terms.

Warnings do just that; they warn you of pitfalls, potential disasters, or other blockades to getting your Web site up and running.

A pull quote is a fact or opinion that appears in the text that is important enough to set off in the margin.

You will notice that pull quote information also appears in the text. This is because we have deemed it important enough to place it off on its own as well as show it as a pullquote. Watch for these to learn valuable tidbits of information when you're in a hurry!

This WebSTAR icon appears when the discussion is specific to WebSTAR server software, by Chuck Shotton. As stated earlier, this book almost always covers Mac Web serving issues without being specific to a particular software package, but when you might need extra information about WebSTAR, you see this icon to inform you that this material is WebSTAR-specific.

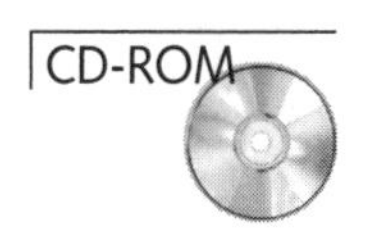

When software or information on the CD is mentioned in the text, you see this icon to inform you that you can find more information on the CD at this time. The appropriate folder or file on the CD is named when applicable.

About the CD

The HOME HTML document on the CD can point you to software demos and information by chapter, as well as provide URLs to more information on the Web. The full contents of the top level of the CD are summarized here:

- **Servers**—This folder contains copies of all the software and installers you need to try out the different Web server applications and demos mentioned in the book. If you want to start installing servers immediately, simply copy this folder to your hard drive and read through Chapter 5 for installation instructions.

- **Software**—This folder contains all the freeware, shareware, and demo applications, scripts, and examples provided on the CD. If you just want to browse through the software by category rather than going through each chapter, you can use this folder to do so.

- **HTML**—This folder contains copies of all the HTML pages on the CD gathered together in one place. This folder is provided so that you can copy all the individual chapters' HTML files to your hard disk at once for editing or updating without having to make room for all the software that appears in the individual chapter folders.

  To begin navigating the contents of the HTML folder, open the "home.html" file with your Web browser and simply follow the links from that page to the chapter-specific pages. All the HTML links work regardless of whether the HTML folder is located on the CD or on another disk.

  To use the chapter folders found in the **HTML** folder effectively, you should use your favorite Web browser application to open the chapter's HTML file located in the **HTML** folder (they are named Cyyhome. HTML, where *yy* is the chapter number). These files contain all sorts of links and goodies relevant to that chapter's topic, both on the CD and on the Internet.

When trying out the software provided on the CD, you should always copy an application's folder to your hard drive before testing it—many applications and scripts need to write information to disk when they first launch, and launching from the CD can cause unexpected problems or even crashes for some shareware applications.

Please also take the time to at least glance through any Read Me files or other documentation that accompany the software provided here—a single sentence can often save you hours of grief when attempting to use a new application.

Software (which includes applications, scripts, and source code for programmers) included with this book can be divided into three areas: demonstrations (demos), freeware, and shareware:

- Demos are normally limited in function or the amount of time you can use them, and are provided as a sample so that you can decide if purchasing the full versions is worthwhile.
- Freeware is software provided free of charge, although many have restrictions about commercial use and re-distribution that still apply.
- Shareware applications are fully functional demos that require the payment of a registration fee after a specified period of usage. The categories that the software on the CD fall into and the terms of any restrictions on their usage are detailed in the documentation accompanying each package.

The people and companies that have allowed their shareware and freeware applications to be included with this book have done so because they want to make trying their applications as convenient as possible for you. Macintosh Web servers have reaped great benefits from the willingness of software developers to make their products available as shareware so that you can try fully functional versions of their software before registering those applications you find useful.

Please help this system work by reading the license terms for shareware and freeware products carefully, abiding by any stated restrictions, and paying your shareware fees when appropriate. The cost is usually minimal compared to the benefits (manuals, support, updates) you receive and you'll be helping to ensure the vitality and productivity of the Mac developer community. It's the right thing to do! Please note that you must send a licensing fee to Peter Lewis in order to use the copy of NetPresenz on the CD.

About the Web Site

Yes, this book has its own Web site! One of your first steps after buying this book should be to stop by http://www.mcp.com/hayden/webserver to check for addenda, errata, and other updates to the printed version of this publication.

The Web site is also the place to leave comments, criticisms, and suggestions about the book (please do!), pick up updated versions of the HTML pages on the CD, find additional information and tips that didn't make it into print before publication, and generally keep this book current with the "state of the Web." I'll be updating the Web site regularly as long as this book is still in print, so be sure to stop by often for the latest information.

Part I

From Surfer to Server

CHAPTER 1

Making the Transition

Reality is more complex than it seems.

—John Gall

Congratulations! You are about to create a server, to become an "information provider" rather than an "information consumer." There is no more rewarding activity than creating a new presence on the World Wide Web, and the opportunities for you to make a personal impact on the Web and the Internet in general have never been greater than they are right now.

As you make the transition from client to server, you'll have to make an internal transition as well. The Web from the administrator's point of view can be a very different place than it was when you were merely browsing it.

The first part of this book is designed to help you make that transition, to give you the knowledge, methods, and tools you'll need to get from browsing the Web to the first live entry from a stranger in your own server log.

This chapter is about taking the first steps to turn your imagination into a Web presence. You'll find some advice about planning a Web site, develop some documentation to guide your later decisions, and hear a few thoughts about what it means to be a professional Web site administrator. It is not particularly technical, but it does require some work and thought on your part. Launching a new server is both a technical and creative activity—I'll supply the technology, but you'll need to supply the creativity!

Cowabunga, Web Serving!

You're not just surfing any more. I wanted to get this word of advice in at the start—the time that you spend on the Web experiencing other sites is one of the single most effective activities you can do to help improve your own site. Of course, you can't be a passive information consumer any longer—you need to be actively seeking out features and effects that influence your own site design and management.

Seek out sites with a purpose similar to your own. If a site or a feature strikes you as particularly effective, or even if you just have a strong reaction to a site (good or bad) without knowing precisely why, add that URL to your bookmarks and make a note of why you did so. Periodically revisit the sites in your bookmarks, review your notes, and try to distill your reactions into lists of dos and don'ts for your own site. When you're satisfied with what you have, use your lists as a basis for your own site and you'll be way ahead of the game.

Making judgments about what qualities of other sites are important to you will depend on your own priorities and predilections, but here are a few examples of the kinds of issues most people are concerned with:

- Aesthetics

  This is perhaps the most subjective part of evaluating sites, but try to record your reactions when a site seems particularly pleasing to your eye or if it seems harsh or otherwise displeasing to you. After you've gathered a few together, evaluate your own reactions: do you prefer simple pages or complex designs? Are some background colors or image types particularly appealing? Try to find patterns in your reactions that will help you guide your own site development.

- Ease of use

  Look at sites with an eye toward how effectively you are led to other links and pages. Are the other portions of the site obvious and easy to reach? Do you find yourself looking for a common link (like contact information) that is difficult to find? Are the important portions of the page highlighted and inviting? Is navigating through the site intuitive, or are you forced to poke around to find what you're looking for?

- Unusual functionality

  Perhaps a site has an animation or other capability that you find particularly appealing, such as a page counter that shows how many people have visited the page or a catalog searching mechanism. Mark these features down for your own site (and turn to Chapter 7, "CGI Applications and Usage," when you're ready to implement them).

To assist you in recording your Web expeditions, be sure to take advantage of the commenting features in most browsers' bookmark listings. You can then export your bookmarks or hotlists to an HTML file that will summarize all your sites and comments on one page for easy reference.

For example, if you open the bookmarks window in Netscape and select a bookmark for editing (the exact method to do this seems to change from version to version, so you'll have to check the current documentation of your browser for details), you can enter about a paragraph of comments like those shown in Figure 1.1.

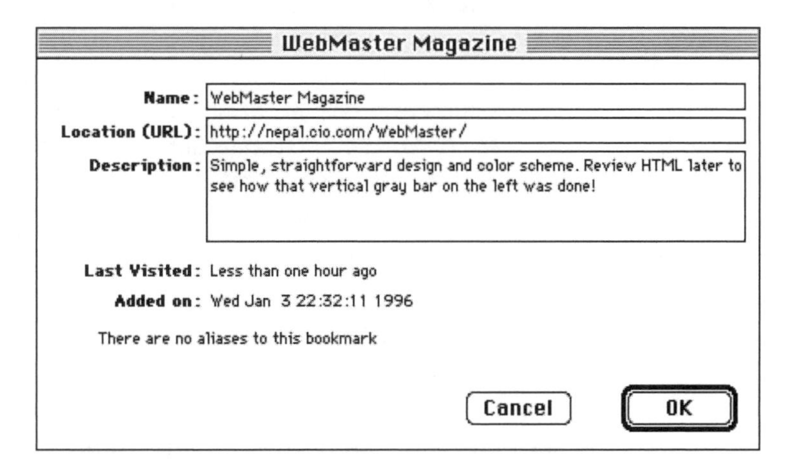

Figure 1.1 *Netscape bookmark editing window.*

Then when you save the bookmark file as HTML, you'll have a page you can load from your disk that looks something like the one shown in Figure 1.2. And bingo, instant reference sheet!

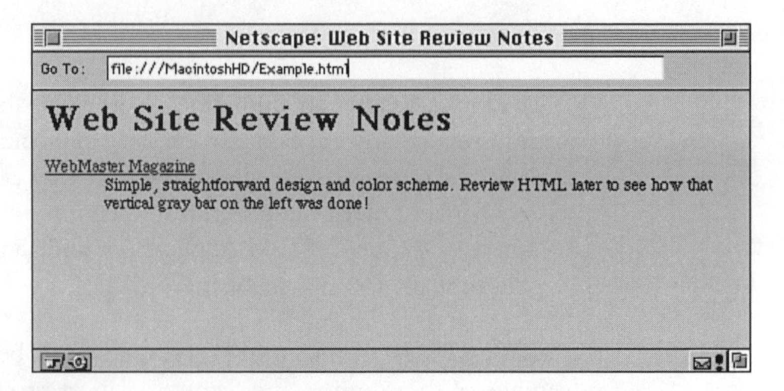

Figure 1.2 *Netscape bookmark file after saving as HTML.*

WARNING

While you are evaluating sites, keep in mind that the vast majority of the people viewing your site will do so using dialup connections, and it is vital to understand what the Web feels like to such a user. A graphic that is a joy to behold over a high-speed connection can drive away clients in droves when they realize it will take five minutes to download over their modems. If you expect to serve information to the general Internet population, and you don't already use a dialup connection to the Internet, the first item on your agenda should be to find one. Most urban areas now have literally dozens of new companies trying to sign up new users. The cost of a dialup connection ranges between 15 and 30 dollars a month, less than most cable TV bills, and a decent 28.8Kbps modem can be had for $100 or less.

If your Web site is a private one where you know that all your potential visitors will have high-speed connections to your server, such as a corporate internal server, you won't need to test your site with a dialup connection, but researching other sites on the Web will still be one of the more productive activities (other than reading this book, of course!) you can undertake to prepare for your own site.

Making a List, Clicking It Twice

Creating and managing a new Web site is not like taking out an ad in a magazine or newspaper—it is more analogous to starting a small company, with its own identity and purpose. It is an enterprise in its own right, with its own unique marketing methods, measures of success, and resource consumption. Seen from that perspective, it is vital that you do some advance planning for your site by outlining your requirements and priorities. In other words, document everything you intend to provide before you commit to your site's design and infrastructure. It will be time well spent.

In this section, you are asked to write down the purpose and goals of your site, make a list of the features you want to see implemented, and review the activities required for ongoing site management. These documents and ideas will be used further on in the book to help you make purchasing and design decisions, so listen closely!

Your Statement of Purpose

Throughout my school career, every writing teacher I ever had always emphasized a single, unbending principle—begin your work with a "Statement of Purpose," a single paragraph that summarizes the message you intend to convey in the following pages. The same principle applies to starting any sort of enterprise or project that requires its elements to serve a common purpose. Your statement provides a rock-solid base on which to build every other aspect of your site, and when you're making agonizing decisions about what size graphics to put on your home page or whether a new PowerPC is a justifiable investment, your statement will provide later guidance.

We'll use your statement of purpose in later chapters to choose a domain name, estimate the resources your site will need, and choose the hardware and software your site will depend on. Your statement will also help you define your needs when designing the "look" of the information served from your site, whether you plan to design your pages yourself or direct someone else to do so. Finally, it will provide a yardstick for you to evaluate your final site against and guide future decisions about upgrades and changes.

Some questions to get you started:

- ☐ How would you characterize the intended audience for your site?
- ☐ What value do you expect your site to produce for you?
- ☐ What larger goal for you or your organization will that value serve?
- ☐ What value do you expect your site to produce for your visitors?
- ☐ What larger goal of your visitors will that value serve?
- ☐ If you are planning to carry existing information (such as a college catalog or technical support database) onto your server, what value does making that information available on a Web server add to its existing form?
- ☐ How will you measure the success or failure of your site in meeting its goals?

Once you've developed answers for those questions, and added whatever elements are appropriate for your specific situation, try to integrate your responses into a cohesive paragraph or two. The key here is to establish your priorities and provide an outline that will guide all your subsequent decisions.

Resources and Commitment

The single most common mistake for new site administrators, whether they are creating their own site or doing so for an organization, is underestimating the time and resources required to start and operate a Web site.

Although it's true that you can simply start up most commercial server programs and be instantly serving a simple home page (assuming you already have an Internet connection), most sites aim for a bit more complexity than that. More importantly, one of my goals in this book is to provide you with the tools and methods to handle server administration on a site of any size or complexity, and I would be remiss if I did not provide an overview for you of the commitment a mature site demands.

The following list combines some of the more common responsibilities of managing a Web site, briefly describes them, and outlines what aspects you need to take into account when estimating what resources ongoing operation of your site will require. Approach this list as a guide and a warning, and return to it when you draw up more detailed procedures and plans for maintaining your site in the long term. Unless noted otherwise, all of the subjects that follow are covered in more detail in Part III of this book, "Site Administration."

Server Content

It's been said that the first and most important measure of your site's value is its content. Content is the accumulation of text, images, and other information that you make available from your server.

You'll need to map out where your content comes from, what form it arrives in, and how it is translated or "flowed" into your site. Your source may be existing documents, databases of information, or new text written especially for your Web site. In any case, you should analyze your sources and budget for your needs. Chapters 6 and 7 of this book, "Serving from Storage" and "CGI Applications and Usage," present detailed methods and tools for moving information into a servable form.

An unwritten rule of content is that it should change as often as possible.

An unwritten rule of content is that it should change as often as possible. The importance of updating the information on your site depends on the type of site you are creating. A directory of faculty members, for example, might only require updating on rare occasions, whereas an online newsletter might want to change at least some of its content daily.

At this point, you should at least be able to identify the types of information sources you will have to work with when managing your site.

Organization

There are two approaches to organizing the files and folders that hold information you're serving from your site—throw everything in as its created and let the links fall where they may, or spend the time to think about how your organization affects the perception and performance of your site, and design it to provide as effective and efficient a design as possible. We'll go into more detail on this later on, but for now, simply be aware that organizing your site can be as important as the organization of the text and images on your pages themselves.

Design

The process of designing your pages in HTML and integrating graphics effectively is, as I mentioned in the introduction, beyond the scope of this book. But I did want to remind you to estimate the resources that the process will require. Ideally, this activity shouldn't take place very often in the course of your server's life, but occasional revamping will very likely be necessary and it will certainly be a major expense when you first get your server started.

Testing

Part of a server administrator's job is regular testing of the server with a variety of different client programs, from different platforms if possible, and verifying that all the elements of the site appear or work as expected. An additional responsibility, especially before a site first opens, or when adding or changing the software running on the server machine, is performing stress testing on your site to avoid nasty surprises later on. (You can learn more about stress testing your server in Chapter 12, "Not Another Audit!".)

Maintenance

Maintenance is a bore, a chore, a hassle, and a pain. Fortunately, it can be automated to a large extent, and I'll be showing you how to do that in later chapters. As a rough guide, you can probably expect to spend at least eight hours a week performing routine maintenance on your site when you first begin "live" activity.

If you plan to update the content of your site often, maintenance requirements can balloon enormously. Delegation of tasks to others, a judicious use of automation tools, and careful planning can all reduce the time required to maintain your site, but an effective estimating technique here is to make a prediction about the time you will need to devote to maintenance—and double it.

Review

How will you know how "well" your site is performing? What milestones do you expect to reach in the first weeks or months after launching your new server? These are the kinds of questions a regular review process is designed to answer. Think about the kinds of numbers you need to evaluate your site on an ongoing basis. Your targets could be in simple counts of total hits, number of repeat visitors, online sales figures, or the percentage of people who move from your home page to another part of your site. Regardless of your specific needs, you will need to establish a system for measuring your server's performance and relating those numbers to your goals. This is also a process that lends itself to automation, and I'll explain how to do so in subsequent chapters.

Professional Development and Education

Ideally, this book would provide all of the education you need to run your site. Unfortunately (or fortunately, depending on your point of view), WWW and Macintosh technology is rapidly changing, even as you read these words. You'll need to subscribe to mailing lists, read newsgroups, review Web-based information sites, and generally maintain a sense of the "state of the art" in the technologies and ideas that are relevant to your site. You may also want to expand your professional skills by learning to create CGIs or other applications that increase the value of your site and yourself as a site manager.

Regardless of your goals, you should at least set aside a regular portion of your workday to review your information sources for items of interest. It's all right to miss a day here and there as your other projects or constraints put demands on your time, but Web serving is a rapidly evolving area of expertise, and those who are unable to keep track of current developments will find themselves having to learn their craft all over again every time they look up.

Considering Form and Function

Your experiences on the Internet and the World Wide Web have probably been entirely client-based so far. You have visited hundreds (if not thousands!) of Web sites already, and probably have at least a vague idea of how you want your own site to look and what message you want your visitors to carry away with them. Now is the time to gather those thoughts together and produce a detailed list specifying the functionality and form you envision for your own server.

At this point, you should retrieve your lists of dos and don'ts culled from your online research (see the previous section "Cowabunga, Web Serving!" in this chapter) and construct a list of the features you want to add to your own site.

Perhaps you want to provide a form for clients to send you messages without using their own email software, or you would like to have visitors fill out a brief questionnaire before being permitted to download software or other information from your server. Whatever you are looking for, write it down. If you found design elements that struck you as particularly inviting or irritating, write those down as well. Detail each and every part of your server as you wish it to appear to the outside world. Lastly, rate these features in order of priority to establish a foundation on which to base decisions about where your resources should be spent.

Don't worry if you don't know how to make these elements work yet. Your responsibility is to identify your needs; my responsibility will be to show you how to meet them.

Ten Elements of Professional Site Management

What is a professional? We usually associate the term with doctors, lawyers, and other individuals who have undergone extensive training and testing to establish themselves as having expertise in a particular area. Generally, the "professions" represent careers with a long history of progression and development. The question then arises, can a "Webmaster," a title that entered the language barely two years ago, be a "professional?"

The answer, of course, is yes. Professionalism has nothing to do with education, corporations, or even experience necessarily. Professionalism is part of your process, your methodology of creating and maintaining your site. Professionalism means contacting your peers and sharing information that increases your efficiency and effectiveness. Professionalism means investing in the time and resources necessary to be current in your field of expertise, knowing what goals your site serves, and generally being in a position of effective and informed control over your site's development and operation.

Professionalism is, at its root, an attitude and an ethic as much as anything else. It comes from a sense of quality—both the desire to create quality and the ability to discern quality.

Professionalism is, at its root, an attitude and an ethic as much as anything else. It comes from a sense of quality—both the desire to create quality and the ability to discern quality. It is a commitment to the ideal of always striving to be a little bit better at your chosen craft or career.

So without further commentary, here are my "Ten Elements of Professional Site Management":

- ☐ You have a "Statement of Purpose" for your site.
- ☐ You understand how every element of your site contributes to meeting your goals.
- ☐ You have a clear idea of who your online clientele are and how your site meets their needs.

- ☐ You have a written plan for expanding your server's capacity when necessary.
- ☐ You conduct regular, formalized audits to verify your site's functionality and integrity.
- ☐ You have a regularly scheduled review process to analyze and report your site's effectiveness at meeting the goals you have set for it.
- ☐ You use automation wherever you can to increase efficiency and accuracy.
- ☐ You can describe the value of your site for you or your organization in less than two minutes to someone who thinks the Web is a dumb idea.
- ☐ You stay abreast of current technology and upcoming events on the Web and on the Macintosh through newsgroups, mailing lists, and trade magazines.
- ☐ You have developed a network of friends and other site administrators *not connected with your own organization* that you can turn to for assistance and advice when things get hairy.

The **Chapter 1** folder in the **HTML** folder on the CD accompanying this book contains a list of sites that will help you get started, including copyright information and general Macintosh resources.

Final Word: At the rate the Web is growing, the supply of professional server administrators is going to fall far short of the demands of sites that need their skills. I urge you to make the effort, both in your own position and with your peers, of striving to make professionalism, at any level, an integral component of your work. We all need more of you.

Summary

Now that you're well-armed with plans and goals for your site, we'll tackle some of the technical aspects of Web servers—how they work and what they can do. We'll also start turning Web pages around to look "behind the scenes" at what server elements work together to create the pages your clients will see. It will be the first step on your journey from thinking like a client to thinking like a server. The Web will never be the same again.

CHAPTER 2

WWW Client/Server: The Short Course

To understand the interaction among all the parts of your Web site, you'll need some background information about what those components actually are and their respective roles in serving information via the Web to clients. This is an important step toward your goal of learning to think like a server rather than like a client. Even when browsing the Web as a client, you'll begin to see Web pages and sites in terms of the elements that combine to create their distinctive appearances and features. The goal is to begin to see results in terms of the context that created them, and reaching that goal will give you tremendous power to conceptualize and develop your own site efficiently and effectively.

The entire Web is built around the idea of simple transactions recurring between clients and a server.

The entire Web is built around the idea of simple transactions recurring between clients and a server—the clients send requests to the server, which then returns responses. More importantly, each transaction occurs independently of all others, with every request considered to be completely new and unrelated to any that occurred before or after it. Everything else about the Web builds on this basic model of a request-response transaction.

For now, I start with the basics—the elements of a Web transaction as shown in Figure 2.1.

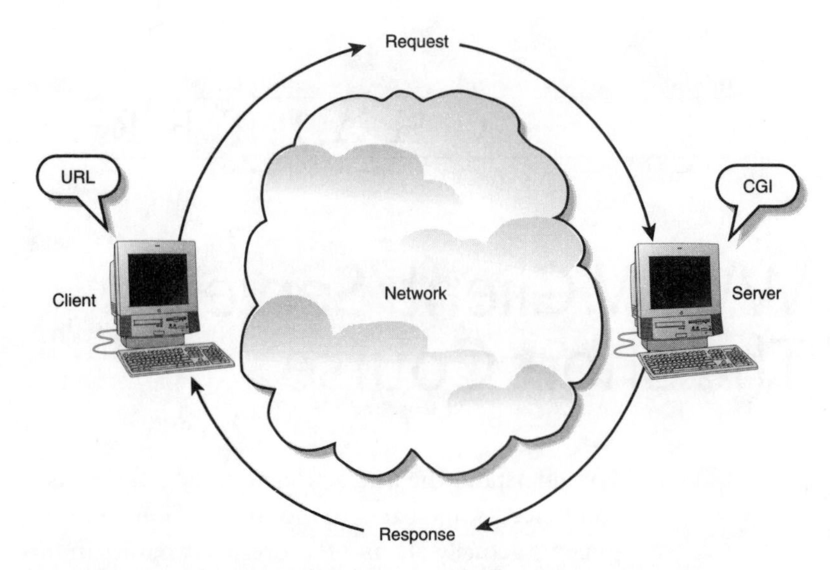

Figure 2.1 *Elements of a typical Web client/server transaction.*

The Client

The client, or browser, is the software that sends a request to your server and to which the server returns information (which I'll refer to in this chapter as the *response*). The client can be a graphical Web browser like Netscape or Mosaic, an automated program that indexes your pages for later searching, such as Lycos or Infoseek, or an automated script that "pre-screens" people's hotlists for pages that have changed since their last visits. Regardless of its ultimate purpose, however, the client's actions always follow the same pattern for any given URL—send a request that your server can understand and interpret the server's response appropriately.

In the Bad Old Days, the only Web clients available were based on character displays that could display only text with a few varieties like boldfaced, underlined, or (shudder) blinking text. Lynx is probably the most popular of these text-only clients, and in the early days of the Internet and the Web, it was the primary method used to view HTML documents. Occasionally, you may notice someone using Lynx trying to view your Web documents, but its use is much less frequent than it once was. The advantage of Lynx and its text-only brethren is that you can use it on a simple terminal account over a text-only connection, like you might use to connect to a BBS via a modem. In areas of the world where Internet access is more limited than it is in North America, text-only browsing is still in appreciable use. In general, though, clients using Lynx-like software will rarely appear at your site.

Graphical Clients

Eventually, a group of programmers at the National Center for Supercomputing Applications (NCSA) created a Web client called Mosaic that could display fully styled text and images on the same page. That single application ushered in the Web as we know it, and its design still influences all clients in use today.

Of course, clients are the single most rapidly changing part of the Web, and such technologies as HotJava (see Chapter 6, "Serving from Storage") and VRML (Virtual Reality Markup Language; see Chapter 6) promise to completely change the way information is viewed over the Web.

Nevertheless, the concept of the "client" in a Web transaction is always the same regardless of the computer or program actually used to implement it. From the server's point of view, every client can be communicated with in essentially the same way. Different clients do have different attributes, but these differences are primarily related to displaying HTML or other data types. That's a concern for site administrators who want their pages viewed effectively by as many people as possible, but not for the server software itself.

To illustrate the differences, take a look at a few screen shots of the same Web page viewed by different browsers, from Lynx to the latest version of Netscape Navigator. Just for fun, Figure 2.2 shows the home page for Macmillan Publishing (http://www.mcp.com/) viewed with Netscape Navigator.

Figure 2.2 *The Macmillan Computer Publishing site viewed through Netscape.*

Netscape's Navigator browser, as shown in Figure 2.2, not only recognizes its own peculiar extensions to the HTML standard (which are usually ignored by most other browsers), but also renders existing standards in its own manner. You can compare the white background and the position of the pop-up menu to the Mosaic window in Figure 2.3.

Although they are slightly different, Mosaic and Netscape at least both allow the full functionality of the site to come through. Now take a look at the same page through Lynx, shown in Figure 2.4.

Hmm, the form doesn't work for Lynx viewers and the site as a whole is quite confusing. Fortunately, you can see a link to a text version that should be designed for text-only clients. If you use a lot of graphics on your own site, you may want to consider providing text versions as well, as was done here.

Figure 2.3 *The Macmillan Computer Publishing site viewed through Mosaic.*

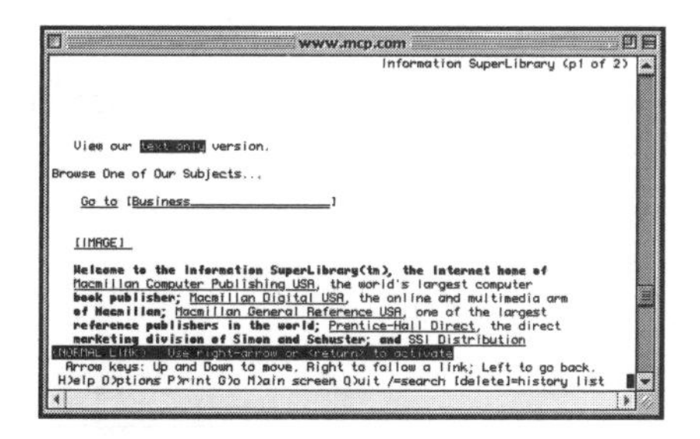

Figure 2.4 *The Macmillan Computer Publishing site viewed through Lynx.*

To Illustrate or Not?

The debate about whether to exert the effort necessary to accommodate both text-based and graphic-based interaction with your Web pages is still raging, so your own approach should be based both on your experiences once your site is in operation and your priorities. If your goal is to accommodate as wide a variety of clients as is humanly possible, you should at least include some textual information to parallel your graphic presentations to enable viewing of your site without using images.

continues

continued

Of course, once average Internet access speeds increase to the point where the time required to download graphics is no longer an impediment, these issues will be moot. The current reality is that some minor proportion of visitors will be unable or unwilling to look at your graphics—how that fact affects your design will depend on the priority you place on serving that minority.

Hopefully, these examples have emphasized the importance of viewing your own site with different browsers.

The first job of most clients is to create properly formatted requests for information. So let's see how that happens!

The URL

A URL (Uniform Resource Locater, also known as a URI, Uniform Resource Identifier) tells the client the where, what, and how of the request it represents. Figure 2.5 breaks up the elements of a URL.

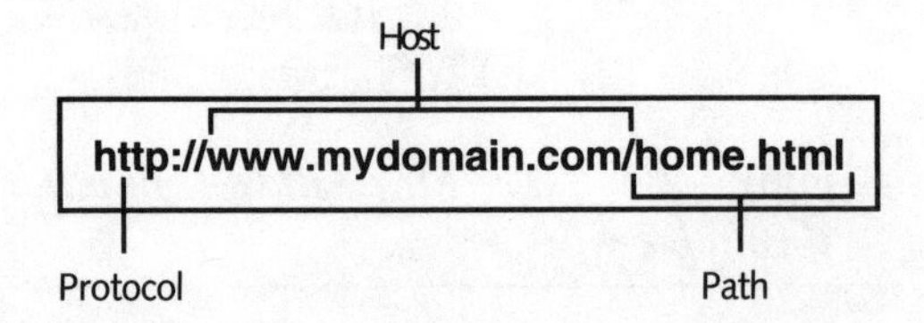

Figure 2.5 *The Essential Uniform Resource Locator (URL).*

The "where" is the server that the request will be sent to, the "what" is the information needed to form the request itself, and the "how" is the protocol used to make the request and receive a response. The parts of a URL as used on the Web (such as the example in Figure 2.5) are fairly straightforward, so let's work our way from left to right to understand how they're put together and how the standard URL can be extended when appropriate.

Protocol

The first part of a URL (everything preceding the "://") specifies the protocol, or scheme, to be used by the browser to connect to the server. The protocol defines both the type of server the URL refers to and the procedure for exchanging information with that server.

The focus in this book is on the HTTP (Hypertext Transfer Protocol) scheme used by the Web and, to a lesser extent, the other protocols that enable both HTTP and other Internet services like FTP (File Transfer Protocol) and email.

Host

The host, or hostname, portion of a URL identifies the machine to which the client's request will be addressed—in other words, a way to find your server on the Internet. Hostnames are also referred to as domain names or FQDMs (Fully Qualified Domain Names). Chapter 3 will expose you in mind-numbing detail to the process of translating a relatively readable name (like www.apple.com) into the numeric form (like 17.254.3.61), called an IP address, that is the actual identity of a specific server. In the meantime, you can think of the hostname as the equivalent of a mailing address because it provides all the information necessary to guide messages to a specific destination on the Internet.

Note that the two rightmost portions of the hostname, mydomain.com in the current example, are required to appear in order to identify your local network on the Internet. This is your site's ***domain name***, and can be broken down into a primary, or root, domain (.com) and a secondary domain (mydomain), which combine to identify your local network as a unique entity. Everything to the left of the secondary domain is normally used internally at your site to identify particular machines, and can be extended if necessary to add additional names.

For example, a company might have a publicly available Web server at www.company.com, while maintaining a separate, private Web server on another machine called www.private.company.com. There is no requirement that the hostname for a Web server begin with www—it's just a convention that allows people to remember URLs more easily.

We'll talk more about domain names when you choose your own in Chapter 4.

Port

The port of a URL refers to a particular Internet service on the host you are attempting to connect to and is indicated in URLs by appending the number to a colon after the hostname. All Internet servers "listen" for incoming connections on particular port numbers—by default, all Web servers answer requests coming in on port 80. In fact the two URLs http://www.mydomain.com/ and http://www.mydomain.com:80/ are exactly equivalent, because the "http" protocol assumes that the port desired is 80 if you don't indicate otherwise in the URL.

Sometimes, you may want to run more than one Web server on the same machine—for example, you may want to have a private server and a public one running side-by-side. You wouldn't want them both to answer the same port number, so you can assign a different port number (8080 is popular) to your second server so that it only answers URLs beginning with http://www.mydomain.com:8080/, while your main server still answers requests coming in to port 80.

You can choose any port number you want for your server, within some limits. Some port numbers are reserved for certain kinds of Internet services, so a good rule of thumb is to keep non-standard Web server ports at numbers between 1024 and 10000.

Path

The "path" of your URLs is everything from the "/" after the host-name to the end of the URL or a "?" character, whichever comes first. The "?" character is used to separate arguments to a URL from the path—don't worry about that just yet—we'll take a closer look at arguments in the next section. The URL's path is commonly used to represent the path you would follow through the folders of your site to find a particular file. However, it's important to realize that there is no requirement that this be the case—for example, you can alias folders and files on a Macintosh and fool the server into thinking items are in one place when they're really in another. In that case, the URL path would be to the alias rather than to the file itself.

But the path of a URL can literally represent anything you want it to—it could contain fields in a database, an ID code to identify a particular client, or data about where the client has last visited. The only requirement of Web protocols is that the server be set up to interpret it and return an intelligible response.

Arguments

When you fill out a form on a Web page and send the information you've entered to the server, the additional information is appended to the URL in the form of an argument. Two types of arguments can be sent as part of a URL: path arguments and search arguments, which are indicated by "$" and "?" characters, respectively.

Path arguments, for example, are used by the Alta Vista searching service to pass information about a request to the application that actually returns the search results. Clicking the "Submit" button in the form shown in Figure 2.6, for example, sends the indicated URL to Alta Vista for processing.

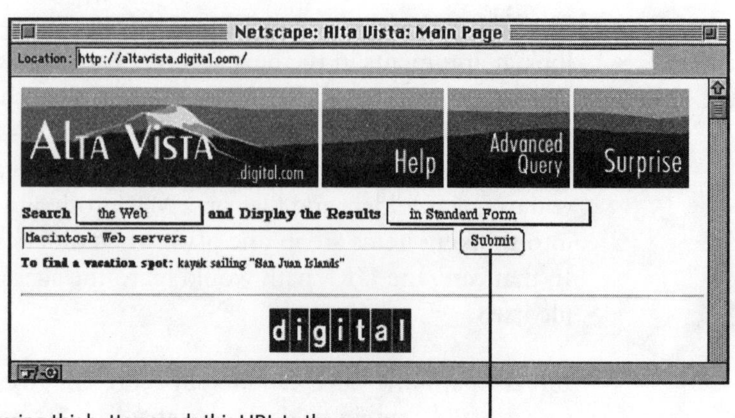

Pressing this button sends this URL to the server:
http://altavista.digital.com/cgi-bin/query?pg=q&what=web&fmt=&q=Macintosh+Web+servers
(underlined part is the search argument)

Figure 2.6 *Using path arguments at the Alta Vista Web site.*

In this case, the search argument consists of four variables, the last of which contains the entered search terms.

Because they are almost exclusively handled by other applications on your server called CGIs, we'll hold off further discussion of them until Chapter 7, which discusses how to use CGIs on your server.

Escape Codes

You may also notice that URLs sometimes contain strange groups of characters with a percent sign, such as "%20." These are "encoded" characters, and they enable the client to send characters that normally wouldn't be allowed in a URL by encoding them using the percentage signs. Each encoding (a percent sign followed by two characters) represents a particular character—"%20", for example, represents an encoded space in a URL. Encoded characters are either characters reserved for other uses (like the "?" character, which is used to indicate where search arguments begin) or special characters such as those used in many non-English languages. All encoded characters in the URL's path are decoded into their proper form by the Web server.

A complete discussion of URL encodings and their usage is available in Chapter 6.

After the parts of the URL are identified, the client uses it to construct a complete request to send off to the server. On its way there, of course, the message must traverse a network to reach its destination.

The Network

The network is, for our purposes, the Internet. It starts at the wire leading away from your Web server and ends at the wire leading into the client's machine. Everything in between is the subject of Chapters 3 and 4, so I'll avoid going into details right now. For the moment, you can consider the network to be one long wire along which messages between the client and the server travel. In my opinion, a more realistic concept is that of the Network as a vast, amorphous cloud of occasionally malevolent intent (as illustrated in Figure 2.1), but you can choose the image that you prefer.

The Server

Finally, we arrive at the server! The server's essential function is to create an intelligible response to return to the client, whether that response is in the form of HTML, an image, or any other kind of information you want to serve to the world. The server doesn't care what it's returning to the client—bits are bits as far as it's concerned.

After a client's request has been received, a Web server needs to find the proper response to the URL the client used. Most of the time, this means simply translating the URL path into a file path on the server's disk. The file referred to can then be read from the disk and returned without modification to the client as part of the response. Some other possible responses are shown in Figure 2.7—you can find out more about their details in the section on writing your own CGIs in Chapter 8.

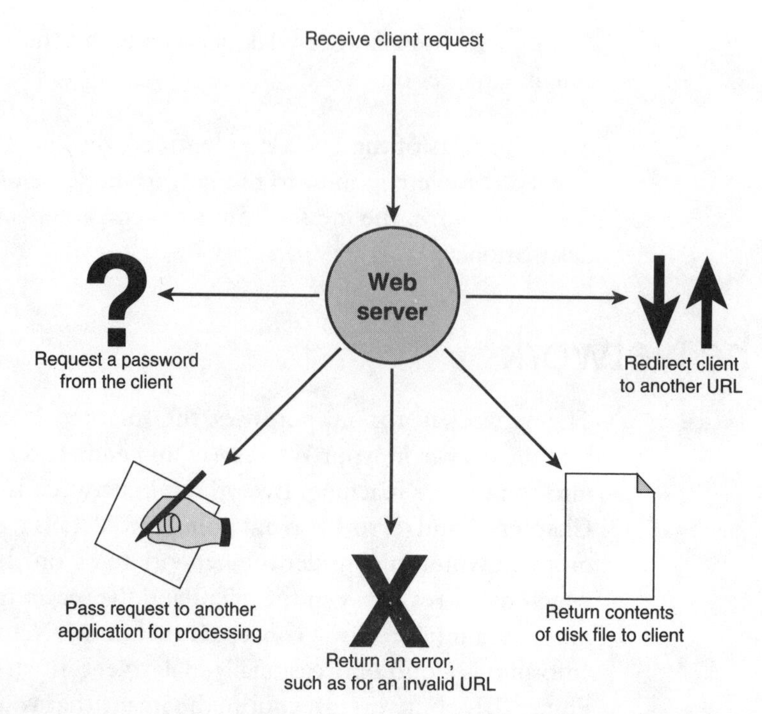

Figure 2.7 *Possible Web server responses to client requests.*

As mentioned earlier, however, there is no particular reason built into the Web's design that a URL must correspond to a file at all. For anything more complex than reading static information from a disk, however, the server application normally needs help from another program to work out what the response should be.

CGIs

CGI (Common Gateway Interface) is a protocol that defines how Web servers can call upon other applications to process HTTP requests.

CGI (Common Gateway Interface) is a protocol that defines how Web servers can call upon other applications to process HTTP requests. This mechanism allows a server's capabilities to be extended without interfering with the server's normal duties. Technically, the term should be used only to refer to the protocol itself, but it's common and fairly standard to use the term "CGI" to refer to the assisting applications as well.

If a URL is to be processed, in whole or in part, by a CGI, the server sends a message to the CGI with the client's request and waits for the CGI to return a response, which the server can then pass back to the client.

> On the Macintosh, messages between applications are sent via a MacOS technology called Apple Events. We'll discuss Apple Events and how CGIs work with them in more detail in Chapter 7, but for now you can think of them as messages passing back and forth between applications.

Normally, a CGI supplies a response to the server that is passed back verbatim to the client. The response can be in any form normally returned by a Web server, which could include requests for passwords, the contents of files on disk, or commands that direct the client to request a different URL.

The power of CGIs rests in what happens after the request is received. Because a CGI can do anything a normal Mac application can do, including communicate with other applications, it allows any imaginable processing of a request to take place. Some possibilities are shown in Figure 2.8.

The only requirement is that some sort of response must be formulated and returned to the server for transmission to the client.

CGIs provide a means for you to completely customize your Web server without actually writing a server application yourself, allowing you to concentrate on providing innovative services without concerning yourself with the details of Internet communications. The proper use of CGIs can transform your site from a simple provider of information into a dynamic, interactive experience for your clients.

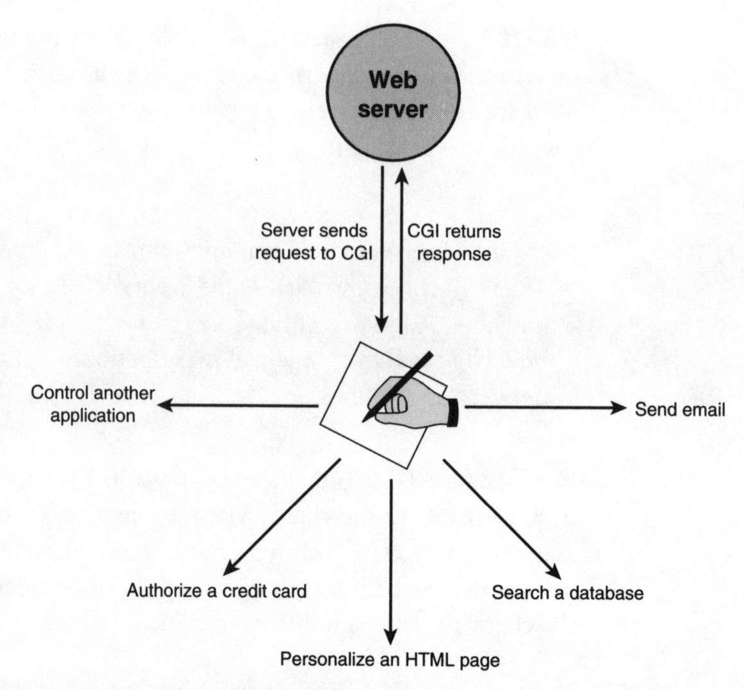

Figure 2.8 *Uses of CGI applications.*

Summary

So in a nutshell, that's the Web. Note that the type of information sent from the server to the client is not important to the structure of the transaction—the Web is a medium rather than a message.

Most importantly, don't confuse HTML with the Web itself. Already, clients are being developed that don't use HTML at all; instead, they may execute programs delivered by a server or use a purely graphical interface, even to the extent of being able to maneuver through a 3-D space defined by the Web server. The Web defines how information is exchanged.

The Web provides an elegantly flexible, reliable, and extensible way to transport information from one point to another through the mechanism of request-response transactions. What is being transported, of course, is entirely up to you.

In the next chapter, you descend into the world of the Internet itself and learn how messages are sent from computer to computer across the world.

CHAPTER 3

Me and My (Internet) Shadow

What is the "Internet?" As Webmasters, we are all utterly dependent upon it, but very few administrators actually understand more than a smattering of how it works. That's a shame, because when something goes wrong on the Net that affects your server, you can be sure that you will be blamed for it—so it behooves you to at least gain enough of an understanding to know when something goes wrong and to deal with the resulting problems effectively.

You don't need to understand all the intricacies of managing the high-speed global communications systems on which the Internet is based, but a basic grasp of how the Web works will push you head and shoulders above many of your peers when a problem with the Internet affects your site.

This chapter is carefully written to provide a view of the workings of the Internet that reflects the needs and interests of server administrators, not network administrators. If you are responsible for maintaining the physical networks and devices that actually route information from one point to another, you should definitely turn to one of the resources at the end of this chapter for a more detailed and general view of Macintosh networking in general and Internet topics in particular.

You should expect to gain enough of an understanding of how information moves between your server and your clients to talk intelligently with the people who provide your Internet connection. Just as importantly, you'll learn the vocabulary and background you'll need to follow discussions and announcements online about the Internet and its development.

Basic Concepts

Before I get into the Internet proper, a brief introduction to some terms common to virtually all networks is in order.

Packets

Packets are the smallest amount of information that can be carried as an individual entity across a network. It is useful to think of them as envelopes, with an address on the outside and some kind of data inside. Most packets also contain other information about their contents, such as data that helps to verify that all the information sent arrived intact. The proper term for Internet-carried packets is "datagrams," but I'll use the term packets throughout this book since the two words are essentially synonymous. The amount of information carried by a single packet commonly varies between 0.5K to 1.5K.

Nodes

In a computer network, a node appears wherever a wire plugs into something. A node can be a computer, like your Mac, a printer, or a device that connects two wires together. A node can be "smart," in that it evaluates the data passing through it, or "dumb," in that it simply passes data from one wire to another. For this book, I'll restrict the use of the term "node" to the "smart" devices—the ones that do more than simply connect wires together.

Networks

A LAN (Local Area Network) consists of a group of nodes that can send data to each other without passing that data through another node. Your LAN consists of every computer or device you can reach solely by following the cabling or wire used by your network.

This is the most common form of network and is the building block on which the Internet is based. Keep in mind that any set of interconnected wires with nodes can be considered a network—even the line between two computer modems is (a very simple) LAN.

The Internet consists of many LANs linked into one gigantic network that can move information from any given node to any other given node.

So what is the Internet? The Internet consists of many LANs linked into one gigantic network that can move information from any given node to any other given node. The methods that these individual LANs use to communicate with each other is the subject of the "Protocols" section of this chapter.

At this point, however, just keep in mind that the Internet is not a particular network or even an entity in its own right—it is a map of the connections between all the LANs that allow information to flow freely. The Internet exists because of the connections between networks, rather than just the networks themselves. The very term Internet expresses this well—"inter," meaning "between," and "net," meaning network—"between networks."

Routers

To move Internet packets from one network to another requires the use of a router or "gateway." Routers, which can be either a standard computer running routing software or a special hardware device used only for routing data packets, are the key elements of the process of moving data across the Internet, as they decide not only which packets move from one network to the next, but also to which network when a choice exists.

Intranets on the Rise

A growing proportion of Web sites (maybe yours?) are being placed on networks that have either no or very limited access to the general Internet. These networks, often confined to a single company or institution, act as mini-Internets that use the same technology as the global Internet, yet are invisible to people outside their private area. For many groups, these "Intranets" ("intra," meaning "within") offer all the efficiencies of Web-based delivery of services to clients without compromising the security of information intended for internal use only.

Fortunately, both Intranet Web servers and Internet servers work on precisely the same principles, so you should be able to transfer experiences from one sort of server to the other without undue difficulty.

Routers maintain tables that they use to check whether they need to pass data packets to another network and if so, where to send them. Because each packet includes the address of its destination node on its "envelope," the router can look at the addresses and determine which LAN is closest to the final destination. This process of forwarding packets repeats when packets leave or enter each intervening LAN until the packet finally reaches the node it was originally addressed to.

Making all this forwarding and addressing work is the subject of the next section.

Protocols

Protocols are the basis of all communication between computers—they define methods and assumptions that are available to anyone creating products that use that protocol, so that one party can, for example, build a Web server while another company produces a Web client with confidence that both products will be able to communicate with each other.

In networking, protocols are normally described in terms of layers, each of which uses the assumptions and methods provided by the layer below it to implement its particular function. The protocols covered in this chapter and their relationships to each other are shown in Figure 3.1.

The rest of this chapter will explore each of these layers from the bottom up, and end with an overview of the present-day organization of the Internet.

Physical Network

There are myriad physical network types and protocols, each of which uses a unique method for addressing and moving packets around. Each LAN on the Internet has its own type of physical network, such as Ethernet or LocalTalk, and its own method of carrying packets from one node to another.

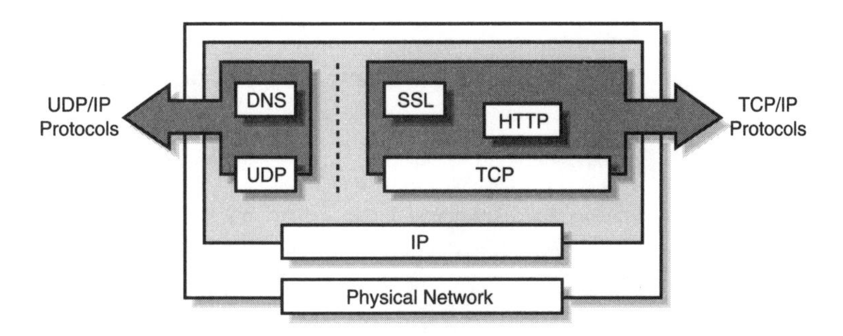

Figure 3.1 *The layering of protocols on the Internet.*

Fortunately, you won't have to be concerned with the protocols used by the physical network, because any network that can connect to the Internet has a method of carrying, or encapsulating, Internet packets within its own proprietary protocol. So as far as the Web server is concerned, all the information it sees that is related to the Internet is in the same format.

Most likely, the physical network your Web server will be connected to locally is some flavor of Ethernet, and should be more than adequate for your needs. For purposes here, assume that the network you're using is capable of moving IP packets around efficiently, although again, if you have a deeper interest or need for more information, I've listed some resources at the end of this chapter that should be helpful.

Internet Protocol

IP, the Internet Protocol, defines the format data packets use for carrying information across the Internet. IP is also the protocol concerned with the routing of packets from their source to their destination nodes, as I described previously in the section on routers.

The IP protocol is wholly concerned with single packets of information—it doesn't know or care whether two packets of information are going to the same destination or if the data two packets carry represent parts of a single, larger file. The IP protocol considers each packet as an individual entity and provides methods to send it on its way as efficiently as possible.

Addressing

One manifestation of the IP protocol you are probably already familiar with is the system of IP addresses used to identify unique hosts or nodes on the Internet. Each node on the Internet (or any other IP-based network) has at least one unique identifying address, consisting of four numbers, each of which can range from 0 to 255 (in practice, you should see addresses that use numbers only between 1 and 254—0 and 255 are reserved for special purposes).

Every IP address can be divided into two sections—the network or domain identifier and the host or node identifier. The point at which this division is made is defined by the class of the domain in which the network resides, with class A networks identified by the first number only, class B by the first two numbers, and class C by the first three numbers. These classes are illustrated in Figure 3.2.

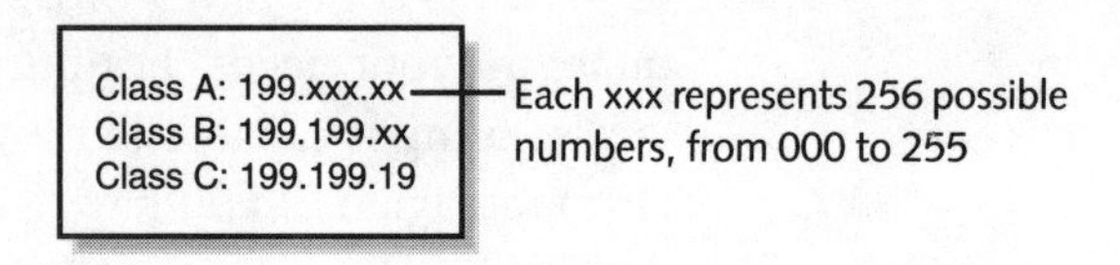

Figure 3.2 *The three classes of IP address.*

Different classes are assigned depending upon how many nodes are planned to exist within a particular domain. Because each "xxx" in Figure 3.2 represents 256 possible node addresses, Class C addresses are assigned to networks or domains of up to 256 nodes, Class B addresses to networks of over 64,000 nodes (256 × 256), and Class A addresses to networks with up to almost 17 million nodes! Needless to say, there aren't many Class A domains around.

IP addresses are classified this way because it reduces the amount of information the rest of the Internet must know in order to forward packets to their proper destinations. For example, Carnegie Mellon University (CMU) has the domain cmu.edu, which corresponds to the B class network of all IP addresses beginning with 128.2. The rest of the Internet needs to know only that addresses beginning with 128.2 are routed to the cmu.edu network, and can ignore the third and fourth number in the IP address.

Once the packet arrives at CMU, however, those last two numbers are used by internal routers to send the packet to its proper destination. CMU is responsible for maintaining the information necessary to locate individual nodes with the 128.2 prefix, while the rest of the world only needs to know where to send the cmu.edu packets. In this way, every CMU IP address is represented by a single entry in the tables maintained by other routers on the Internet.

Were it not for this system of "summarizing" entire networks, every router on the Internet would need to maintain table entries for each of the thousands of CMU IP addresses!

Routing

When an IP packet is sent out to a local network from your Mac, it contains two destination IP addresses—the address of the point of its final, intended destination, and the address of the router or gateway node on your local network that is responsible for forwarding the packet to the next network on the way to its final destination. If the destination is on the same LAN as the sender, both IP addresses on the packet are the same.

More likely is the situation where you are sending data off to a distant destination. In that case, at least one node on your network is designated as a router, meaning that it has the responsibility of accepting the IP packets and forwarding them to whichever network is next along the path to the destination.

At each LAN, or "hop," across the Internet, this process is repeated, with the IP packet being transferred from network to network by routers until it finally reaches the end of its trip.

All Internet applications and protocols use IP addresses and IP routing to send and receive information, making IP the critical "transport" protocol that allows the Internet—a network of networks—to operate.

Domain Name System

DNS (Domain Name System) is the protocol that defines the methods of translating domain and host names (like www.mydomain.com) into the numeric IP addresses that the IP protocol needs to route packets correctly across the Internet. DNS is implemented solely to assist humans in remembering and using IP addresses and is not, strictly speaking, part of the process of communicating across the Internet.

DNS is implemented as a distributed, hierarchical database—that is, the information required for translating domain names into IP addresses is distributed throughout the Internet, so that there are just a few machines that need to hold the information necessary to translate domain and hostnames into IP addresses for each domain. These machines are called domain name servers, or DNS servers, and assigning particular DNS servers to a given domain is one of the main purposes of registering your domain name (see Chapter 4, "Jacking In," for more information on registering domain names).

Normally, your DNS server is maintained by your Internet access provider and its functioning is their responsibility. Your primary concern is therefore simply to verify that the DNS servers for your domain are correct and available to the rest of the Internet. Look to Appendix A, "Internet Troubleshooting," for more information on how to identify and solve DNS problems for your clients.

Transmission Control Protocol

TCP (Transmission Control Protocol) is the second most ubiquitous protocol on the Internet after IP. In fact, you'll often see Internet-related networks referred to as TCP/IP networks, because the two are so closely related.

TCP is responsible for three aspects of Internet communications: guaranteeing that data sent arrives at its destination correctly, combining the data from IP packets together in their original order as sent, and maintaining multiple channels of communication that can operate simultaneously. Let's look at each task independently:

Connections and Ports

Communication via TCP requires the establishment of a "connection" between the two communicating nodes on the Internet. Establishing a connection requires a series of brief messages to be passed back and forth, much like the "handshaking" a modem goes through to connect to another modem. In general, the client is the one that initiates the request for a connection and the server is the node that answers. Once a connection is made, a bit of memory is set aside on each node to handle their TCP communications. Ultimately, of course, the connection is closed and that bit of memory is released for other uses.

> You may have heard that MacTCP allows a maximum of 64 connections—this limit refers to how many TCP connections are able to exist at any given time. This may seem like a small number for a busy Web server, but if your server is handling anywhere near 64 connections simultaneously, it's time to buy a second Mac. Even a fast PowerPC will have trouble juggling that many tasks simultaneously, and such a server will appear quite sluggish to your clients.

Your Web server also has the additional responsibility of listening for incoming requests for connections by clients—if the server isn't waiting for a request to arrive, requests that are sent are simply unanswered and a connection never opens. You will configure your server (in Chapter 5, "The Show Begins—Choosing a Server") for a maximum number of "listens"—thus establishing the maximum number of connections your Web server can handle at one time.

Ports are a kind of extension to IP addresses that identify types of connections and allow multiple Internet servers to operate simultaneously on a single machine. Just as each node on the Internet has a unique IP address, each TCP connection on a node is assigned a port number. This allows servers (like your Web server software) to "listen" for connection requests addressed to particular port numbers.

For example, most Web servers answer requests for connections to TCP port 80 by default. You could also run another copy of the server software that was configured to answer requests for port 8080. Each copy of the Web server responds only to requests addressed to its specific port number, allowing you to run two separate servers on a single Mac. The same idea can be extended to other Internet services, so that you can simultaneously operate FTP, email, and Web servers on one Mac, just as long as each server application uses a unique port number.

Packet Ordering

When a file is sent via TCP/IP from one node to another, it is broken into smaller pieces, each of which is placed in an IP packet and sent separately. Because IP routing treats each packet as an individual entity, it is possible and even probable that packets may reach their destination in a different order than that they were sent, depending on how busy particular networks and routers are at any given time.

TCP, fortunately, numbers each packet that it sends over a particular connection. This allows the node receiving the packets to rearrange the packets if necessary to maintain the correct ordering. If TCP didn't handle this for you, your clients might find themselves displaying the bottom of an HTML page above the top!

Delivery Guaranteed

Besides arriving out of order, some IP packets may not arrive at all. Every IP packet has a "lifetime," or period during which routers will continue to attempt to forward it on to its destination. If a particular network or router is very slow or busy, however, the packet may be delayed long enough that it exceeds its lifetime (usually about two seconds) and is then no longer forwarded by routers and simply disappears.

To cope with these missing IP packets, TCP keeps track of the packets sent and requires the destination to return another IP packet to the sender acknowledging that the original one was received (see Figure 3.3). If the sender does not receive the acknowledgment, it resends the original packet until it is either acknowledged or the TCP connection is broken.

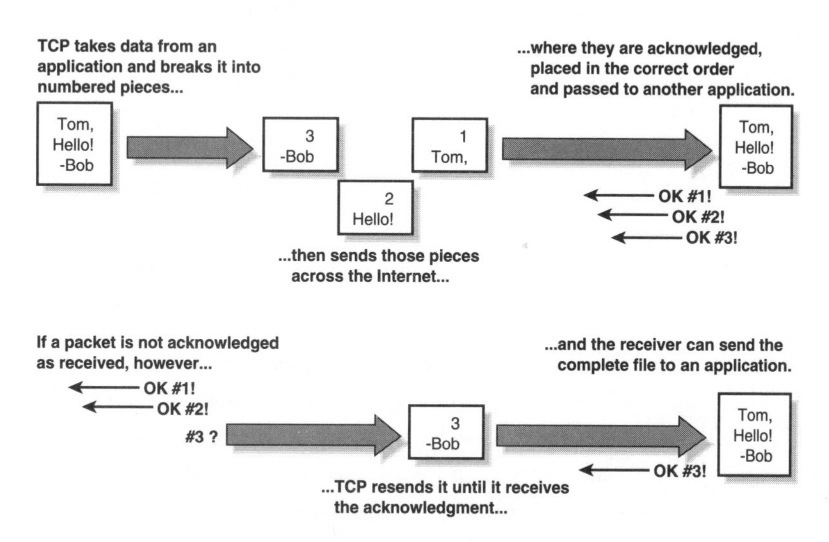

Figure 3.3 *How TCP handles missing packets.*

Note that neither TCP nor IP cares about what sort of information is being communicated—their concern is solely with moving packets from point to point (IP) and managing the overall flow of data between nodes (TCP). Together, they establish the foundation upon which almost all other Internet services are built.

Universal Datagram Protocol

UDP (Universal Datagram Protocol) is little more than the IP protocol itself. UDP dispenses with all the TCP methods of guaranteeing that received packets can be put back together in their original order, and has no facility for recovering from the loss of packets during transmission. It does allow for verification of the integrity of the data carried in each individual packet, but even that is optional. Also, the ports used by UDP connections are different from those used by TCP connections, even though they may have the same number. So UDP port 25 can maintain a completely different connection than that run over TCP port 25.

Because of the lack of error-correction, UDP is used for data transfers that can tolerate the loss of some data or the arrival of out-of-order packets. This would be useless for downloading software or an HTML page, but is perfectly fine for other applications, such as voice transmission, that can tolerate noise, or "static" in the transmission. UDP is used, for example, in the RealAudio http://www.realaudio.com technology that streams sound over the Internet using UDP. The lack of error correction and other overhead inherent in UDP allows a much more efficient data transfer rate, so even a 14.4Kbps modem can play intelligible speech if a small number of packets arrive out of order or are even lost entirely.

So why does a Web server care about UDP protocols? Because UDP is also used by Domain Name System translation requests, since a request to translate a domain name into an IP address (or vice-versa) can be contained in a single packet. If the request is not answered because the packet was lost, it can simply be sent again, and there is no need to worry about the order of IP packets since each request and response consists of a single packet.

HTTP

HTTP, the HyperText Transfer Protocol, is the protocol that makes the Web different from other Internet services, like email or FTP. Be careful not to confuse it with HTML, which affects how documents are displayed and structured. HTTP defines the interaction between a client and a server on the Web.

In Chapter 2, you looked at an overview of how the Web works. That overview was a summary of the HTTP protocol. If you're planning to write your own CGIs (see Chapter 7, "CGI Applications and Usage"), you'll need to understand more of the details of the HTTP protocol, but I'll put that discussion off until the pertinent chapter.

The salient points here are that HTTP opens a TCP connection to your server, sends a request for information (as defined by the URL), and receives a response. As soon as the response is sent, the server closes the TCP connection. The client only gets one chance to ask. If the response wasn't what was expected, or if it directs the client to make a different kind of request, the whole process begins again. Open connection—request—respond—close connection. That's HTTP in a nutshell.

Secure Sockets Layer

SSL (Secure Sockets Layer) is a protocol developed by Netscape and others that encrypts the data being sent between a client and a server using a TCP/IP connection. Because it is actually encrypting all the data in each packet, it can theoretically be used to provide secure communications for any protocol that uses TCP/IP communications, from HTTP to email to FTP. A downside is that encrypting and decrypting data under SSL is a highly compute-intensive task, and tends to slow down communications even on PowerMacs.

SSL is also able to authenticate servers and clients, so that an SSL-based Web server identifying itself as that of "Joe's Internet Bargain Barn" is in fact that belonging to Joe, and not an impostor attempting to collect credit card numbers for misuse. The card numbers still aren't safe, but at least you know who stole them.

Other TCP/IP Protocols

Table 3.1 shows some of the other TCP/IP-based services that appear on the Internet. There are many others, but remember that each of these are no more than different methods of managing communication over a TCP/IP connection for their own specific purposes. The port numbers indicated are the ports on which servers for a given protocol listen for requests—if you attempt to connect to a POP server on port 100, for example, you'll fail because POP servers listen only for connection requests on port 24.

Table 3.1 *Commonly Used Internet Server Protocols*

Abbreviation	Port	Protocol	Used By
SMTP	25	Simple Mail Transfer Protocol	Servers that receive email messages for forwarding or delivery.
POP	110	Post Office Protocol	Servers that email clients connect to for downloading email.
FTP	20, 21	File Transfer Protocol	Servers that allow browsing of file systems and the transfer of file contents.
NNTP	119	Network News Transfer Protocol	Servers that deliver Usenet newsgroup articles to clients.

Putting It All Together

As I mentioned earlier in this chapter, the Internet is made up of huge numbers of individual LANs linked up by routers that move IP packets from one address, or node, to another. The actual structure of the Internet is closer to a tree arrangement, where a group of very high-speed networks form a "backbone" that carries most IP packets ("traffic") between the local networks you are familiar with, such as from one university to another or from your local Internet access provider to another provider halfway around the world (see Figure 3.4).

Backbone networks are maintained by the large telecommunication companies such as Sprint, MCI, and UUnet, among others. These providers supply connections (via routers) to each other's networks and sell connections to their backbones to smaller Internet access providers, who in turn sell portions of their access to others, including yourself. The backbone networks are usually maintained exclusively for the use of Internet traffic—that is, almost all the nodes are routers rather than clients or servers.

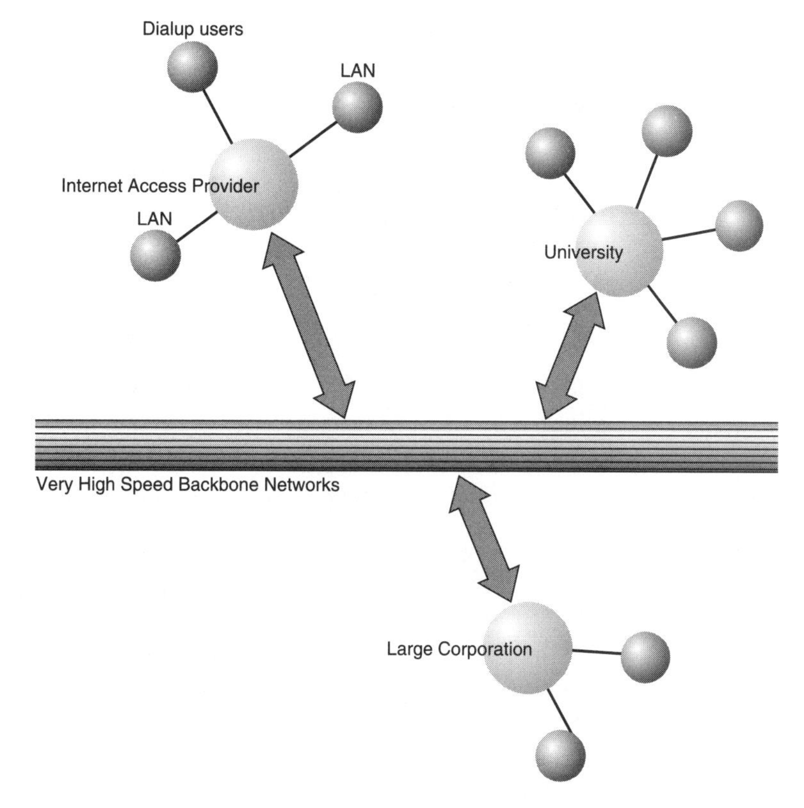

Figure 3.4 *Network interconnections on the Internet.*

Each step away from the backbone tends to be to a slightly slower network, and also tends to correspond to an increase in the number of nodes. The closer your server is to a backbone, then, the better off your server tends to be, because there are fewer intervening networks between you and your clients.

Resources

All Internet protocols and definitions are found in a constantly evolving series of documents called RFCs (Request For Comments), Internet-Drafts, and other names that all refer to quasi-official statements of how protocols and standards on the Internet are to be implemented. These documents are publicly available on the Internet and are produced by different groups of interested and qualified individuals that work together to reach a consensus on how the Internet should operate.

Table 3.2 lists some URLs that should get you started if you'd like to learn more about the Internet protocols.

Table 3.2 *URLs of Internet-Related Resources*

URL	Description
http://www.dns.net/dnsrd/docs/rfc.html	List of DNS-related RFCs.
http://www.con.wesleyan.edu/~triemer/network/docservs.html	Useful list of TCP/IP port numbers and protocols, with links to definitions of commonly used protocols.
http://www.netscape.com/newsref/std/SSL.html	Netscape's SSL reference page.
http://lcweb.loc.gov/global/internet/inet-pubs.html	Book listings and links to Internet-related sites, maintained by the Library of Congress.
http://www.ics.uci.edu/of, pub/ietf/http/	Home page for the current state and proposed changes to, the HTTP (Web) protocol.
http://www.cis.ohio-state.edu/hypertext/information/rfc.html	Links to searchable indexes of RFCs and a number of other relevant documents.
http://www.yahoo.com/Computers_and_Internet/Networking_and_Communications/	A smorgasbord of links....

I also promised earlier in this chapter to point you to other resources that discuss Macintosh networking and LANs in more detail. These are the two books I recommend out of those I've come across so far—but there are many others and you should certainly browse through a few at the bookstore in case the style I appreciate isn't to your own taste:

Live Wired: A Guide to Networking Macs
Publisher: Hayden Books, by Jim Anders
ISBN: 1-56830-015-8

Understanding Local Area Networks, Fifth Edition
Publisher: SAMS Publishing, by Neil Jenkins and Stan Schatt
ISBN: 0-672-30840-1

Summary

That's a lot of work just to get one home page out to a Web client! And you can run a Web site perfectly well knowing very little of it. But every move your server makes depends on all these protocols and parts working in unison, and understanding what goes on behind the scenes can be of immense help not only in troubleshooting problems, but also in your ability to use your server more effectively. If you would like to learn more about how the Internet works and how it's changing, please take a look at the resources I listed previously.

The next chapter shows you how to get your server hooked into the Internet and how to register and use your own domain name. This will require you to make your first decisions about implementing your site, so be sure you have your list of site requirements (from Chapter 1) in front of you before continuing.

CHAPTER 

"Jacking In"

Now that you're an Internet guru (if you're not, you must have skipped the previous chapter), the next step is to actually build yourself a connection between the Internet and your server.

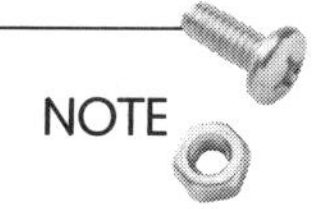

NOTE

If you already use a local Ethernet or other TCP/IP network, and you plan to run your server directly off that network with an existing Internet connection, you can skip ahead to the section entitled "Selecting and Registering a Domain Name." You may want to come back here and skim through the rest of this chapter at a later date.

If you do not already have an Internet connection, or need to upgrade your current access to a dedicated (as opposed to a SLIP/PPP connection) or higher speed connection, this chapter provides the background necessary to choose both the right type of connection for your needs and an Internet Service Provider (ISP) to handle your link to the Internet.

The Internet Connection

As you learned in the last chapter, the Internet uses gateways, or routers, to move TCP/IP messages from one local network to another. When you connect your server to an Internet access provider from a remote location, the line between you and your provider is considered a network in its own right, so both you and the ISP need a router in place at either end of the line.

So when you evaluate the performance and appropriateness of a given connection to the Internet, you're really concerned with at least three different networks:

- ☐ Your own, which may consist of one or many machines.
- ☐ The line between you and your ISP.
- ☐ The ISP's connections between you and the rest of the world.

Your main concern is with your end—the interface between your network and the line coming in from the telephone company—but the performance of your site is always dependent on all three parts working together.

Let's take a brief look at the players in this scheme.

Your LAN

"Your LAN," in this case, could be either a single server or a local network of many machines, all of which need Internet connectivity and individual IP addresses. I use the term LAN to refer to either possibility unless noted otherwise. The only real difference in terms of the equipment you'll need is that running a local TCP/IP network requires the use of a router, or gateway, that knows about your local network and can manage moving IP packets back and forth between your network and the routers at your access provider.

You also need to install an interface between the telephone line and your local network to take a role similar to that of a modem, in that it provides a bridge to your network for the signals traveling in from the telephone company. This device is often referred to as a terminal adapter or CSU/DSU (Channel Service Unit/Data Service Unit), depending on the context and type of connection.

In practice, many companies are beginning to offer combined functionality in a single device, so you could have one box that serves as a router and terminal adapter or CSU/DSU all together. Your access provider will probably recommend equipment for you to use, but be careful if it offers to sell you the equipment, as there may be a conflict between what equipment is best for you and what the ISP finds profitable to sell. On the other hand, an ISP may be able to offer discounts that are to your advantage or have a configuration that works best with certain manufacturers' equipment, so don't hesitate to ask why the ISP makes certain recommendations before accepting its advice.

The Telephone Company

The telephone company is normally the provider of the physical line and switching equipment necessary to move data from your local network to your access provider's network. Different types of Internet connections utilize different capabilities of the telephone system, but in general you will always end up paying the telco something for the use of its system to carry your connection. This charge is completely separate in most cases from the bills you receive from your ISP, and can consist of flat-rate monthly fees and usage fees, depending on your location and type of connection. In addition to these repeating fees, the telephone company will assess setup charges for the installation of your line.

You'll read about these issues further when you look at specific connection types later in the chapter.

Internet Service Providers

ISPs (Internet Service Providers—also referred to as NAPs, or Network Access Providers) are the folks who take responsibility for connecting you to the Internet. Some ISPs are national (or even international) organizations that maintain geographically large, high-speed networks that are the "backbone" of the Internet, whereas others are local organizations that supply expertise and a local connection point for others connecting to a larger provider.

In terms of the organization of the Internet, ISPs usually take the role of purchasing an expensive Internet connection from a larger provider that can handle huge amounts of data, and then reselling portions of that capacity to customers like you. The role of ISPs is therefore that of a buffer between the general public and the primary high-speed network managers like Sprint, MCI, and others.

This situation is rapidly changing as the large providers, including the local telephone and cable television service providers, are preparing to offer Internet access directly to consumers or businesses. Because so many ISPs are small, local organizations, there will likely be a severe shakeout in the industry in the coming months as many local ISPs find themselves unable to compete on pricing or efficiency with the large telecommunications firms beginning to enter the Internet access market.

I talk about some of the consequences of this shift in the industry when I discuss choosing access providers later in this chapter.

The Connection to the ISP

The most critical part of your link to the Internet is usually the portion between your premises and your ISP's location. Because it's the part of your connection that has the most effect on your server's perceived speed as well as the part that will cost you the most over time, you should evaluate your alternatives carefully before settling on a particular type.

Connection Speeds Revealed

Most connection types are described in terms of speed, or bandwidth, meaning the amount of data they are theoretically capable of transferring in a given amount of time. Bandwidth is usually listed as some number of K, like a 28.8K modem, where 1K indicates 1,024 bits passing over the line each second.

Note that network connection speeds, despite being quoted quite often as some number of "K," are in units of kilobits, not kilobytes, as you might be used to from seeing file sizes reported as K in the Finder. For the rest of this chapter, I'll use the term "Kbps" to indicate the bandwidth of a particular connection and "K" to indicate the kilobytes per second measure, just to avoid confusion. Because one byte is made up of eight bits, a 28.8Kbps connection speed is equivalent to a file transfer rate of 28.8/8 kilobytes per second, or 3.6K. So when you talk about different kinds of connection types and you're trying to estimate how much information you can actually move over a given line, be sure to convert the quoted speed in kilobits per second into the more familiar kilobytes per second to estimate the time required to transfer files (divide the Kbps number by eight to determine the speed in units of kilobytes).

Most connections also take advantage of some sort of compression scheme that can increase the amount of information they can carry—the actual bandwidth doesn't change, but more information is being packed into each bit. A good 28.8kbps modem can move raw data files at nearly 5-6K (kilobytes) per second with compression. Nevertheless, there are many factors that reduce the actual maximum transfer rate over a particular line well below the theoretical maximum—as a rule of thumb, you can expect actual average bandwidth to run at approximately 75 percent of the rated bandwidth. On a 28.8Kbps modem (theoretically rated at 3.6K), for example, you can plan on being able to use about 2.5K reliably.

Now, let's take a look at what's available!

Modems and Dialup Lines

If you are on a very limited budget, or otherwise want to experiment with a Web server without committing a great deal of money to the project, you can use a 28.8Kbps modem over a standard phone line, just as most people do when accessing the Internet as clients. The primary difference is that, as a Web server, you need to obtain a static IP address from your ISP.

Normally, when you use SLIP or PPP connections to reach the Internet, your Mac is assigned a new IP address from a pool maintained by your provider every time you dial into the ISP's modems. This is unworkable for a Web server, because your location on the Internet (as represented by your IP address) will change every time you call into the ISP and none of your clients will be able to find your server from one day to the next.

Normally, obtaining a static IP address means that the ISP installs a phone line and modem just for you that nobody else can use, and you receive a phone number for that modem. Then, every time you dial the ISP, you connect over the same line and receive the same IP address.

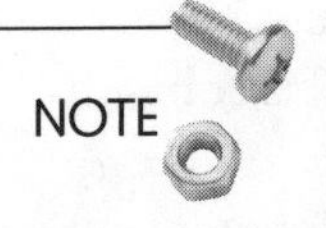

If you want to get the maximum amount of bandwidth over your connection, both you and your ISP should be using the same brand and model of modem, if at all possible. The throughput obtained by matching modems can often be significantly higher than that available when different brands talk to each other, even if they both are supposedly using the same protocol.

Finally, even if you need to connect only one Mac to the Internet, look into adding a router between your Mac and the modem. Routers have the capability to manage TCP/IP traffic in such a way as to keep your modem running at peak efficiency, and also have the capability to detect when the phone connection drops and will automatically redial to keep the line open.

Let your Mac do what it does best—Web serving—and let the router handle what it does best—managing TCP/IP traffic and maintaining your connection to the Internet.

If you've spent much time working with PPP or SLIP connections, you know that the Mac sometimes has difficulty knowing when the modem is in trouble—keeping the line open (and your Web server up) can be a real hassle without using a device designed for that task, like a router. Let your Mac do what it does best—Web serving—and let the router handle what it does best—managing TCP/IP traffic and maintaining your connection to the Internet.

28.8Kbps service is most appropriate if you have only one computer you need to connect to the Internet, and if you are willing to limit your server to a fairly low volume of traffic, although you may be surprised how well such a setup actually performs. The investment is fairly minimal, and it can be an excellent way to experiment with serving the Web without spending several hundred dollars each month on your connection.

ISDN

ISDN, or Integrated Services Digital Network, is nothing more than a digital phone line. In the past, if you wanted to transport the digital on/off signals of computer communications over the types of lines you use for voice communication (called POTS, for Plain Old Telephone Service—a lot friendlier name than what ISDN stands for), you needed a modem at each end of the phone line to translate signals to and from an analog form.

ISDN still requires a kind of modem (called a Terminal Adapter, or TA) and usually a router as well, but allows data to travel over the same phone lines you are using now in a digital form, thereby increasing both the amount of data that can flow over the line and the types of communication, such as video-based teleconferencing, that can be performed. You can also use an ISDN line to carry low-volume traditional telephone service (hence the name "Integrated Services...") at the same time as it moves your TCP/IP traffic back and forth—look for this capability when you shop for TAs and routers if it interests you. You may be able to plug your existing phones directly into the ISDN interface, or you might need to purchase new ISDN-capable phones to conduct voice conversations, depending on the model of TA/router you choose.

Unlike standard telephone service, ISDN lines require an external source of power to operate. In the event of a power failure, ISDN phones will no longer work. If you use an ISDN connection for both voice and data communications, I advise maintaining a traditional POTS line as well for emergencies.

ISDN lines are normally sold by telephone companies in the form of a BRI (Basic Rate Interface), which consists of two data, or "B," channels (that actually carry data) and one "D" channel, which carries signaling information and other overhead. All three "channels" co-exist on the same telephone line, much like a television cable carries sound and video information simultaneously. The two B channels are each capable of carrying 64Kbps of data and can work together on a single connection, so that a single ISDN BRI interface can carry up to 128Kbps at a time.

ISDN BRI connections require you to purchase a device called a *terminal adapter* (TA), which translates the signals from your phone line into IP packets for your server or local network. You can plug the ISDN line directly into your Mac using an ISDN TA Nubus or PCI card, but most people find that they gain more flexibility and use out of the ISDN line by attaching the TA to a router that can be connected over an Ethernet network to their server and any number of other computers on a LAN. Some manufacturers are beginning to offer combined ISDN routers and TAs, which makes life a lot simpler and a bit less expensive. You should ask your ISP or local telephone company about this when discussing its equipment recommendations.

One important point is that you should decide on your ISP and find out what brand of ISDN router it is using before purchasing your own. Just like modems, you'll generally find that having routers from the same company talk to each other produces much better and more reliable throughput than communication between two different brands of equipment. This isn't absolutely critical, but if you want to get the fullest possible use out of your ISDN connection, matching manufacturers is the simplest method of doing so.

> You should definitely choose a provider before purchasing your communication equipment, as it may have requirements that limit your options.

In terms of Internet connections, ISDN offers by far the most flexibility and opportunity for upgrades in the future, and is being pushed hard by some phone companies as the next stage in residential telecommunications. In many metropolitan areas, ISDN connections from the local telephone company can be had for about $30.00 a month plus a per-minute usage fee, and many ISPs are offering flat-rate 128Kbps ISDN service for $100.00–$150.00 per month. Installation and setup charges can vary quite a bit, from free to the hundreds of dollars, so you'll have to ask around to find out what's current in your area.

Because ISDN is so new, monthly pricing is unpredictable from one area to the next. Some telephone companies are still adding per-minute surcharges to ISDN line usage, whereas others allow you to make unlimited numbers of local calls for free (flat rate service) once the monthly standard bill is paid. If you live in a flat-rate area, you can easily save hundreds of dollars per month by not paying usage fees. You'll have to ask the telephone companies and ISPs about the current local tariffs.

Frame-Relay versus Leased Lines

Other than ISDN, most connection types that are faster than a standard modem can handle fall into either the frame-relay or leased-line models.

A leased line requires the phone company to reserve a physical connection through its switching centers for communication between you and your ISP. In other words, there's a bunch of transistors with your name on them. It also normally requires that your ISP install a line between the ISP and the telephone company's offices that is reserved for your use. This model offers the advantage of maintaining a connection all the way through to your ISP that is exclusively yours, but the extra line installations can be very expensive.

Frame-relay service follows the same model between you and the telephone company, but with frame-relay you then share a single line between the telephone company and your ISP with your ISP's other frame-relay customers. This is usually less expensive to set up, because only one line needs to be installed rather than two. The disadvantage is that because you are sharing a single line into your ISP, your usage plus that of the ISP's other customers may exceed the capacity of the single line to the ISP—so if you choose frame-relay service, be sure to ask your ISP how many other customers use the same line, and at what point the ISP would plan to upgrade its connection to handle an increased amount of traffic.

Either option requires you to install a device called a CSU/DSU (Channel Service Unit/Data Service Unit), which is functionally similar to an ISDN TA, plus a router, on your end of the connection.

You may be offered another type of service than a straightforward leased line or frame-relay connection. New models for network connections (and new acronyms) seem to sprout up almost daily, but most are just variations on these two types.

With that bit of background, let's look at some of the pricier (and faster) options for Internet connections.

56K Service Connection

56Kbps service was once the most common type of connection for those who wanted more speed than a traditional modem could provide yet could not justify the high price of a T1 (see the next section). It has been supplanted in most areas by ISDN service, and there really is very little to recommend it at this point. The initial startup costs of a 56Kbps connection are usually quite a bit higher than for ISDN, and the CSU/DSU you'll need to purchase for your side of the connection isn't often usable for any other type of service. The monthly prices for 56Kbps service from an ISP tend to be close to that of ISDN, if not a bit more, although the actual cost will depend somewhat on how busy the line is if your monthly ISDN cost is based on usage rather than a flat rate.

The advantages of 56Kbps service are that it may be available in areas where ISDN is not and that your monthly bills may be less than those for an ISDN connection with per-minute charges. It's also the fastest type of connection you are likely to use with frame-relay service.

T1s and Beyond

A T1 line is rated at 1.5Mbps—that's the equivalent of about 24 standard 128Kbps ISDN lines, and is more than all but the highest traffic Web sites really need. Just like 56Kbps connections, T1s require their own CSU/DSU equipment, a router, and the installation of new phone lines. They also usually require the use of leased-line service rather than frame-relay. If you do need a T1 or faster connection, I would suggest talking directly to the major NAPs, such as BBN, Sprint, UUnet or MCI, to see whether you can skip the local ISP and connect directly to a backbone network.

You can also obtain a "fractional" T1, which is sold, like ISDN, in pairs of data channels. The advantage of the fractional approach is that you'll already have all the necessary equipment installed for a full T1 if you decide to upgrade at a later date without paying monthly fees for the full T1 when you're just starting.

Most people using a fractional T1 are setting their bandwidth at 256Kbps, which should handle even a large organizations' needs nicely.

If your site needs multiple T1s or an even faster connection, you'll need the services of a professional network administrator to set yourself up effectively. Table 4.1 compares T1 lines with other common connection types and can be found later in this chapter.

Single-Server Options

All the previous options assume that you are trying to establish a connection from your home or place of business to an ISP. This is a common situation for people establishing a new Web server. If you're interested in maintaining only a single server, and don't need a high-speed Internet connection for other purposes, you might want to consider using one of the following two options instead.

Colocation

Colocation refers to the practice of placing your server physically on the site of your ISP, normally with a connection to the Internet through the provider's own internal high-speed network, such as an Ethernet network. Most people choosing colocation do so because it's cheaper (no telephone company costs or expensive routers to install at your own site) and more reliable, because there are fewer hops, or intervening networks, between your server and the rest of the world. It also tends to provide more bandwidth to your site than you might be able to afford otherwise, and providers often have power and data-backup systems installed that would be expensive for you to set up on your own.

The tradeoff is that you no longer have direct access to your server and that others may be able to obtain access to your server without your knowledge. Placing your server at your provider's premises, whether it is in the open or in a secured area, requires a significant degree of trust in your provider. This is a special concern for Macintosh servers, and is discussed in more detail in Chapter 10, "Security."

It is possible and feasible to manage a server remotely over TCP/IP or other types of connections from your home, work, or elsewhere. The details are discussed in Chapter 13, "Walkaway Serving."

Forming a Co-Op

Another option is to engage in cooperative sharing of a high-speed line with other server administrators by establishing a local network with everybody's server at one location and then subscribing to a single high-speed connection to an ISP. Because everyone involved is interested solely in an inexpensive connection rather than making a profit from the provision of the connection itself, a shared T1, 56K, or ISDN line will usually offer significantly more bandwidth per dollar spent by the individual participants than they would receive when purchasing their connections individually.

A side benefit of establishing a co-op is that you can get together with other Macintosh Web servers and form an all-Mac site. Many ISPs are unfamiliar with Macintosh-specific issues, and working with an all-Macintosh network can make troubleshooting easier and more efficient.

Generally, a single individual is designated as the main administrator and is responsible for network problems, contacting the ISP in times of trouble, and so on. Many co-ops also make arrangements to share some administrative responsibilities among the co-op members, use a common backup system, and generally help each other work more efficiently. Effective sharing of responsibilities is dependent upon the expertise and trust that members share, but if you already know a few people in your area who might be interested (or are willing to make new friends!), forming a cooperative can be an innovative and effective solution to your Internet connection needs.

Estimating Your Bandwidth Needs

Estimating the bandwidth your site will require is still a bit of a black art—and I'm not even going to pretend that I have a magic formula to plug all the numbers into that will report your ideal type of connection. Table 4.1 summarizes some rough guidelines, but remember that you can serve any site through any connection—the type that you actually need depends on the relative priorities you place on speed and on your budget.

Table 4.1 *Internet Connection Types*

Type	Bandwidth	Hits/Day	Type of Site
Modem	28.8Kbps	Several hundred	User groups; small non-profits or businesses with little Web presence.
56K	56Kbps	Several thousand	Small business with an active Web site; small commercial Web site.
ISDN	128Kbps	Tens of thousands	Small schools; mid-sized commercial sites.
Fractional T1	256Kbps	Fifty thousand	Elementary school or small college; more than one Web server.
T1	1500Kbps	Hundreds of thousands	Large organization; several Web servers.
T3	45000Kbps	Are you insane?	Netscape's home page.

One nice way to experience different options yourself (and meet a few Mac Web site administrators in the process) is to visit http://www.brad.net/, which maintains lists of Macintosh-based Web sites organized by location, type of connection, and type of Mac used. Figure 4.1 shows the home page, which displays most of the options available for exploring the listings.

Browse around and visit a few configurations to get a feel for their performance. If you have questions, email the site administrators—most will be willing to share some of their experiences and impressions with you.

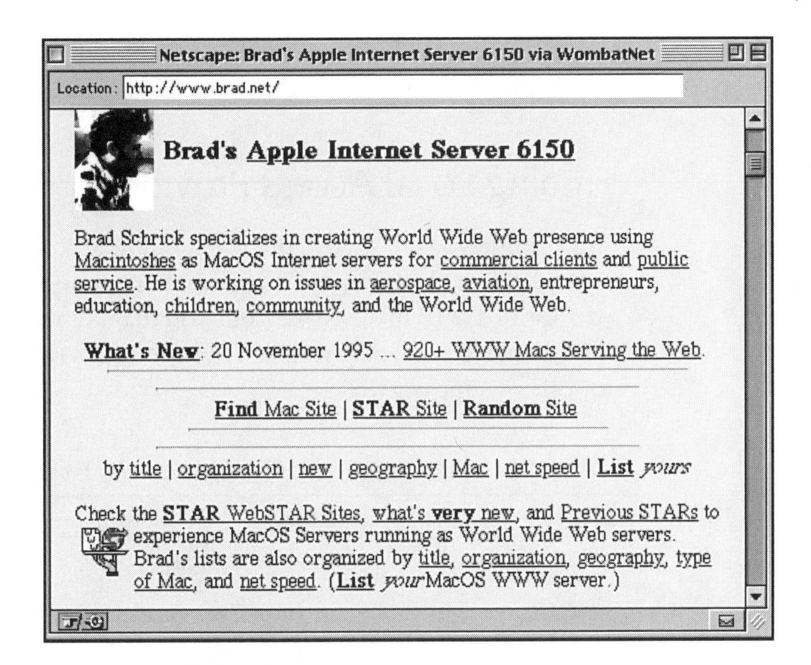

Figure 4.1 *The* brad.net *Macintosh WWW server list.*

Choosing an Access Provider

Internet access providers (synonymous with ISPs) are the folks you will pay (and pay, and pay...) to create and maintain the connection between your premises and the rest of the Internet. The level of support and professionalism displayed by your ISP is absolutely critical to the success of your Web site. Fortunately, ISPs are now becoming ubiquitous in most urban areas and even some rural areas now have a choice of two or three local ISPs, so you should have some real options to explore.

Unfortunately, many of these providers are understaffed, underfunded, and generally underpowered for the services they offer. Establishing a functional ISP is fairly straightforward, but establishing a quality operation is neither trivial nor inexpensive.

In this section, I'll show you how to find local providers and evaluate them before committing to a particular one.

Finding Local Access Providers

After you have Web access, there are a number of sites that list providers by area code, city, or even local telephone prefix. I've provided a list of URLs in Table 4.2, but you may want to search one of the Internet directories, such as Yahoo! http://www.yahoo.com/ for other listings as well.

Table 4.2 *URLs to Access Providers on the Web*

Site Name	URL
The List	http://thelist.com/
POCIA	http://www.celestin.com/
CommerceNet	http://www.commerce.net/directories/products/isp/
ISP Meta-List	http://www.herbison.com/herbison/iap_meta_list.html

Comparing Providers

After you have a list of ISPs to investigate, you can proceed to "interview" them before making a decision. Look very carefully at your list and set aside the time to investigate all the ISPs thoroughly—a good ISP will allow you to focus on your server rather than its problems, whereas a bad one can easily ruin your site's performance and budget.

Consider the following issues when making your provider decision:

- ☐ Topology of provider's connection
- ☐ Reliability of the ISP's internal and external connections
- ☐ Capacity of the ISP's connection to the Internet compared to the amount of capacity it sells to its customers

- ☐ Terms of service agreements
- ☐ The availability and skill of the ISP's technical support personnel
- ☐ Current customers' comments
- ☐ Commentary in local newsgroups
- ☐ Startup costs

The sections that follow discuss these issues in detail.

Topology

What is the bandwidth of the provider's connection to the Internet? How many routers and networks will your site's traffic need to travel across to get from the Internet into your site?

These are the kinds of questions that an examination of an ISP's topology can answer. Your provider should be able to produce a map of its connections and internal networks that shows the path that TCP/IP traffic will take between your proposed site and the world outside your provider's domain. This map should identify all the routers used by your ISP and indicate the bandwidth of each local network your site's traffic will need to cross.

If you're uncomfortable with analyzing this information, you should take it to a friend or consultant who can make a quick evaluation of the information your prospective ISP has provided. A full tutorial on analyzing ISP network topology would take up a couple more chapters of this book and you probably have enough to read already. In general, the fewer routers between you and the Internet, and the faster the intervening networks are, the better off you'll be.

Redundancy

As you know, your connection to your provider depends on a router or gateway at your provider's site that moves data to and from your own site—but what happens when that router experiences a problem or otherwise fails to perform? Your provider should be able to tell you how it would cope with router failure, and hopefully it will be able to assure you that it has backup devices or software that can take over the functions of the failed router should that become necessary.

Another aspect of redundancy is in the ISP's connection to the outside world—the best ISPs will have multiple access points to the Internet (using different providers) so that if one were to fail, the others can be used to maintain connectivity. This is still a bit of an unusual situation, but can be a big plus if you must reduce downtime on your server to the absolute minimum.

Capacity

If you've ever used commercial airlines, you already know about the concept of overbooking—the idea that because some percentage of tickets tend not to be used, the airline can sell more seats than exist on the plane in hopes that all the ticket holders won't show up at once.

Internet access providers, unfortunately, often subscribe to the same principle of overselling their capacity. For example, a T1 line is equivalent to 24 ISDN 64Kbps data channels—that's 12 basic ISDN customers. But because it's unlikely that all 12 customers will be using their full 128Kbps bandwidth at any given moment, the provider may feel perfectly comfortable selling ISDN to 10, 20, or even 30 different customers like you, all being pumped through the one T1 line.

This is a big no-no, so be sure and compare the information the ISP provides about what connections they provide to customers to the bandwidth of its Internet connection. If the sum of the customers' bandwidth is anywhere near that of the ISP's own connection, be warned that you may end up with less speed than you expected.

Terms of Service Agreements

Do not, and I must repeat myself, **Do Not** sign on with a provider that does not use written, signed contracts that detail its agreements with you. Ideally, there should be performance clauses such that your placement in its internal network (your topology) is guaranteed and some penalty or escape clause if you suffer more than a tiny amount of downtime due to its equipment failures.

You must protect yourself—lack of a written service agreement is a giant, red, flashing, stop sign for your continued association with such a provider.

Technical Support

The single most reliable indicator of an ISP's professionalism and commitment to its customers is the availability and skill of its technical support. When your connection to your provider has a problem, you need someone to be aware of the problem immediately and have the resources to solve it as soon as possible. Senior technical people need not be on-site 24 hours a day, but at least one senior person should always be available during business hours, and someone should always answer the phones whenever you call.

Talking to current and former customers is probably the best way to research the quality of a provider's support, but you can do a little investigating on your own by simply calling the technical support lines at odd hours.

Current Customers

Ask for a list of names and phone numbers for current customers of the providers you are considering. If they cannot or will not provide one, move on. If you do receive one, call them up and bend their ear as much as they will allow you to do so. Ask them about downtime they have experienced, technical support, and their general satisfaction with service. Most network and server administrators are happy to share their experiences, good or bad, so don't be shy.

WARNING

Do be careful not to compare apples to oranges—if all the current customers are using 56K frame-relay connections and you are

continues

intending to open up an ISDN line, their experiences with reliability may be no indicator of your own. Many providers will, upon realizing that a new service like ISDN is in demand, buy the equipment without sufficient expertise to manage it effectively. Try to find individuals whose setup is as similar as possible to the one you plan for yourself.

Local Newsgroups

Local newsgroups can be a great resource for soliciting real-world opinions of a provider's reliability and support. Most cities have a local newsgroup or even several (here in Pittsburgh, they are all under the alt.pgh.* hierarchy), so be sure and ask for opinions before committing to a particular provider.

One caveat—many people on the local newsgroups are accessing the Internet via dialup connections like SLIP or PPP. Experiences with these types of services may not necessarily be indicative of how a provider performs with its dedicated customers who access its system through entirely different means. You should probably discount reports of problems with busy modem lines, dropped connections and the like, but pay close attention to how people feel the provider treats them when there is a problem. Again, support is a critical part of the package an access provider is offering you.

Startup Costs

Any full-time connection to the Internet requires a hefty investment in networking equipment at your end of the line to the provider. Some providers, however, also seem to take it for granted that you will bear the cost of its purchase of similar equipment at its own site. Such equipment is necessary to maintain your connection, but if the equipment, like an ISDN router, is intended solely for use by you, your service agreement should make it clear that you own said equipment and can take it with you if you ever decide to switch to a different provider. If you do not obtain such a clause, you should be equally clear that you are not willing to bear the full cost of such equipment. If the provider is able to re-use the equipment with other customers, you should not pay the full price of such investments unless you also obtain ownership.

NOTE

The Internet, and Internet service opportunities, has produced the biggest crop of get-rich-quick hucksters since the telephone was invented. Look for established providers with an existing customer base and remember that you generally get what you pay for in connectivity. Maintaining a reliable Internet connection is not technically difficult, but it does require an investment in personnel and equipment that can be substantial. Most providers are UNIX-based, and UNIX systems require a great deal of expensive expertise to manage effectively. An inexpensive monthly access fee may not be so inexpensive if your site is inaccessible on a regular (or even irregular) basis.

Selecting and Registering a Domain Name

The first contact any client has with your site is with your domain name. An easy to use and remember domain name will help immensely in assisting clients to find your site and to recall your URL when they want to return to your server.

This section reviews each step of choosing, registering, and verifying a new domain name.

NOTE

If you are setting up a Web server within an organization that already has Internet access, you probably already have a domain name to use, something like `mycompany.com`, which you just stick a www. in front of to name your server. Talk to your network administrator about naming your server if you are attaching it to a pre-existing local TCP/IP network.

Choosing a Good Domain Name

Unless you are running a server on a very large internal network, such as might be found at a university, the complete hostname for your server will likely consist of only three parts—such as www.mydomain.com. The mydomain.com portion is the part you are registering, and is the domain name for your server. After your domain name is registered, you (or the person handling your DNS services) can add or change hosts in that domain easily, with updates going into effect within a day or two. Hosts are indicated by the portion of the server name preceding the domain name, like the www part of www.mydomain.com.

The Root Domain

The last part of your domain name (the "root" domain) is determined by your location and the nature of the organization requesting the new domain. In the United States, this portion normally reflects the type of organization responsible for that name, as shown in Table 4.3.

Table 4.3 *Common Root Domains for Internet Service in the United States*

Root Domain	Organization Type
.com	Commercial or personal domain
.net	Network access providers (including ISPs)
.edu	Educational institutions
.org	Private non-profit organizations
.gov	Governmental organizations
.mil	Military domains
.ito	International Treaty Organizations

Outside of the United States, the last part of the domain name is usually based on the nation in which the domain exists—some examples are presented in Table 4.4, but the full list is much longer and can be found at the URL ftp://ftp.rs.internic.net/netinfo/iso3166-countrycodes.

Table 4.4 *Examples of International Internet Root Domains*

Root Domain	Country
.uk	United Kingdom
.jp	Japan
.au	Australia
.de	Germany

You will occasionally see domain names that reflect a geographic location within the United States, such as pgh.pa.us, meaning Pittsburgh, Pennsylvania, USA. This is a fairly uncommon usage now, and I don't recommend using this scheme unless you are advised to by your ISP.

The next part of your domain name (the mydomain portion of mydomain.com) is the one you are most concerned with choosing carefully. You can choose virtually any name that has not already been registered, with the following restrictions.

Domain Name Guidelines

Follow these restrictions to avoid picking an improper domain name:

- The total length of the domain name should be less than 25 characters, including the periods—mydomain.com is 12 characters long. Shorter is always better and is strongly encouraged.
- The domain name should consist solely of standard alphanumeric characters (A–Z, a–z, 0–9) and dashes ("-").
- The domain name may not begin with a dash, although it may begin with a number. I strongly recommend you do **not** begin your domain with a number (such as 9isfine.com) because many programs check the first character of a hostname to determine if it is an IP address (all numbers) or a domain name (which must be converted to an IP address before use). You've been warned!
- You may not use underscores ("_") or spaces.

What name to choose is up to you and your own creativity, but any domain name should be fairly short, easy to remember and to type, and should express some aspect of your organization that allows the domain name to be guessed should it slip someone's memory (or bookmark file!).

Most business entities can simply use a variation of its corporate name, such as att.com for AT&T, ibm.com for IBM, or apple.com for Apple Computers. The goal, if practical, is to allow someone who knows of yourself or your organization, but not your Web site, to guess the domain name and connect to your site without ever seeing a link or URL to the site. Failing that, the domain name should at least be catchy and memorable—http://www.suck.com/ is a good example of the latter approach.

Registering a New Domain Name

All of the standard root domain names (*.com, *.edu, and so on) in the United States are maintained by a central registry called Inter-NIC (managed by Network Solutions, Inc.), which prevents duplicate domains from being used and maintains master tables of the domain name servers responsible for each domain.

The InterNIC provides two types of services you'll need to use—the Whois service, and domain name registration and updating. *Whois* is a program to provide information about existing domain names, so that's where you should look first to make sure that the domain name you'd like to use has not already been assigned.

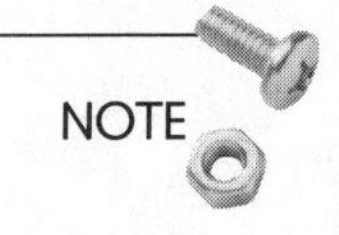

NOTE

> You do not need to actually have your server connected to the Internet before requesting a domain name—you can request one any time you like, and considering the backlog in processing requests at InterNIC, it's probably never too early.

Is it Available?

The first step in registering a new domain name is to ensure that your domain hasn't already been registered! From a Macintosh, the simplest way to use InterNIC's Whois services is via the Web:

Just for fun, let's try to register my name as a domain—Stewart.com.

First, use a Web browser to connect to the URL http://rs.internic.net/rs-internic.html. The page returned will look something like Figure 4.2.

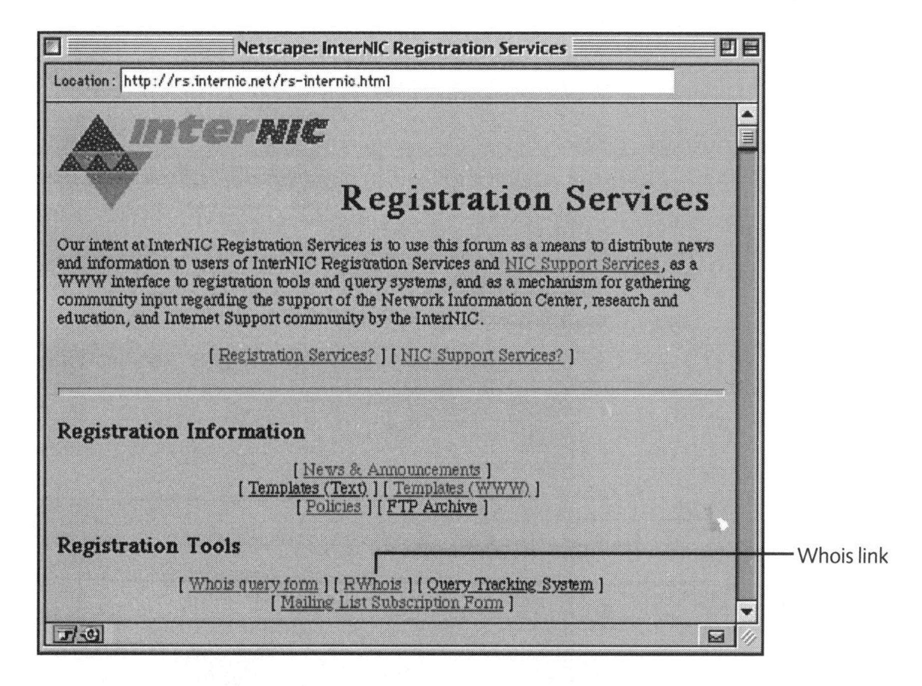

Figure 4.2 *InterNIC Registration Services home page.*

Now click the "Whois" link as indicated in Figure 4.2. You'll see a form with a single text box available for entering the domain name you'd like for yourself, as shown in Figure 4.3.

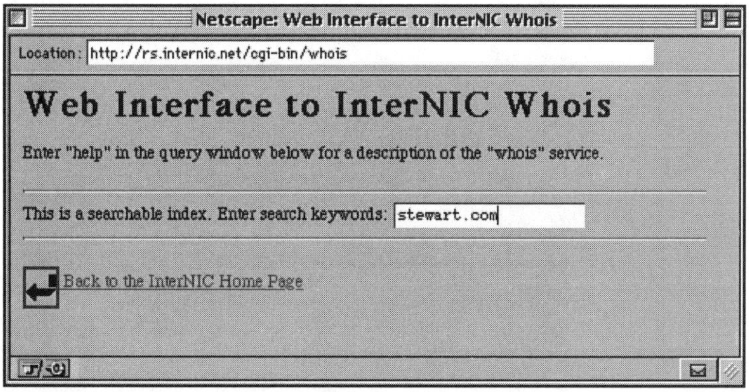

Figure 4.3 *Whois query form.*

Enter the domain name you are interested in and press Return. You see the screen shown in Figure 4.4.

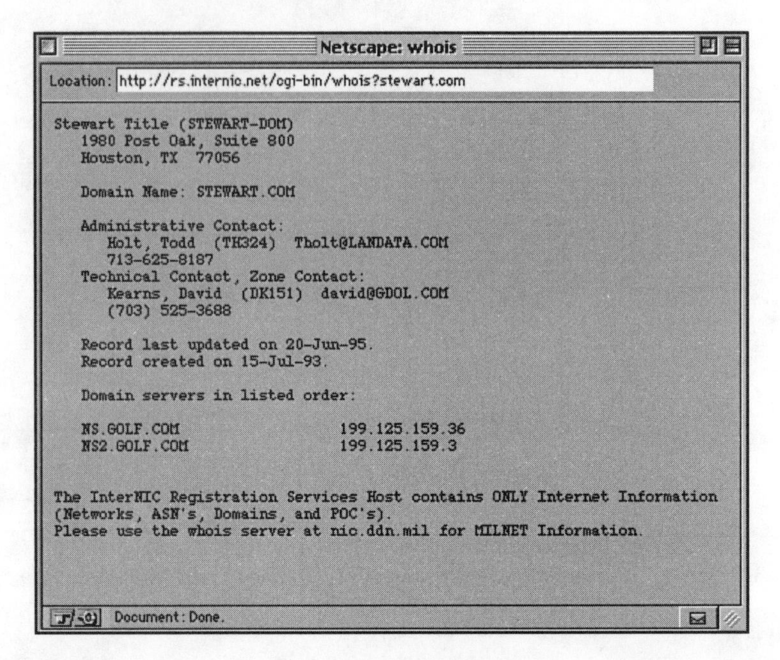

Figure 4.4 *Whois Response for* stewart.com.

Oh, well. It was worth a try. The response shows that stewart.com is already registered, and displays contact information should I want to reach the owners or administrators of the domain, as well as the IP addresses of the DNS servers for the domain.

Let's try the same process again for a new domain, Buskirk.com. The results appear in Figure 4.5.

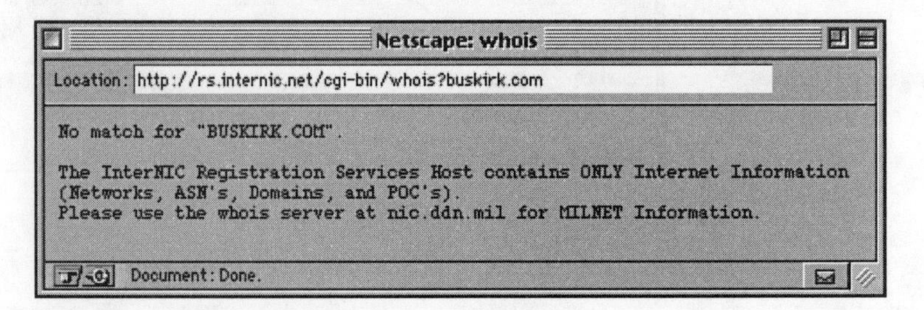

Figure 4.5 *Whois Response for* BUSKIRK.COM.

Hey! What a surprise—now I can request registration of my new domain...well, almost. There's a few details to take care of first.

> If your desired name is already in use, you can try contacting the administrative contact found in the Whois listing for that domain to investigate having the domain assigned to you. Any arrangements you make to take over an existing domain name are entirely between you and the existing domain name holder—InterNIC will not participate or mediate in domain name disputes, except that it will grant registration for disputed names to anyone who can provide evidence that they hold legal rights (in the form of a trademark) to that name.

What You Need

Before you can request a new domain name, InterNIC requires that a primary and secondary domain name server be configured to provide DNS lookup services for that domain. These DNS servers are the ones that appear in the Whois results shown in Figure 4.4. If you are working with an ISP, it normally will perform the DNS configuration and InterNIC request on your behalf, sometimes for a small fee. You can, in that case, skip the rest of this section as well as all of the next section and go directly to "Checking on Registration Progress" once your ISP has submitted your request.

If you want to request your domain name yourself, you will need your ISP or any other person who maintains a DNS server to provide you with the hostnames and IP addresses for the primary and secondary DNS servers that are responsible for your new domain *before* you fill out the request forms.

The exact request to make of your ISP is this:

> "I am going to register mydomain.com with InterNIC. Please configure your DNS servers to respond authoritatively for that domain name, and tell me the hostname and IP address each of the primary and secondary DNS servers when they are ready. I will also need the name, phone number, postal address, and email address of the zone contact for my domain."

You should receive a hostname and IP address for the two DNS servers within a day at the outside—maybe even while you're on the phone if the ISP really knows its stuff. The work necessary to accomplish this merely consists of editing a text file to add a couple of lines—don't let the ISP get away with claims that this is a major service or drawn-out affair.

By the way, you'll also need to be able to send the InterNIC 100.00 U.S. dollars to register your new domain. Registration fees are $50.00 per year, so this fee will pay for the first two years of usage of the domain. After two years, you'll need to pay another $50.00 every year to keep the domain active, otherwise it will be released back into the available pool.

Filling Out the Forms

To actually register your domain, return to the main InterNIC page (refer to Figure 4.2) and choose the "Templates(WWW)" link, which will take you to Figure 4.6.

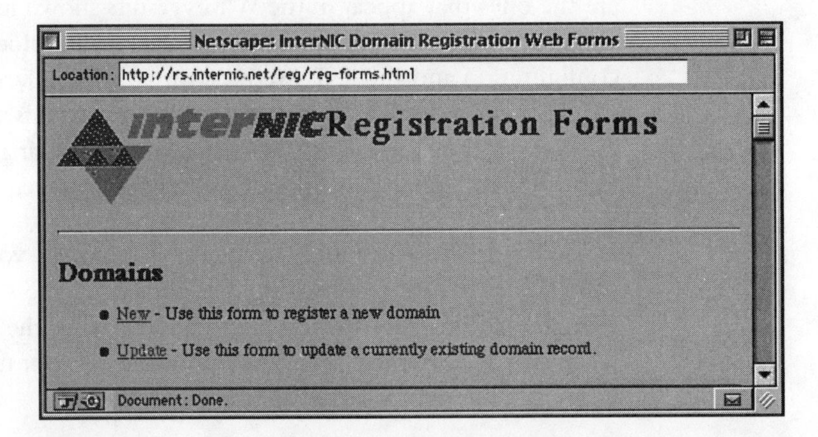

Figure 4.6 *Links to the InterNIC Registration request and update forms.*

Choose the "New" link. This will take you to the actual registration form, shown in Figure 4.7.

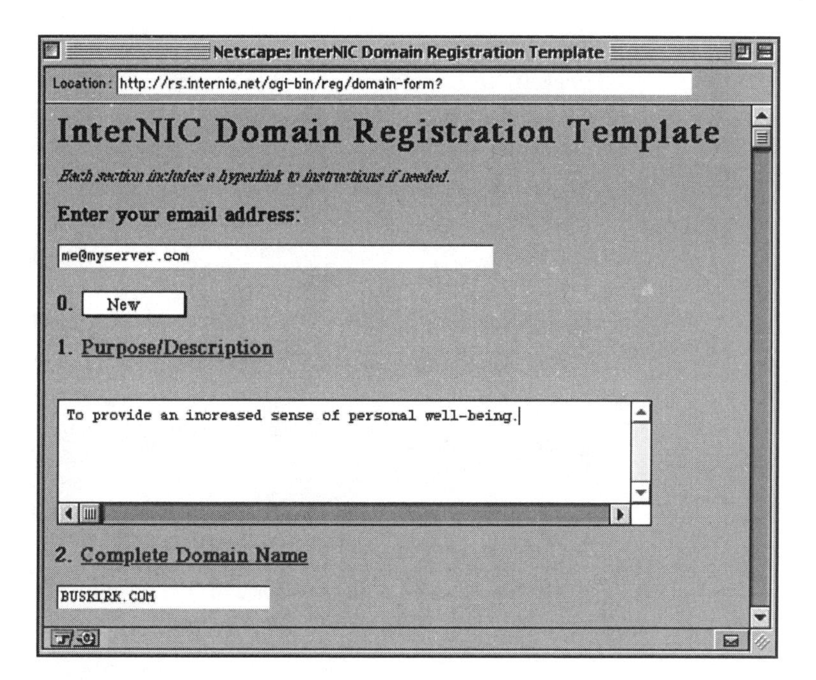

Figure 4.7 *Top of the InterNIC domain name request form.*

Enter your email address, a brief description of the use you plan to make of your domain in section 1, and the full domain name you are requesting (like buskirk.com) in section 2.

The next part of the page asks for contact information for the administrative and technical/zone contacts. Enter your own information in the administrative contact areas, and the information you received from your ISP in the technical contact areas. When you continue to scroll, you will find yourself at the screen shown in Figure 4.8.

Now you can enter the hostnames and IP addresses for the DNS servers that you received from your ISP. The popup menu has choices of "Postal" and "Email," which allow you to specify the method by which you would like to be billed for registering your domain name. Go ahead and specify your choice, and scroll on down the page. There is a contractual agreement there you should read over, and then click the "Submit" button on the bottom of the page.

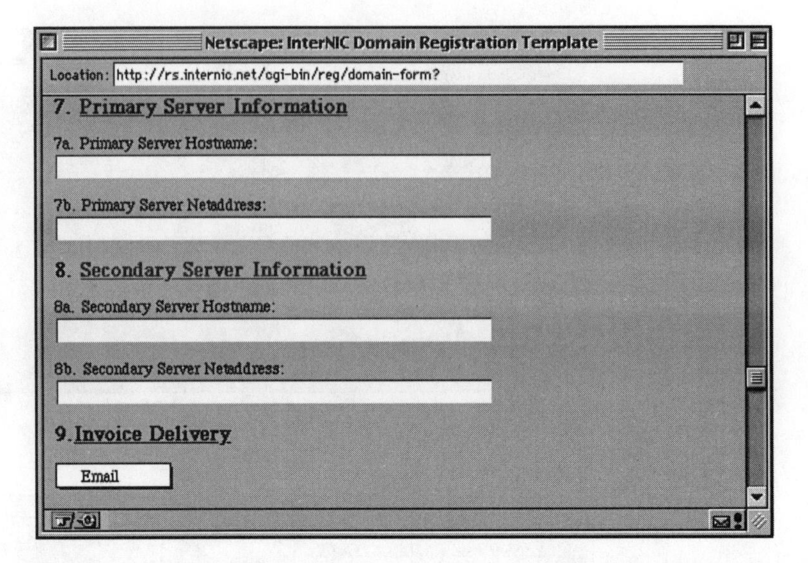

Figure 4.8 *Second part of the InterNIC domain name request form.*

If all went well, you will receive a response page with a tracking number for your request. Be sure to record it so that you can track the status of your request.

Checking on Registration Progress

After your request is accepted, you should check occasionally on your registration as it is processed. InterNIC provides a Web form for you to do so, but you will need a tracking number to perform the request—you should have received this number from whomever submitted your original domain name request.

With the tracking number in hand, go to http://rs.internic.net/cgi-bin/finger. Figure 4.9 shows this site.

Type the tracking number in the area provided and press Return. You should receive a status update like the one shown in Figure 4.10.

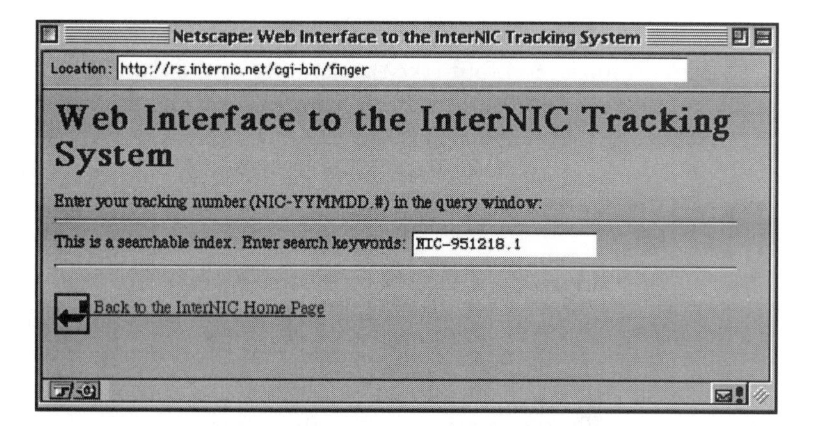

Figure 4.9 *InterNIC Request tracking form.*

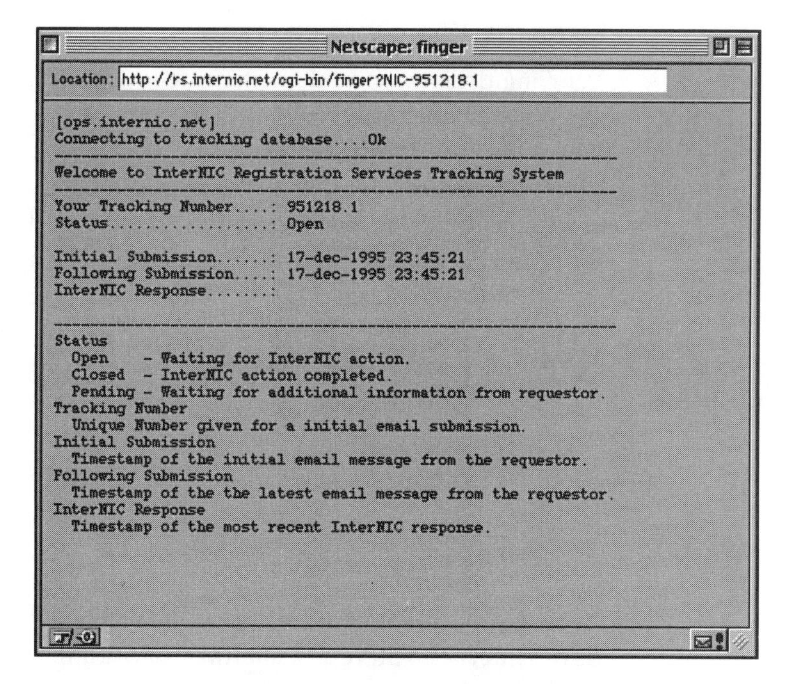

Figure 4.10 *Domain name request status display.*

The results are fairly self-explanatory (this request is still in progress), but take special note of the dates indicated for email communications both from and to InterNIC. You can use this information to verify that any email you send InterNIC in reference to your request was received properly, as well as verify that you haven't missed any email sent to you regarding your request.

If your domain name was already requested but is still being processed when you requested it for yourself, you may receive a message from InterNIC stating that the domain name is unavailable. If so, you'll need to either request a new domain name or use the Whois command to find and contact the holder of the domain to discuss transferring it to you.

Verifying Your Domain Name

Verifying that your new domain name is ready is as simple as using the Whois service again to look at its entry in the InterNIC database. Once the domain is listed there, you can expect to wait one to three days before your domain name is generally resolvable by other Internet hosts, as the information about your domain must be distributed across the Internet before everyone can use it in a URL.

> You may want to review Chapter 15 after you receive your new domain name to prepare for publicizing your site across the Internet. It's never too early to start planning your marketing efforts!

Summary

By now you should have an ISP, a domain name, and a connection to the Internet. You're sick and tired of reading about the Internet and are ready to install your server.

Well, that's a happy coincidence, because the next chapter is all about choosing and installing the Web server of your choice!

CHAPTER 5

The Show Begins—Choosing a Server

Finally, you get to the actual servers! Now that you have an Internet connection, or are in the process of obtaining one, it's time to take a look at the different HTTP servers available.

All of the servers discussed in this chapter are available in demo versions on the CD that came with this book (in the **Servers** folder), so you'll have an opportunity to try them for yourself before deciding which is best for you.

Besides reviewing the available Mac HTTP servers, I'll also explain some common methods of expanding a site's capabilities when necessary and show you how to test the demo servers on the CD. I encourage you to experiment with all of them before making a final decision about which your site will be built around.

Testing Servers

When experimenting with new Web servers, you may need to obtain information about your TCP/IP configuration that wasn't necessary when you were just using client programs like Netscape. Please read through this section before installing any HTTP servers on your Mac to ensure that you will be able to test them properly.

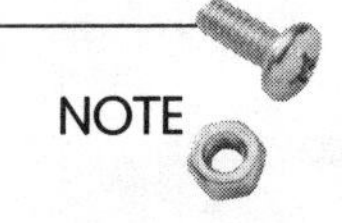

NOTE

Open Transport should have been released by the time you read this book, but the following instructions are for MacTCP only. If you have Open Transport installed on your Mac, you should check the Web site associated with this book for an updated tutorial (at `http://www.mcp.com/hayden/webserver`).

Net-Connected

If you can already use TCP/IP applications like Netscape from your Mac, you won't need to make any changes to your MacTCP or Open Transport configuration. You will, however, need to know your IP address or domain name to construct URLs to test your server.

To find out your IP address, open the MacTCP control panel shown in Figure 5.1.

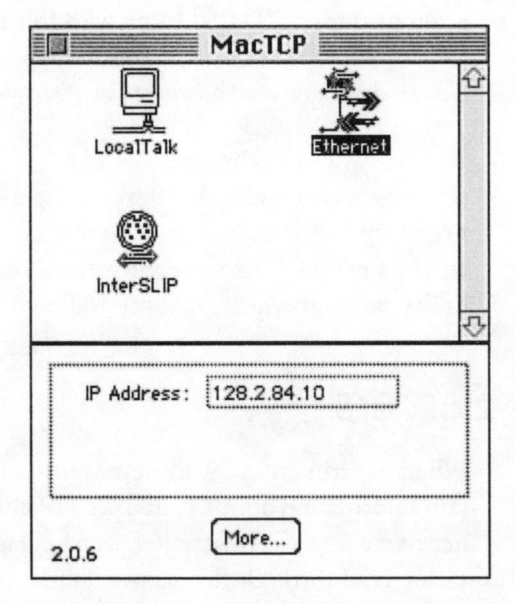

Figure 5.1 *The MacTCP control panel.*

Your IP address is shown in the lower half of the MacTCP window. In this case, your IP address would be 128.2.84.10. To determine your domain name, launch the IPNameTool utility (shown in Figure 5.2) found in the **Software Utilities** folder on your CD. Updates to this software can be found at http://www.aggroup.com/mm/d_n_g/goodies/goodies.html.

Type the IP address you obtained from MacTCP into the upper entry box and click the button marked "Address To Name." Your domain name should appear in the lower entry box within a few seconds. If an error message appears, your IP address may not be assigned to a domain name and you should ask whoever provides you with TCP/IP services how to obtain one. You can still test your server by using the IP address in place of the domain name in your URLs, such as http://128.2.84.10/.

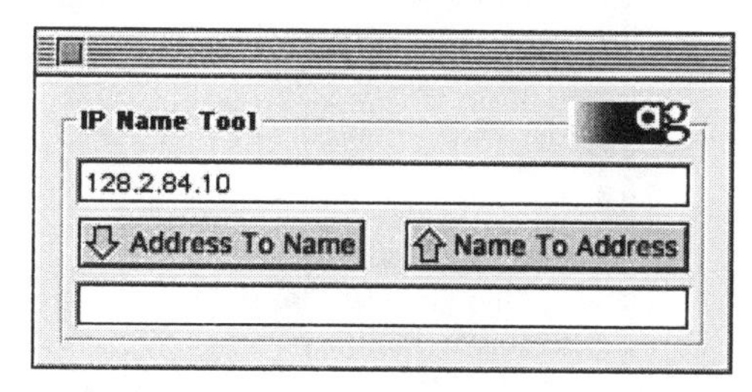

Figure 5.2 *You type the IP address into the upper entry box, as shown here.*

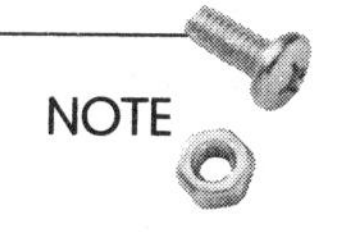

If you access the Internet via a dial-up connection that assigns a different IP address to your Mac every time you connect, you will need to find your current IP address, as previously explained, every time you dial up your service provider.

On a Single Machine

If you have access only to a single Mac for testing, you can test your server by using the steps that follow.

Configure MacTCP

Make sure you know how to re-create your current MacTCP configuration before making changes! Write down all the settings, making a little diagram of the dialog box if necessary, before changing anything.

Open the MacTCP control panel and click the "More" button. The MacTCP configuration window should appear, shown in Figure 5.3.

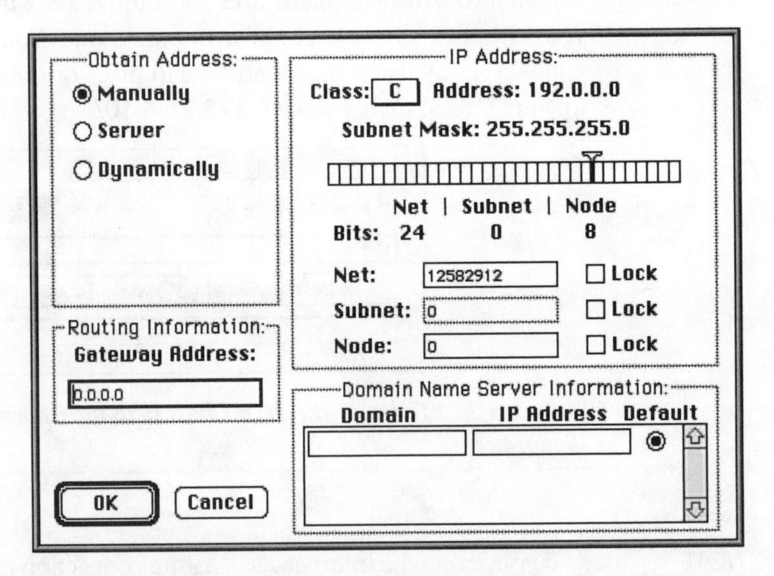

Figure 5.3 *MacTCP Configuration window.*

Your window should look like Figure 5.3 when you are finished with the following steps:

1. Click the "Manually" radio button in the upper left part of the window.
2. Type **0.0.0.0** in the "Gateway Address" input box.

3. Use the popup menu next to the word "Class" on the upper right to change the class to "C".

4. Blank out all the input boxes on the lower right by selecting and deleting any text that appears there.

The configuration window should appear as shown in Figure 5.3. Click the "OK" button to return to the MacTCP window, as shown in Figure 5.4.

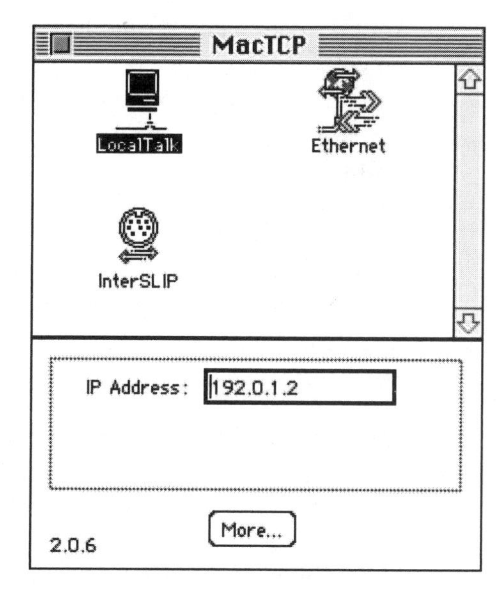

Figure 5.4 *The MacTCP main window.*

5. If the LocalTalk icon is not selected, click it to highlight it.

6. Type **192.0.1.2** in the IP Address entry box.

Your window should now look like Figure 5.4. Close the MacTCP window.

Create a Hosts File and Turn on AppleTalk

You'll also need to create a "Hosts" file for MacTCP so you can use a domain name in your URLs rather than an IP address. Follow these steps:

1. Create a new file in your favorite text editor (SimpleText works fine) with a single line as follows:

   ```
   <domain name>.  A     192.0.1.2.
   ```

   Your domain name should be whatever you anticipate using on your live server, such as www.myserver.com. Note the trailing dots appended to the domain name and the IP address—you must include them even though they aren't part of the hostname in a URL.

2. Save the file with the name "Hosts" in the top level of your System folder. If there is already a Hosts file there, replace it with your new one. Note that if you use a word processor like Microsoft Word to create the Hosts file, you'll need to save the file as text only, or MacTCP won't be able to read it.

   OK, almost done! The last thing you'll need to do is to make sure that AppleTalk services are active on your Mac, even if you aren't connected to a network.

3. Open the Chooser from the Apple menu and either verify that AppleTalk is turned on or click the "Active on restart" radio button on the lower right of the window. Click "OK" on any window that pops up when you click the radio button.

4. Now, restart your Mac, and you should be able to launch both server and client TCP/IP applications simultaneously. When typing in URLs, you should be able to use either the domain name you assigned in the hosts file, or the IP address "192.0.1.2" as the hostname, such as in http://192.0.1.2/.

You will need to have enough RAM available to run both the client and the server applications simultaneously, but the server should respond just as though you were an actual client accessing your server through the Internet, if a bit more slowly.

Netscape's browsers sometimes get confused when using this kind of configuration. If you start to experience problems, you can try restarting Netscape or use a different browser for your testing.

Choosing a Server

A year ago, there were only two HTTP servers available for the MacOS, neither of which was really high-performance applications. Today, new Web servers are being released every few months and there's a server application available that's suitable for just about any budget or type of site.

One of the primary decisions you'll need to make is whether you prefer using a single server application that can handle multiple Internet services like email, FTP, or common CGI functions internally, or if you prefer a bare-bones HTTP server that can have additional functionality by adding other server software or CGIs. Keep in mind your plans for the future as well as your current needs when you review the available applications. What is fine for now might not be the best choice in a few months.

All the Web servers described here are in rapid development, with prices and feature sets changing almost monthly. Please visit the Web sites I've listed for each server for more information. Updates are also available at the Web site for this book, `http://www.mcp.com/hayden/webserver`, if you'd like a "one-stop" overview of the current state-of-the-art in Mac Web servers.

Keep in mind as well that you can run multiple servers at a single site, either on different Macs or on the same machine. It is not uncommon to use the WebSTAR/SSL Security Toolkit. (…which should really be called the Security Server, in my unasked-for opinion. The "Toolkit" name is confusing.) to serve encrypted pages on the same machine as another, unencrypted server application if the secure server is not utilized often.

The following section describes each of the programs currently available for Macintosh-based Web serving. I've tried to confine my editorial comments to the end of each description so that you can compare the applications objectively before being subjected to my rants and raves. Once you get a server running, look through the documentation accompanying it to explore more advanced features.

> The QuickStart section for each server is designed to provide a simple way to start each server serving a few basic HTML pages and graphics. This is provided so that you can experiment with the performance and interface of each of the demonstration HTTP servers provided on the book's CD.

WEBSTAR

WebSTAR/MacHTTP/Commerce Toolkit

The first Mac-based HTTP server that saw widespread use was MacHTTP, a shareware program that rapidly became the HTTP server application of choice (out of all two of them!) for Mac Web sites. Ultimately, MacHTTP development was confined primarily to bug fixes, and it spawned a full-fledged commercial application, WebSTAR, distributed by StarNine Technologies. WebSTAR development has been rapid and robust since it went commercial, and has split into the standard HTTP version and an SSL-encrypted version (SSL refers to the Secure Socket Layer protocol, which was introduced by Netscape to enable secure communications over the Internet).

MacHTTP is still available for the Mac on a shareware basis, but is missing most of the high-performance features of WebSTAR and is suitable only for low-volume sites.

Overview

Contact: http://www.starnine.com/

Cost: About $500.00

Requirements: Macintosh running System 7.0.1 or later, with at least 8M of RAM.

Notable Features

Notable features include:

- Completely scriptable
- Highly advanced CGI support
- Remote logging options
- Background-only version included
- Can be administered from any networked Mac using the included administrative application
- User-defined log data
- Huge user/developer community

Potential Problems

Potential problems include:

- HTTP server only—no built-in FTP or email support
- Requires the use of AppleScript or the included administrative application to configure and administrate
- No built-in CGI functions
- Rudimentary activity summaries built-in
- Rudimentary user/password protection

QuickStart

Install WebSTAR on your hard disk by following the Installation Guide on the CD. Doing so will install a folder on your hard drive containing WebSTAR, the WebSTAR administrative application WebSTAR Admin, and HTML documentation and references.

Launch the WebSTAR application from the copy on your hard drive. You should see a window appear like the one shown in Figure 5.5.

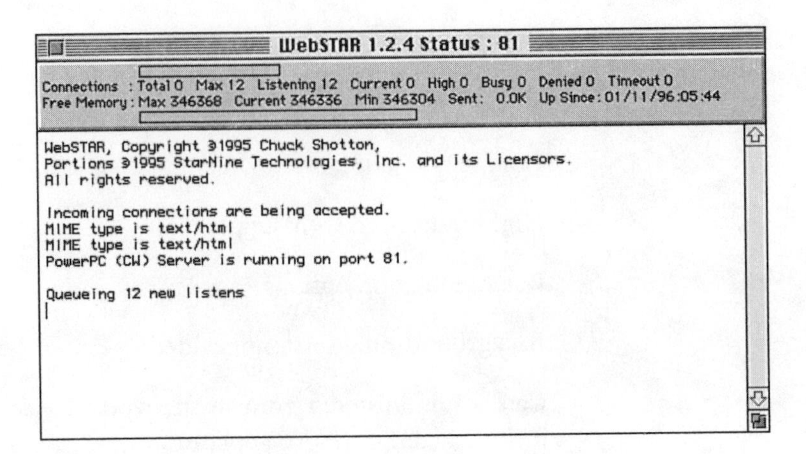

Figure 5.5 *WebSTAR server monitoring window.*

Using the domain name for the server if you have one, or the IP address if you do not (see the previous section, "Testing Servers," if you're not sure), request the default home page from the server with a URL like http://www.myserver.com/.

That's it! You're serving the Web.

Adding Content

When sending a URL to WebSTAR, the first file or folder name following the server's domain name refers to filenames of items in the root folder and its subdirectories. To serve files, you can either move the files or their folders into the root directory, or make aliases of them and place the aliases within the root directory. An example of two files and their URLs are shown in Figure 5.6.

Commentary

WebSTAR and its kin are designed with a minimalist philosophy—they are bare-bones HTTP engines that aim at performing one task (serving Web sites via HTTP) as rapidly and efficiently as possible. Not that they don't implement a bunch of great features to make that task easier and more efficient, but WebSTAR has always been aimed at creating a strong center that you and others can build upon and enhance, rather than attempting to anticipate all your needs and provide solutions in advance.

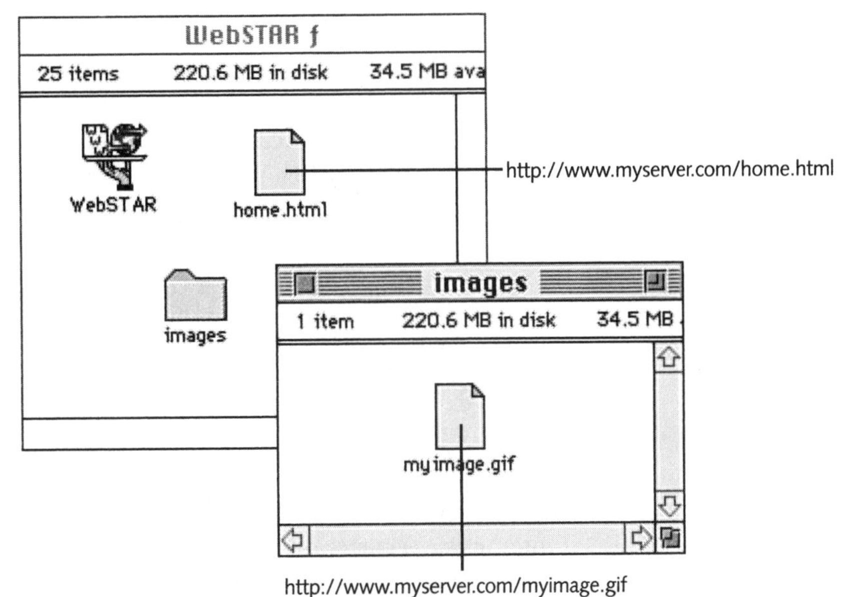

Figure 5.6 *URLs for files in WebSTAR root directory.*

The downside to this approach is that to add even the most rudimentary CGI functions to your site, you need to install and manage various other applications to provide those services. The upside is that there are many commercial and shareware applications that can be added to WebSTAR, because its design encourages development of CGI applications.

NOTE

Upcoming versions of WebSTAR have the capability for CGI authors to add CGI functions directly to the WebSTAR application, which will increase the efficiency and speed of many sites that depend on CGIs for their operation. Look for the "plug-in" version of WebSTAR at StarNine's Web site (`http://www.starnine.com/`) to take advantage of this feature when it is released.

WebSTAR is currently the most popular general Web server application for the Mac.

WebSTAR is currently the most popular general Web server application for the Mac. It has a huge and supportive user base, an excellent reputation for robust (read "crash-free") serving when used alone, and influences the standards and conventions of Macintosh Web serving similarly to how Netscape influences the development of Web browsers. A big thumbs-up!

InterServer Publisher

InterCon, who also produces Web browsers (NetShark) and other Mac TCP/IP applications, sell InterServer Publisher, a combined HTTP, FTP, and Gopher server with CGI interaction capabilities. InterServer is currently the only alternative to WebSTAR with robust CGI support, although many CGIs written for WebSTAR may not work with InterServer due to small differences in the way information is passed between the server and the CGI.

The SSL-Capable Version of WebSTAR

WebSTAR development has been rapid and robust since it became commercial, and has split into the standard WebSTAR version and an SSL-encrypted version (SSL refers to the Secure Socket Layer protocol, which is used by the Netscape browsers to enable secure communications over the Internet).

The Security Toolkit version of WebSTAR provides this SSL-capable version of WebSTAR. The SSL version can interact only with SSL-capable browsers—if you need to serve both encrypted and unencrypted content from your site, you'll need to use the Security Toolkit in addition to a standard server application. Serving SSL-encrypted Web pages also requires the purchase of a "digital ID" from Verisign, Inc. You can find out more about serving via SSL and the Verisign IDs at http://www.starnine.com/webstarssl/webstarssl.html and http://www.verisign.com/.

In all other respects, the SSL server is identical to the normal version and can use the same CGIs, and serve the same kinds of files, as WebSTAR.

Overview

Contact: http://www.intercon.com/newpi/InterServerP.html

Cost: About $500.00

Requirements: Macintosh 68030 or higher running System 7.0 or later, with at least 4M of RAM.

Notable Features

Notable features include:

- ☐ Supports HTTP, FTP, and Gopher services with one application
- ☐ High level of scriptability
- ☐ Automatic binhex or MacBinary file transfers
- ☐ Built-in macros for inserting information in HTML files at the time they are served
- ☐ Built-in imagemap functions
- ☐ Works in background via a system extension

Potential Problems

Potential problems include:

- ☐ CGI support not as robust as WebSTAR's—not compatible with many CGIs written for WebSTAR
- ☐ Poor logging capabilities
- ☐ No configurable MIME types
- ☐ Rudimentary user/password security
- ☐ Must be administered from server machine

QuickStart

Install InterServer Publisher by following the Installation Guide on the CD. Restart your Mac to activate the server extension.

Launch the InterServer Publisher Setup application you just installed on your hard disk and choose "Configure Servers..." from the Setup menu. You should see a window like the one shown in Figure 5.7.

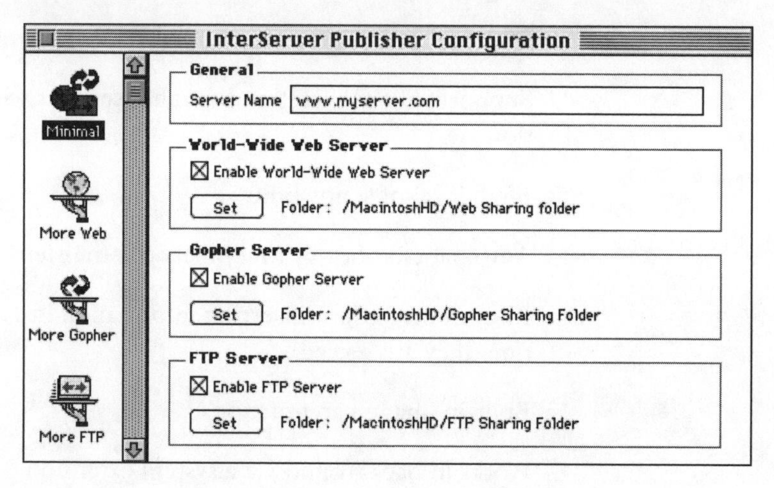

Figure 5.7 *The InterServer configuration window.*

Check off the boxes for the Internet services you want to activate. Each service is assigned the contents of a single folder on your Mac for serving—the default folders shown were automatically installed on your hard disk during the installation process. If you like, you can reassign all the services to a single folder to allow multiple services to access the same files.

Close the configuration menu and launch the application "StartServer" in the InterServer main folder. This activates the system extension that performs the actual HTTP serving functions for InterServer. When you're finished testing, be sure to launch the "StopServer" application and remove the InterServer Extension from your Extensions folder before rebooting.

Adding Content

To experiment with your own files and images, you can move the files into the "served" folders shown in Figure 5.7 and InterServer will make them available immediately. The folder designated for Web sharing is the equivalent to the WebSTAR root directory, so please refer to the end of the WebSTAR QuickStart section for more information on constructing URLs to access your documents.

Commentary

InterCon has always been known for combining multiple TCP/IP services in single applications, and InterServer Publisher is no exception. It is the only commercial server to include FTP services in its repertoire, which can be a great boon for sites that need to allow users to upload files to protected directories for serving via the Web.

InterServer also has subsumed some of the most common CGI functions into the server itself, such as imagemap support and page counters. The use of a system extension rather than a normal application for the server engine is unusual, but seems to work well.

The lack of MIME types can be more of a problem for servers that wish to provide a variety of file types to clients, such as QuickTime movies. Common file suffixes such as .html, .hqx, .bin, and so on, are sent with the appropriate MIME types automatically. Anything unrecognized, such as the .pdf extension of Adobe Acrobat files, however, is served with the plain binary MIME type, which can prevent some client applications from recognizing the file as belonging to a particular application and disabling automatic launching of a viewer for the file.

Most clients will look at the file suffix to determine how to handle unknown file types, so this may not be a major problem in practice, but it certainly deviates from the norm for Web servers.

On the other hand, InterServer can be set to automatically serve normal Mac files in binhex or MacBinary formats simply by adding the appropriate extension to the URL, that is, the application "myapp" would be served as a binhexed file by either the FTP or

Web servers simply by changing the URL on your pages to "myapp.hqx."

I would recommend InterServer for sites that need to offer multiple Internet services to their clients, but don't require CGI functions beyond those included in the InterServer package. The system's features are particularly well-suited to the needs of Web publishers, such as schools or other organizations that would like to provide information and basic CGI services but don't necessarily need to take advantage of the more flexible CGI interface in WebSTAR.

Web Server 4D

Web Server 4D combines the functionality of a database with Web serving functions in a single application. Built upon the 4th Dimension (4D) relational database system (http://www.acius.com/), it is also available in a Developer version, which is the uncompiled 4D database Web Server 4D is based on—it is thus the only commercial MacHTTP server that allows you to customize it for your own purposes!

To use the Developer version, you'll need to purchase a copy of 4th Dimension (about $600.00, version 3.2.6 or later) and, for maximum performance, the 4D Compiler (about $800.00, version 2.3.5 or later), which converts a 4D database from an interpreted script into a compiled application that runs three to ten times faster. If you aren't already familiar with programming in 4D, I strongly recommend you purchase the 4D application and experiment with it before committing to the Developer version of Web Server 4D.

Overview

Contact: http://www.mdg.com/

Cost: About $400.00

Requirements: Macintosh running System 7.0 or later, with at least 16M of RAM

Notable Features

Notable features include:

- Built-in email functions (sending only)
- Tracks visitors by IP address
- File and folder-based security for up to hundreds of thousands of users
- Large number of server statistics summaries
- Built-in configurable database for serving or recording information
- Built-in HTTP forms processor for transfer to email or recording in database
- Built-in page counter displays

Potential Problems

Potential problems include:

- Does not work with CGIs
- Limited access to raw log information
- Not scriptable
- No remote administration capabilities
- High RAM requirements

QuickStart

Install Web Server 4D on your hard drive by following the instructions in the Installation Guide file in the **Web Server 4D** folder in the **Servers** folder on the CD.

Launch Web Server 4D, and choose the “Start Server” item from the Setup menu. The Web Server 4D monitor window will appear, as shown in Figure 5.8.

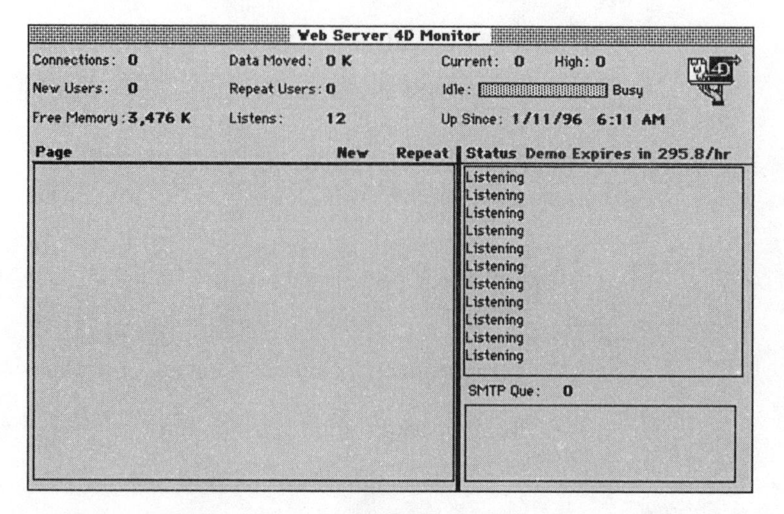

Figure 5.8 *The Web Server 4D monitoring window.*

That's it!

Adding Content

Web Server 4D will serve two kinds of information—data from its internal database and files from within the directory in which it resides, just as WebSTAR does. Refer to the WebSTAR QuickStart for more details on constructing URLs to reach files in the server folder. Please refer to the Web Server 4D documentation for details on using its user-configurable database to serve information.

Web Server 4D is "wicked fast."

Commentary

Web Server 4D is "wicked fast," as a friend of mine would say. I was surprised at its speedy response times, which are roughly the equal of WebSTAR without CGIs, and are even faster than WebSTAR running simultaneously with the types of CGIs necessary to implement a similar level of functionality.

The lack of a CGI interface could be hobbling if Web Server 4D did not already include so many CGI functions internally. The availability of the Developer version somewhat counters this lack of functionality, because the source code can be altered to fit whatever needs you may have in terms of CGI functions—assuming, of course, you can invest in the tools and skills necessary to program 4D.

Because 4D is easily capable of handling hundreds of thousands of records, the internal database should be able to serve most people's needs without a problem.

> 4D's response times can slow dramatically when very large (tens of thousands) of records are returned from a search, so if you use Web Server 4D's database functionality you may need to organize your searching criteria to avoid large numbers of returned records.

Although both Web Server 4D and NetWings (see the next section) are built upon 4D and share many common features, I found Web Server 4D's interface and functions to be much more intuitive and easier to use. Of the two 4D-based servers, I recommend Web Server 4D unless you have a particular need for the unique features of NetWings.

NetWings

NetWings, like Web Server 4D, is an HTTP server built upon 4D, so all my 4D-related comments above apply to NetWings as well. It's a bit older than Web Server 4D, and adds gopher, SMTP/POP email, and mailing list management to its available Internet services. It also is aimed more at the non-HTML savvy administrator, as it contains extensive functions for creating pages without any HTML coding.

Overview

Contact: http://www.netwings.com/

Cost: About $300.00

Requirements: Macintosh running System 7.0 or later, with at least 8M (16M highly recommended) of RAM

Notable Features

Notable features include:

- ☐ File or volume-based access control
- ☐ User-definable database fields
- ☐ SMTP/POP email server
- ☐ Mailing list manager
- ☐ HTML coding not required to create a Web site
- ☐ Censor function—blanks words from user-defined list when serving pages
- ☐ Comprehensive server logs
- ☐ Built-in imagemap functions
- ☐ User-defined macro codes for insertion of boilerplate HTML into served pages

Potential Problems

Potential problems include:

- ☐ Email services may interfere with HTTP performance
- ☐ Interface requires relatively long learning time
- ☐ No remote administration capability
- ☐ CGI interface available but not recommended

QuickStart

Install NetWings on your hard drive by following the Installation Guide in the **NetWings** folder within the **Servers** folder on the CD.

Launch NetWings, and choose the "Start Server" item from the Setup menu. The NetWings monitor window will appear, as shown in Figure 5.9.

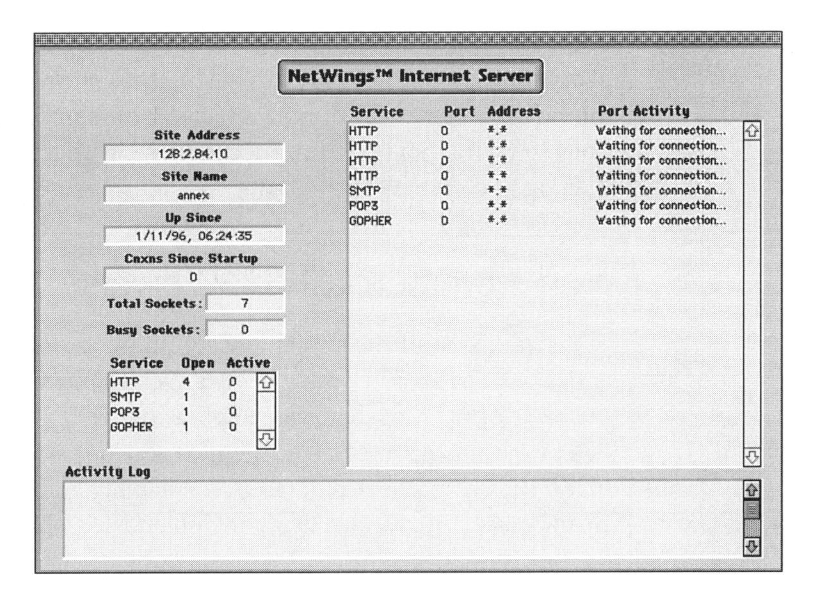

Figure 5.9 *The NetWings monitoring window.*

That's it!

Adding Content

Drop any files or images you want to serve into the folder called **NW_Pages** that was installed with the application. The URL to refer to files in this folder is http://<domain name or IP address of server>/NW_Pages/<filename>.

Commentary

The main thrust of NetWings is to provide a product that, with a single Mac, can provide all the basic Internet services a small organization needs to quickly set up an Internet and Web presence. It contains an extensive toolset for automatically creating HTML pages that does not require any HTML coding on the part of the administrator.

Although NetWings is similar to Web Server 4D, I found the administrative interface to be a bit more intimidating, although well-documented. You will definitely want to keep the manual handy when working with NetWings.

Because email and Web services are the primary needs of most organizations looking to establish an Internet presence, NetWings can be an effective solution to the desire of many small organizations to establish a basic Internet presence with a minimum of training and administrative costs.

Non-Commercial HTTP Servers

In general, I don't recommend using non-commercial products for critical applications like a company's Web site because the support and development of shareware applications is often unpredictable. Peter Lewis' NetPresenz (see the next section) is an exception, in that it has an excellent reputation for stability and steady bug fixes. In any case, you can give them a whirl and see what you think!

NetPresenz

NetPresenz (formerly FTPd) (http://www.share.com/peterlewis/), by the ever-helpful Peter Lewis, is a basic Web, FTP, and Gopher server available as shareware for a measly ten dollars (see Figure 5.10). It's a great way to quickly put up a few pages on the Web, but lacks most of the more advanced functions of the commercial HTTP servers. Nevertheless, it's a nice adjunct or emergency server, and is the most popular way of adding FTP services to an existing HTTP server.

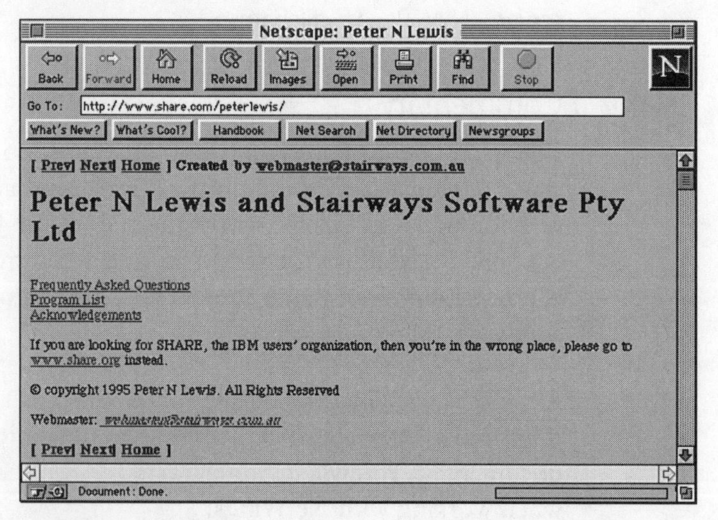

Figure 5.10 *Peter Lewis' NetPresenz site.*

If you do install NetPresenz, pay very close attention to the manual's instructions about controlling access to your server via the Users and Groups control panel. It's easy to accidentally make your entire hard disk available to the entire Internet if you're not careful. When you do make FTP services available, immediately take the time to thoroughly test the server with an FTP client to ensure that you haven't allowed unauthorized access to your files or accidentally allowed clients to upload or delete files on your server.

NetPresenz is actually very functional and a great way to get started on the Web. Its primary weak point is that it uses the Mac's file sharing system to access your hard disk, which prevents it from being suitable for sites with high usage levels. NetPresenz now also supports CGIs. Note that you must pay Peter Lewis the Shareware registration fee in order to use this product.

httpd4Mac

The other original HTTP server for the Mac, httpd4Mac (http://sodium.ch.man.ac.uk/pages/httpd4Mac/home.html), also offers basic no-frills Web service and is free, so the price/performance ratio can't be beat....

The current feature set is too limited for the server to be considered in the same class with the commercial applications, but you might want to keep your eye on it, as the author plans to continue upgrading its capabilities.

TeleFinder

TeleFinder, from Spider Island Software (http://www.spiderisland.com/) began life as a BBS (Bulletin Board System) application, but has added email and Web serving functions to its software. Figure 5.11 shows Spider Island's home page. TeleFinder allows you to create an entire "online service," and is primarily useful for organizations that wish to create a local dialup service for clients or members similar in concept (albeit smaller in scale) to services like America Online. BBS systems are unusual enough that TeleFinder's Web serving capabilities are almost ancillary to its main purpose, but if you are planning to implement both email and Web services at your site, TeleFinder may offer a fresh perspective on possible solutions.

Figure 5.11 *Spider Island Software, makers of TeleFinder.*

Coming Soon…

The following servers were both in beta testing at the time this book was written, and may very well be available by the time you read this paragraph—check their URLs for updated information. Both products promise to provide capabilities for Macintosh Internet servers that have been previously confined to other platforms, but promises are just that—I'll be keeping my fingers crossed. Note that the names may change by the time they are released.

One/Site

One/Site, from Delphic Software (http://www.delphic.com/) promises to be the end-all Macintosh Internet solution, with DNS,

HTTP, NNTP (Network News Transport Protocol, AKA Usenet newsgroups), FTP, Gopher and email servers all running in a single package. Wish them luck.

NetWings Proxy Server

The next version of NetWings plans to bring the first caching proxy server (see Chapter 9, "Statistics and Usage," for an explanation of caching proxy servers) to the Mac, which will be a real boon to companies and other large organizations that currently need UNIX machines to provide proxy services to their clients. NetWings has been due for an update for some time, so a new version may add additional functionality as well. You can check on the current NetWings product line at http://www.netwings.com/. See Figure 5.12.

Figure 5.12 *The NetWings home page.*

Securing Your Server

Once you activate a server that's available to the Internet, you've done something potentially dangerous that you probably haven't had to think about before—granted the world access to your Mac. Fortunately, Macs are much less vulnerable to "accidental" security problems than UNIX platforms, but paranoia has always served me well.

All of the QuickStart instructions given in this chapter set their respective HTTP servers to only allow files to be served out of a single folder on your hard drive, so maintaining Internet security is simply a matter of making sure that the Web-served folder doesn't contain any files you wouldn't want the world to see. Once you are sure of this, you can check through the documentation of your server application to determine how to control access to portions of your site via IP addresses or username/password checks.

If you are on an AppleTalk network and are using WebSTAR (or a WebSTAR variant) on your site, its remote administration capabilities allow anyone on your AppleTalk network to control and reconfigure your server application, which may present a problem. You can prevent unauthorized control of your server by opening the Users and Groups control panel, double-clicking the "Guest" icon, and making sure that all guest access to your server is unchecked. This will require a username and password from anyone attempting to control your server or mount your hard drives from a remote Mac.

Upgrading Your Site

Hopefully, the traffic on your site will soon build to the point where you start thinking about upgrading your Internet connection or your site. For your connection, you can use two methods to determine when an upgrade is necessary—either you notice from examining your server logs (see Chapter 9) that your transfer rates are starting to fall, indicating that your traffic is beginning to exceed your capacity to handle it, or your server reports increasing numbers of "busy" connections, each of which represent a client's request that was denied because your server was already handling the maximum number of simultaneous clients allowed.

Distributed Sites

An easy upgrade for many sites is to simply begin distributing your content among two or more individual servers.

An easy upgrade for many sites is to simply begin distributing your content among two or more individual servers. If your pages are graphic-intensive, you may be better off dedicating a single server to just serving image URLs, whereas your main server continues acting as the source for the bulk of the content of your site. The same approach can be used to move very large files off your main site, such as QuickTime movies. Transferring large files tends to hold TCP connections open for long periods of time and prevent your server from answering requests for smaller files, such as your home page, efficiently.

Apple Computer uses this approach on its main home page at http://www.apple.com/ (see Figure 5.13). It utilizes no less than five servers to serve the home page and two graphics, and to handle each imagemap's response when visitors click one of the two graphics to navigate to another part of its site.

Once you set up additional servers, all you need to do to begin distributed serving is change the URLs for the files you've moved to reflect their new location!

Server Arrays (RAICs)

You may see the term RAIC (Redundant Array of Inexpensive/Independent Computers, pronounced "rake") mentioned on Mac-oriented newsgroups and mailing lists. A RAIC consists of two or more Web servers that contain identical contents (also called "mirrored" servers), so that a URL directed at one server always returns the same information as does a URL directed at any other. This enables the traffic of any particular site to be evenly distributed across the individual servers, thereby increasing the capacity of the site overall to handle requests.

Figure 5.13 *The Apple Computer home page.*

NOTE

Outside of the Mac world, this kind of server arrangement is called a server array rather than a RAIC. In fact, I highly recommend you try to use the term "server array" rather than "RAIC" when talking to other people because your UNIX and Windows friends won't know what a RAIC is and, when you explain it, they'll laugh at you for coming up with such a cute name for a server array.

Implementing a server array requires two new activities—incoming URL requests need to be distributed among the different servers, and you need to provide a way for all the members of the array to keep their contents coordinated with each other.

You'll recall that, normally, each domain name corresponds to one IP address, and that a single Internet host machine can have multiple domain names, or aliases, that all resolve to the same IP address. Implementing a server array requires adding the reverse situation to your DNS configuration—namely, that each domain name can be resolved into one of any number of IP addresses so that, for a two-server array, 50 percent of the requests sent to www.myserver.com end up at the IP address of one of your servers, and 50 percent of the time the request ends up at the other IP address.

Accomplishing this little trick requires the assistance of your DNS administrator and the BIND (Berkeley Internet Name Domain) software on their DNS server. BIND can be configured to answer each request to resolve a particular domain name with a different IP address, distributing the number of IP address "aliases" evenly among the incoming requests. Simply assign as many IP addresses as there are servers in your array to your domain name, and your traffic will automatically begin distributing itself evenly across your servers.

NOTE

> If your DNS administrators claim ignorance of BIND and server arrays, just point them at `http://www.ora.com/gnn/bus/ora/item/dns.html` for educational assistance.

Now that your clients are helping out by distributing themselves across your array, your job is to make sure that they always perceive your site the same way no matter which particular server they happen to end up using. For static files, the simplest method is to use a synchronization utility or AppleScript to keep folders and files on different servers updated with each other. The version of AppleScript installed as part of System 7.5 includes a script called "Synchronize Folders" that will work nicely, or you can find a utility like Synchronize! Pro (Go to http://hyperarchive.lcs.mit.edu/HyperArchive/ and search for "synchronize" to find the most current version) to handle the task for you. Figure 5.14 shows this site.

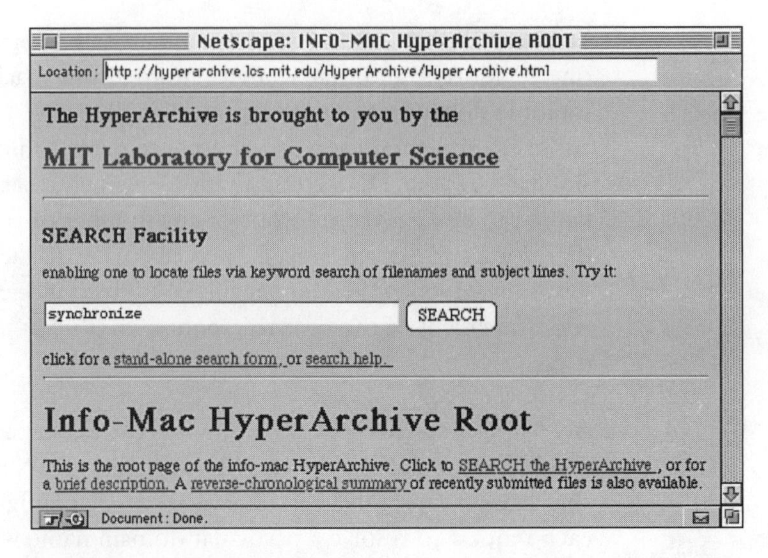

Figure 5.14 *The MIT HyperArchive search form.*

NOTE

Many sites use databases or other CGIs to implement functions like shopping carts or discussion forums. This can present a problem for server arrays, because the information captured or held on one server may not be available to another. You have two solutions:

- Maintain these kinds of functions on a single server and use your array for your static content alone.
- In the case of databases, use a client/server solution that keeps all the data on one commonly accessible machine and use the database system's client software on the individual Web servers.

Because all the information is being held at one location, your CGIs will always be in sync with each other.

Lastly, don't forget that you need to collect all your server logs together to analyze the activity of your site as a whole!

Summary

At this point, you should have a server application installed and ready to build your site around. Congratulations! The core of your site is in place.

The next part of this book will show you how to serve different kinds of information to clients and how to implement the specialized functions that give your site its distinctive look and feel. In other words, you're about to learn how to perform the most critical part of your Webmaster duties—creating and managing the content of your Web site.

Part II

How May I Serve You?

CHAPTER 6

Serving from Storage

After you have a server installed, you'll begin adding files to your site and creating the content that gives your site its unique value to your clients. Whether you are serving HTML code, images, or QuickTime movies, you need to answer three questions:

- ☐ How do I create files for serving?
- ☐ How do I serve those files correctly?
- ☐ How do I manage my site's content efficiently?

Fortunately, you've come to the right chapter to get your answers!

Creating Content

There are dozens of fine tutorials and guides available both online and in bookstores that offer excellent advice and guidance for writing HTML pages, creating graphics, and designing your pages for effective communication with your clients. People whose careers are in graphic design and communications are your best sources for advice in designing the "look" of your site, whether that appearance is in the form of HTML text or images.

There are, however, a number of more general issues that come up when creating the content of your site, discussed next.

HTML Compatibility

One of the biggest headaches in producing a publicly available Web site is deciding which HTML markup tags you will use for your pages. Although a mechanism for establishing and evolving a common standard for HTML exists, some browser manufacturers (notably Netscape and, to a less successful but no less earnest degree, Microsoft) are attempting to "push" the standards in different directions by implementing support for novel HTML tags in their browsers.

Because these new tags are often added in response to perceived needs on the part of clients and page designers, they quickly gain widespread use despite the fact that other Web browsers not made by the company originating the new tags will not display pages using them correctly.

For example, most HTML writers love the table-formatting tags introduced by Netscape. They vastly increase the flexibility of page design and became so popular that some other browser manufacturers began adding support for displaying tables despite the fact that no Internet standard for their display had been agreed upon. Figure 6.1 shows an example of a sophisticated use of table tags (you can see this site in action at http://www.intellinet.com/CoolTools/CalendarMaker/).

Most measurements of browser usage put Netscape's share of clients on the public Web at between 60 to 80 percent of browsers used.

Most measurements of browser usage put Netscape's share of clients on the public Web at between 60 to 80 percent of browsers used, so using Netscape-only tags does serve the majority of your clients well. But the problem goes beyond Netscape-specific page design, as there's no particular reason why another company might not release a new browser that also becomes hugely popular, with its own set of idiosyncratic display capabilities that fragments the browser market even further. It seems that the problem of serving different browser types will be with us for a long time to come, so you should establish your strategy to deal with the situation early on.

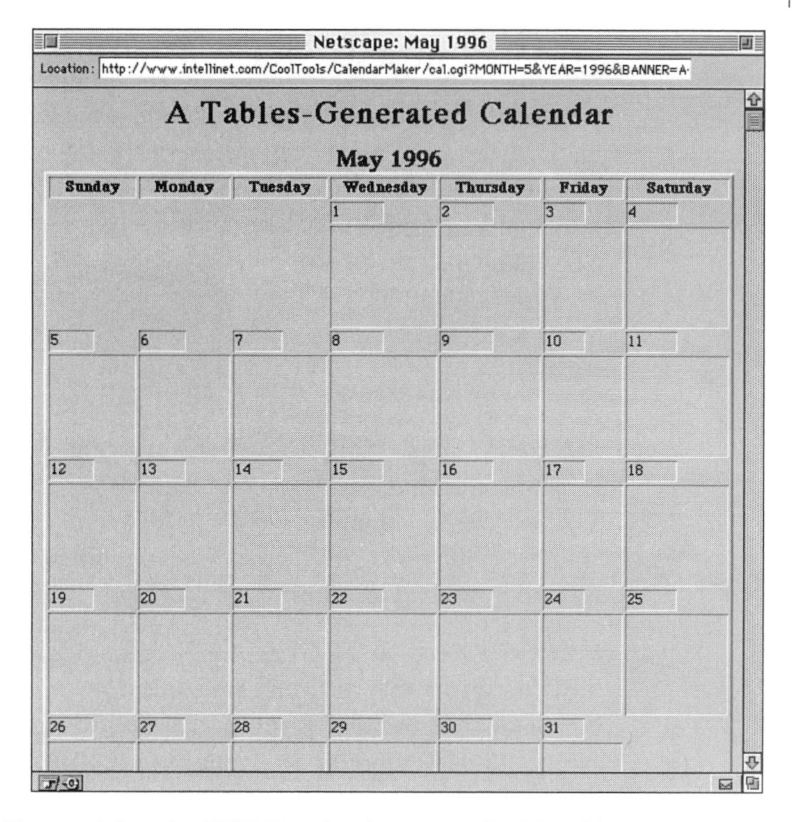

Figure 6.1 *An HTML calendar created with table tags.*

You have five options for coping with nonstandard HTML tags:

- Don't use them.

  Simple and effective. Not always an option, as it reduces your flexibility in page design dramatically, but is guaranteed to work with virtually every client likely to visit your site.

- Only use nonstandard tags that don't affect standard browsers significantly.

  A good example of this approach is the Netscape <CENTER> tag, which centers page elements in the browser window. If the browser used doesn't support <CENTER>, the elements being centered will usually default to flush left on the page which, while not as pretty to look at, generally doesn't detract from the functional aspects of your site and maintains the usability of your pages for clients.

- ☐ Offer alternative pages.

  Many sites have links on their home page for versions of their site designed to use different levels of graphics or support different browser types (usually divided into Netscape and non-Netscape areas). This is probably the most convenient method from the client's point of view, but it can be a real headache from your point of view to maintain parallel Web sites.

- ☐ Notify clients of your site's requirements.

  Some people think seeing "This site enhanced for Netscape" or something similar on your pages is rather rude, but it's increasingly common to simply design for Netscape and ignore other browser types. Such pages often also include a link to download the latest version of Netscape.

- ☐ Use a server or a CGI that will automatically detect what browser is being used by a client and serve different HTML code back to them as appropriate for their capability to display it. I'll have more to say about this in the next two chapters.

HTML Editors

Any word processor or text editor, even SimpleText, will do as an HTML editor in a pinch. But if you've ever had to write a complex HTML table manually, you know that manual HTML coding can be terribly time-consuming.

The CD contains reviews and links to literally dozens of HTML editing tools, utilities, and applications, but I'm going to confine my comments here to some general issues you'll face in using any HTML editor, and briefly review a couple of products that seem to stand out from the crowd.

Just as you must take into account different browsers when writing HTML, you will need to take into account the limitations of different editors. To some extent, the same problems with nonstandard HTML tags that browsers face are also faced by editors, which must constantly strive to keep up with the latest HTML tags to remain effective.

Adobe PageMill

The first of the true WYSIWYG HTML editors, PageMill (http://www.adobe.com/PageMill/), has been hailed as the first application to put HTML page creation within the reach of people unwilling to learn the arcana of HTML tags. PageMill allows most standard HTML layouts, including the placement of images on pages, to be created without ever asking the user to actually view the HTML code itself. The figure below shows the beginning of a page being built in PageMill.

Professional HTML coding, however, is often a process of small adjustments by a knowledgeable designer who knows how to manipulate HTML layout commands in unexpected ways. PageMill is most suitable for quickly mocking up pages for later adjustment in a text editor or for people who want to create straightforward HTML pages with a minimum of fuss. Professional HTML designers or others who need to manipulate their page layouts for unusual effects will probably continue to need to manipulate the HTML tags directly for some time to come.

Although in theory the best editors would divorce the user entirely from the markup tags that control the display of their pages, this is unlikely to be practical for professional HTML designers for some time to come. Completely hiding the actual HTML from the page designer requires that the editor understand every current markup tag, even conflicting ones, and make choices about which approach is best for coding a particular design. Because of the difficulty of doing so, completely graphical (WYSIWYG) editors will always be limited to some subset of the available HTML options at any given time.

Some sort of hybrid approach is therefore necessary for most HTML designers, whether that means manual editing of files produced by the editor, or a facility for the user to define the attributes of new markup tags as they become available. In any case, try out the various packages on the CD until you find one that works well with your work style. New editors and enhancements to existing ones are being produced almost as fast as Netscape introduces new markup tags, so you should certainly check with the makers of any application you particularly like for more current versions of their products.

Converting to HTML

Many word processors and page-layout programs have been extended to allow these traditional desktop-publishing tools to export their contents in the HTML format for Web serving. Some formatting information is usually lost in the process, primarily information that simply doesn't exist in HTML such as font choices and some types of text placement, but most of these utilities will at least automate the first step in turning an existing set of documents into a set of HTML pages, complete with links to inlined images.

A number of utilities are included on the CD for converting information already in Microsoft Word or Excel, PageMaker, QuarkXPress, ClarisWorks, or NisusWriter formats into HTML pages. There are also a few extensions that allow HTML editing tools to be incorporated directly into these applications and other text editors, such as BBEdit.

As more organizations begin adapting their documents to be viewed through both traditional and online media, you can expect support for "HTML-izing" existing publications to be an increasingly standard feature for these types of applications.

Images

The nature of the modern Web, and its explosion of popularity, can be traced back to the first use of graphics on Web pages. Despite the fact that many clients still browse the Web without loading every image they come across, much of the impact of your site derives from its use (or misuse) of graphics.

Lessons in graphic design are beyond the scope of this book, but I do want to mention a few issues that every site designer must cope with.

All static images served over the Web are compressed to save time in downloading to clients. Two types of compression are commonplace—GIF and JPEG, usually identified by the file suffixes .gif and .jpg or .jpeg. Some other compression schemes are growing in use, such as Progressive JPEG, but the vast majority of graphics are likely to remain in one of these two formats for a long time to come.

The GIF graphic-file format results in pictures that are somewhat larger than the same file compressed under JPEG, but is much less likely to distort the final image, at the expense of reducing the number of colors you can use in a given image. It is also the only file compression format that allows "transparency," the process of indicating a single color (usually the background of your image) that should be treated as transparent by the client's browser, so that the normal background color of the page shows through the transparent regions of your images. GIF is best suited for line drawings and other images that need to be displayed just as they were created. It is also the only format supported by just about every graphical browser currently in use, so GIF images are the best way to reach the largest number of clients with your images.

Because the GIF compression scheme is relatively inefficient at compressing images, the JPEG format is often used for efficiency. JPEG is a "lossy" compression scheme, meaning that the image the client sees is somewhat degraded from the original image. JPEG compression looks best when used on images that contain many soft edges, such as photographs, as the small amount of degradation JPEG introduces in the image is usually unnoticeable or at least minimized.

The CD contains a number of image manipulation and conversion utilities that will help you convert images from one format to another and provide some simple image-editing tools. It also contains a list of sites with more information and tips for creating Web graphics, as well as links to sites that collect graphics you can use freely on your own server.

Other File Types

Do you want to serve Java applets from your Web site? How about Adobe Acrobat or sound files? No problem! Your Web server can serve any file whatsoever from your disk to your clients without any special modifications or upgrades to the server application.

A common misconception about Web servers is that they are somehow capable of altering or editing files that they serve, but that couldn't be more wrong. HTTP servers, unless specially configured to do so, do not examine, alter, edit, or care what passes through them and off to the client. The sole concern of the server application is to try to determine the type of file that is being served so that it can inform the client's software of its identity. The data itself, however, is essentially irrelevant to the server.

When a visitor to your site complains that a file you've served is somehow mangled or truncated, chances are that the problem is with the file itself or in how the server or client applications are configured with respect to MIME types (see the next section for more info on MIME types) rather than with the server application.

If the information is being processed by a CGI, or if your server is able to insert or modify HTML macros in your documents, you should look to these areas for the possible source of the problem.

Serving Files

Now that you have your files, how do you get them to your clients? For the standard file types, like HTML, your server is already configured to serve them correctly. If you plan on transferring applications or archived information, though, you'll need to do a little more work to make sure that they arrive safe and sound on your client's machine.

All about MIME

MIME (Multipurpose Internet Mail Extension) types were developed to answer the need to send information other than text through email. MIME provides a method of attaching notes to information that defines what type of information it contains, so that the software reading the file can translate or save the data appropriately.

Web servers and clients use MIME types to inform Web clients what sort of data is being sent by the server so that the client can display the information, save it to disk, or pass it on to another application to handle, whichever is most appropriate.

MIME types are indicated by including a line in the HTTP response that includes the MIME type information, which appears as follows:

```
Content-Type: <type>/<subtype>
```

The <TYPE> portion of the MIME type is used to indicate what general category the information falls into, such as sounds, images or text. The <SUBTYPE> portion indicates more specific information, such as the name of the application that should be used to open the document being transferred. Some examples of MIME types appear in Table 6.1.

Table 6.1 *Common MIME Types*

Document Type	MIME Type
HTML file	text/html
GIF file	image/gif
QuickTime movie	video/quicktime
Acrobat file	application/pdf

The MIME type definition also allows the creation of novel MIME types by using a MIME type of application/x-<special type>, where <special type> is any string of characters that uniquely identify the type.

A list of the canonical MIME types is available at http://www.netscape.com/assist/helper_apps/media-types.html, but the best resource is probably the "Helpers" configuration window in Netscape Navigator, which contains a list of most current MIME types and their corresponding file suffixes.

For example, when RealAudio (http://www.realaudio.com/) introduced its system of playing compressed sounds over the Internet, it needed a way for Web browsers to recognize the new file type and automatically launch the player application when downloading a RealAudio file. It defined a new MIME type of application/x-realaudio, and instructed clients and servers wishing to use its software of the new MIME type so that they could use RealAudio files correctly.

Of course, this begs the question of how your server recognizes file types so that it can send the correct MIME type to clients. That process is called *suffix mapping*.

Suffix Mapping

The primary means by which MIME types are assigned and interpreted is by suffix mapping. Suffix mapping became a standard in the non-Macintosh world because the Mac concepts of file type and creator codes don't exist on other systems. Instead, the standard is to use one- to three-letter suffixes on both binary and text files to indicate what type of application the file belongs to, or if the file is itself an application.

Suffix mapping refers to the process of examining the suffix of a file to determine what type of file it is, and then assigning it the appropriate MIME type. On Macintosh systems, you can also use the file type and creator codes to assign the MIME type, but the suffix itself must still be correct or some clients will not be able to correctly use the files you've served them.

All the Web servers on the CD are already configured with the proper suffix-mapping information for the vast majority of files you might want to serve. As new formats become available, however, like Java applets or VRML files, you will need to modify the default settings to support the new file types. You should refer to the documentation on your server for more information on how to do this.

If you are serving files with unusual MIME types, you will also need to advise your clients of the file suffixes and MIME types you are using so that they can cope with the files when you send them.

Filenames

UNIX and Macintosh systems both benefit from being able to use long filenames, and you may be so used to it by now that you don't appreciate the advantages of the Mac file-naming conventions. If you start serving files to clients on other platforms that they need to save to disk, however, you'll quickly learn the differences!

UNIX-based files can have long names like Mac files, but are not permitted to include some characters in filenames. Windows 3.1 and earlier users are even more limited, as they are usually constrained to filenames of no more than eight characters and suffixes of three characters (also called "8.3" filenames). If you serve files that might be downloaded by non-Macintosh users, you should change the name of the file (using an alias also works well) to conform to their limitations. The best guideline is to use alphanumeric characters and to use no more than eight of them in the filename plus up to three characters in the suffix. This will ensure the least amount of potential problems for your clients.

Which Fork Was That Again?

When you deliver HTML text or graphics files over the Web, you don't need to worry about what operating system or computer the client is using—HTML and graphics formats are interpretable by every client you're likely to serve. When you start serving executable files like applications, or special kinds of information like QuickTime movies, however, you quickly run into a key difference between the Macintosh and other computers.

The MacOS stores information about files and applications in two distinct places on your disk, referred to as the data fork and the resource fork. Simple files like HTML pages keep all of their information in just one place, the data fork, so those files can be served directly over the Web to any client. Applications, however, and some data files like QuickTime movies require that their data and resource forks be combined into one file before they can be used by a Windows or UNIX user.

Even for Macintosh users, any file that needs a resource fork to work, like an application or even some document types, must be converted into a single file before serving. The standard method of doing this is to *binhex* the file, which combines both forks into a single file that can be transferred as text and then translated back into a normal Macintosh file on the client's computer.

Files can also be transferred to Macintosh users using a special protocol called MacBinary, which also combines the forks together, but typically creates smaller files than does the binhexing process. Tools and references for converting Mac files into servable formats are available on the CD, and in general I would recommend using binhexed files exclusively, as MacBinary transfers are less reliable.

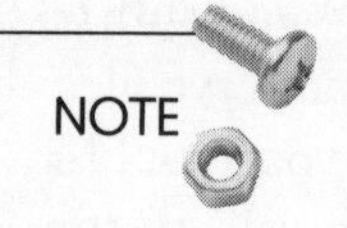

NOTE

For QuickTime movies, you need to use a special application to "flatten" the movie's resource and data forks into a single file that clients not using Macintoshes can understand and play on their systems if they have QuickTime installed. A utility called "Flatten-Moov" is included on your CD just for this purpose.

Content Management

The content of your site will undergo continual changes no matter what type of site you are developing—your design is changing, you're updating links to offsite resources, altering or adding to your own content, or reacting to changes on the Web to keep your site compliant with the current state of the art. For even a few dozen pages, the time required to maintain links and design elements through all these changes can be daunting.

Fortunately, this need is recognized and products are beginning to appear that assist site administrators in updating sites effectively and efficiently. Site management tools will enable you to maintain and change common elements like page headers and footers, navigation bars, and links without manually editing all the pages involved, and will guarantee that your site never suffers from dead links or other unexpected by-products of changes.

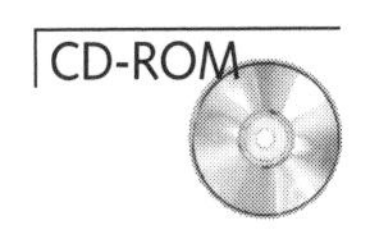

Unfortunately, none of these products had seen the light of day at the time this was written. I've included links to the sites that will provide you with more information on these applications on the CD, but I am unfortunately unable to review them yet. Do keep your eye on the Web site for this book, however, as I'll be sure to keep you updated there!

The most promising of these applications are Adobe's SiteMill (http://www.adobe.com/Apps/SiteMill/), and Heyertech's WebMaster Pro (http://www.heyertech.com/products/toc.html).

Summary

The vast majority of work on your server will probably involve organizing and editing static information. The difficulty of doing so efficiently is dependent on the complexity of your particular site, but is always a large part of any site administrator's time on the job.

Eventually, you will develop your own "toolkit" of applications and techniques that enable you to meet your own needs efficiently, but this chapter should have given you a head start in understanding the issues you'll face. The tools available to assist you are wonderful, and content design and management is probably easier on the Macintosh than on any other platform, as you'll find out when you review the applications and resources available on your CD.

The next chapter will introduce you to the world of dynamic information on Web servers, and will explain how to build a site that not only serves information, but uses interaction with your clients to enhance their experience and your site's value.

CHAPTER 7

When a Disk Is Not Enough: CGI Applications and Usage

Whether your site is commercial, nonprofit, or purely personal, you will very likely want to add more interactivity to your site than that provided by simply serving files to visitors. CGI applications (as introduced in Chapter 2, "WWW Client/Server: The Short Course") are the primary means of adding "personality" to your site and allow you to interact with your clients in a variety of ways, some silly and some profound.

This chapter explains:

- ☐ How CGIs work
- ☐ General usage guidelines
- ☐ Common CGI services and applications
- ☐ Troubleshooting CGI problems

Keep in mind that of the Web servers reviewed in this book, only the MacHTTP/WebSTAR line and InterServer Publisher offer what I consider to be reliable CGI support. If you plan on developing or using any but the simplest CGI applications, I strongly recommend choosing WebSTAR as your HTTP server application because of its superior CGI support and the fact that most commercial and shareware CGI applications are designed to work with WebSTAR. If a CGI is described as "compatible with MacHTTP," however, it should work essentially as described even with InterServer Publisher.

If you plan on using any but the simplest CGI applications, choose WebSTAR as your HTTP server application because of its superior CGI support and the fact that most commercial and shareware CGI applications are designed to work with WebSTAR.

NOTE

Many common CGI functions have been built into the non-WebSTAR Web servers, and basing your site on an application such as Web Server 4D or NetWings may eliminate the need to use any CGIs at all. If you do begin working with one of these servers and later discover a need for CGI support, you can always run a copy of WebSTAR on another Mac solely for your CGIs and continue working with your original Web server for the rest of your site. This is also a nice way to "divide the load" at your site among different machines and maintain quick responses to client requests.

Technically, servers that offer "CGI services" built into the server application aren't really using CGIs, because they aren't communicating with other applications to provide their functionality. However, rather than write out the entire phrase "CGI applications or services built into your Web server" throughout this chapter, I'll just use the term "CGI" to refer to either type of implementation.

When you see the term CGI, think "CGI applications or services built into your Web server."

How CGIs Work

Traditional CGIs are applications that work in tandem with your Web server to "take over" the process of creating a response for your clients when they send a URL to your server. If your server determines that an incoming URL is intended to be handled by a CGI, it passes the URL and other information about the request to the CGI application, which can perform whatever action it wants before returning a response to the server. Figure 7.1 illustrates this process.

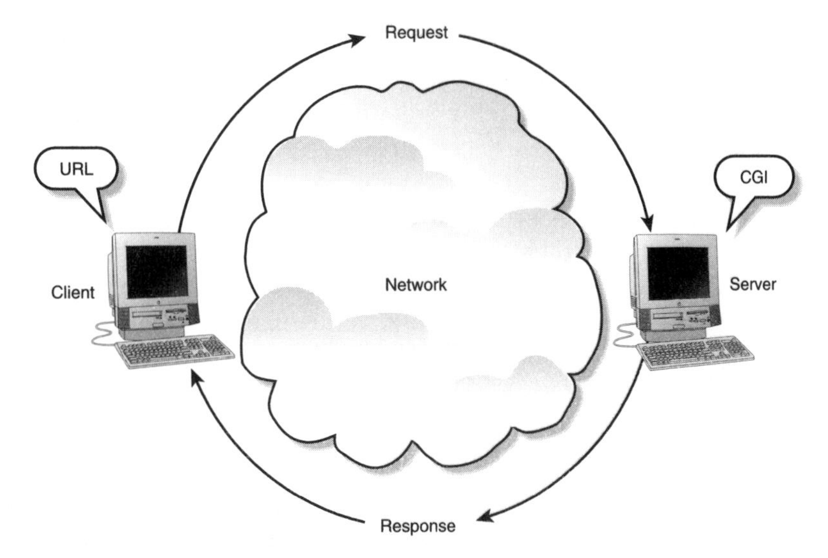

Figure 7.1 *How CGIs work with your Web server.*

Apple Events and CGIs

If you're not already familiar with how Apple Events work on the Mac, you'll need a little background to understand how CGIs function and to troubleshoot potential problems.

All Mac applications respond to your actions by interpreting "events" you create, such as typing on the keyboard (a keyboard event) or clicking your mouse (a mouse event). So when Apple wanted to create a way for applications to communicate with each other, they created the concept of "Apple Events," which carry messages between applications by using the excess RAM on your Mac to hold the information about the event. Note that the concept of "message" has been extended for Apple Events, which can transmit any sort of information, not just equivalents to user actions such as mouse clicks.

When a Web server receives an HTTP request destined for handling by a CGI, an Apple Event is sent to the CGI with all the information available about the request contained in the event. When the CGI is ready to respond, it sends a second Apple Event containing the complete HTTP response back to the server, which passes the response through and closes the TCP/IP connection to the client.

Because all this "passing" of messages occurs in RAM, Apple Events are extremely fast, with hundreds of events capable of being passed back and forth every second, depending on the speed of the sending and receiving applications. For a single HTTP request, the additional time required is barely measurable, although the actual impact will depend somewhat on how often your CGI is being called upon to perform its duties. Apple Events do have a finite lifetime, however—generally, your CGI has to respond within two minutes or the event will "time out" and the Web server will return an error response to the client. The exact time is usually adjustable by changing the appropriate settings on your Web server application.

Apple Events are also limited in size. Although they "officially" can carry up to 64K of information, sending messages over 32K in size—whether to the CGI or back to the server tends to be unreliable.

Overview

With that information in hand, you can look at how a generic CGI request is handled on your server:

1. The server receives a URL request from a client.
2. The server compares the suffix on the URL (if any) to its table of suffix mapping to determine whether the URL should be handled by a CGI.
3. If it is a CGI URL, the server packages up any data sent by the client, along with other information about the connection such as the client's IP address or domain name, into an Apple Event and sends it to the CGI, first launching the CGI application if necessary.
4. The CGI examines the event and performs whatever processing it is designed to do, and then constructs a valid HTTP response for the client, normally in the form of a Web page.

5. The CGI returns another event to the server with the HTTP response attached, which the server then sends back verbatim to the client, closing the TCP/IP connection afterward.

The next section helps you pick out where a CGI connection might have trouble.

CGI Response Types

The vast majority of CGIs return an HTML page to the client. This is exactly analogous to the server finding a file on disk and returning it (and nothing prevents a CGI from performing the exact same action), except that the HTML returned has usually been created specifically for the one request, rather than being the same for every visitor. CGIs can also return other types of information, such as inline graphics or HTTP responses such as those described in the following sections.

Redirections

CGIs can return a "redirection" command, which instructs the client's browser to immediately retrieve a new, CGI-specified URL without the client's intervention. This kind of response is useful in a variety of situations:

- When screening URLs for authorized requests of information.
- When sending a client to a standard response page while allowing the CGI to perform another action—such as sending email—without keeping the client waiting.
- When distributing time-consuming URLs, such as file download requests, across alternative servers.

Authorization Requests

An authorization request is the HTTP response that triggers the client's Web browser to throw up a dialog box asking for a username and password. An authorization request is normally accompanied by an HTML page that is displayed if the client cancels the request in the dialog window.

Error Responses

Just as your Web server can return messages to clients indicating that a file cannot be found or that it is too busy to handle another connection at the moment, a CGI can return the same error messages if they are applicable. Remember, CGIs simply move the process of determining the proper response to a given URL from the server application to the CGI application—from the client's point of view, any response a server could provide itself is indistinguishable from a response constructed by the CGI, because both responses look exactly the same to the client.

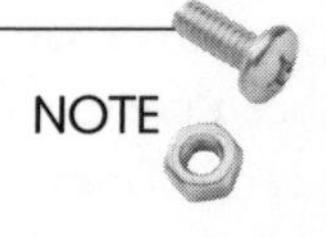
NOTE

> You can find more detailed information about HTTP responses and how to create them in the "CGI Development Reference" section of Chapter 8.

A final word: the definition of a CGI as a standalone application that runs concurrently with your Web server is becoming increasingly obsolete. Most new Web servers for the Mac are adding functionality previously reserved for CGIs into the server application, eliminating the need for the CGI at all. CGIs themselves are also becoming increasingly sophisticated, so that rather than installing a different application for each CGI function you need, you can just install a single program that can be configured to handle multiple types of CGI functions.

Using CGIs

In general, adding CGIs to your server is no more difficult than running any other kind of application. Because the primary user of CGIs is your Web server rather than a person, the user interface, especially for shareware CGIs, is often minimal or nonexistent.

All CGIs require that AppleScript be installed in the extensions folder on your Mac. If you are using a MacOS version earlier than 7.5, you may not already have AppleScript installed. If this is your situation, try installing the Web servers available from the CD. They should add AppleScript to your Extensions folder as part of their normal installation process.

If you place aliases to your CGIs and your HTTP server in the **Startup Items** folder so that they will automatically launch when your server starts up, I advise you to rename the aliases so that all the CGIs launch before the Web server does. This avoids possible problems with your Web server accepting connections and sending Apple Events to your CGIs before they are ready to receive them. Because aliases in the **Startup Items** folder will launch alphabetically by name, simply renaming the aliases "1," "2," "3," and so on will launch them in the indicated numerical order.

Intermediary CGIs

Many applications that respond to Apple Events are not able to interpret the particular types of Apple Events CGIs use. You can still use these kinds of applications with your Web server by installing an intermediary CGI, which acts as "middleman" to translate messages from the Web server into Apple Events understandable by the other application.

This approach is used most often with databases like Butler or FileMaker Pro that are not able to understand CGI events themselves but are controllable from other applications or scripts designed to work with them. Intermediaries are also used when a CGI needs to communicate with multiple applications to process a request, and to allow communication with applications running on other machines, such as a database server or email host.

One benefit of using an intermediary CGI with an application running on another machine is that you can separate the processor time required by the other application from the server machine itself.

Synchronous and Asynchronous CGIs

Both WebSTAR and InterServer Publisher support asynchronous CGI processing—that is, they are able to send an Apple Event to a CGI and continue processing other HTTP requests while waiting for a response to come back from the CGI. They also support an older method of interacting with CGIs, synchronous processing, in which the server sends an event to the CGI and waits, suspending all other activities, until the CGI responds or the Apple Event times out.

Synchronous processing is very rarely used any more, as it completely locks up your server for the duration of the CGI's activities. About the only reason to use it is if your CGI requires complete control of the Mac's processor in order to complete its processing before the Apple Event times out, and if that is the case, I strongly recommend finding another solution to your CGI needs or moving the CGI to a server used only to handle requests for that CGI.

WARNING

To determine whether a CGI should be called synchronously or asynchronously, Web servers check their tables of suffix mappings against the URL being requested. By default, most servers are set up to recognize ".cgi" suffixes as synchronous and ".acgi" suffixes as asynchronous, although you can usually change the assignments to whatever mapping you like. If you suspect that your server is treating a CGI synchronously when it should be asynchronous, double-check your suffix mappings to be sure you have named the CGI correctly.

Because servers can send a new event to your CGI before it's finished processing a previous one (or two or three previous ones…), CGIs need to be specially written to handle multiple events simultaneously before they can be used asynchronously. Virtually every CGI you are likely to find is designed with asynchronous processing in mind, but you may stumble across very old shareware CGIs that are not. If you suspect your CGI of having problems when multiple events are sent to it, try looking for a newer version or checking with the author to determine whether it supports asynchronous operation.

NOTE

CGIs written in AppleScript are notorious for being unable to handle multiple events simultaneously. If an AppleScript-based CGI is showing odd behavior, try renaming it to force your server to treat it synchronously or better yet, replace the CGI with a non-AppleScript version that is designed to handle multiple events properly.

RAM Requirements

A good rule of thumb is that you'll need at least 8MB of RAM to effectively use any but the most minimal CGIs with most Web server applications (although some, especially those built around databases, may need much more), depending on the number of simultaneous connections you are allowing to your server. You should always try to leave at least 1MB of RAM unallocated (more won't hurt), because this "unused" RAM is needed by the MacOS to pass information to and from your CGIs.

Processing Time

Most CGIs coexist quite nicely with a Web server and don't add significant loads to your Mac's processor. Some CGIs, however, especially those dependent on databases or any other processor-intensive application, can slow down your server's non-CGI responses significantly if they are used often. The usual solution is to either use an intermediary CGI (as previously described) to connect to an application running on a different Mac or to set up the CGI on a separate server, with its own copy of the Web server application, and use the hostname of the secondary server solely in URLs that reference the offending CGI.

Sending Information to CGIs

You can specify information to be sent to your CGIs when clients click a link or a button in a variety of ways, depending on your needs and how your CGIs are designed. You can use either the URL, an HTML form, or both at once!

Sending Information in a URL

You already know that a CGI application is specified in a URL by typing the file path to the CGI application, such as http://www.myserver.com/myCGI.acgi for the CGI "myCGI.acgi," located in the root folder of your Web server. A CGI, however, often needs more information than a basic URL provides in order to fulfill its purpose. Such additional data are called "arguments" to the URL, and can be sent in two ways.

- The first type of argument is the "search" argument, which is sent by appending any information you need to pass to the CGI to the URL after a "?" character. For example, sending the word "hello" as a search argument is done with the URL http://www.myserver.com/myCGI.acgi?hello.
- The second type of argument is the "path" argument, which consists of any characters following a "$" character, such as http://www.myserver.com/myCGI.acgi$hello. Any characters after the first "$" in a URL, up to either the end of the URL or a "?" character, whichever comes first, are called the "path argument" of the URL and can be used by a CGI.

Both types of arguments can be combined, and they will be read separately by any CGI designed to recognize them. Keep in mind that URLs are usually limited to no more than 1024 total characters, including any arguments, and that there is no guarantee that some browsers might not truncate the allowed length even further. To send large amounts of information to a CGI, the preferred method is via forms.

Sending Information from Forms

When you write a form in HTML, the first markup tag contains a specification for the "method" by which the form information is to be submitted, which is usually GET or POST. If you use the GET method, the form values will be appended to the URL as search arguments, and are subject to the same length limitations mentioned above (and they make for ugly-looking URLs).

The POST method, however, appends the form data to the HTTP request rather than the URL, much like a file attachment in an email message. Not only is this invisible to the clients (all they see is the basic URL), but it enables you to send much greater volumes of information with a single request, up to 24K with WebSTAR, but that value may vary a bit among servers. You can combine POST arguments with URL arguments if your CGI supports it, although most do not.

Minimum criteria for CGIs are that they handle multiple connections at once, are actively being developed and supported, and are known to run stably in a variety of environments.

CGIs in Action

In this section, I describe many of the most common uses for CGIs and review some solutions that have impressed me with their capabilities. All the CGIs mentioned here meet what I consider to be minimal criteria for worthy CGIs: they can handle multiple connections at once, are actively being developed and supported, and are known to run stably in a variety of environments.

With a just a couple of exceptions, I have avoided mentioning any CGIs that utilize AppleScript. Although AppleScript was once the most popular means for creating CGIs, developers quickly found that its speed (or rather, lack thereof) and inability to handle multiple requests concurrently severely limited its usefulness in most environments.

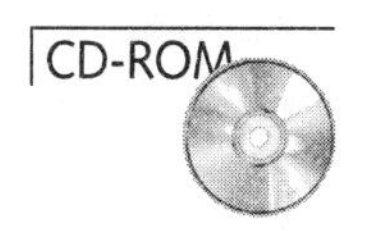

The HTML pages included in the **HTML** folder on the CD have more information on a variety of AppleScript-based CGIs, but I would advise using other types of CGIs whenever possible.

Testing New CGIs

Once your Web server is in operation, I strongly recommend that you set up a separate Mac, if possible, to test new CGIs and experiment with your server configuration before modifying your main site and possibly introducing new problems. Ideally, your development machine should be the same model and configuration as your Web server so as to duplicate the actual server's environment as closely as possible. If that's not possible, you should at least try to imitate the Web server's configuration as closely as you can.

This provides the added benefit that if your main server should suffer some sort of catastrophe, you'll have a backup Mac ready to go.

Imagemaps

Imagemaps are those graphics that allow clients to click portions of an image to go to different URLs on or off your own site. They are often used in navigation bars, home pages, or wherever a graphic interface (as opposed to text-based anchors) is desirable.

Imagemap CGIs work by receiving the coordinates of the point on the graphic clicked by the client, translating those coordinates into a URL, and returning a redirection response to the clients that send them to the proper page. To accomplish the translation of a coordinate (such as "120,60") into a URL, you need to create a map file for each imagemap to specify which areas of the image correspond to which URLs. Depending on the imagemap CGI you are using, these areas can be rectangles, ellipses, or irregular polygons. Using imagemaps, therefore, requires the use of a program to create the map file as well as the imagemap CGI itself.

I'll describe a few CGIs and map-file creation programs at the end of this section, but first, I'd like to mention an alternative to imagemap CGIs that is gaining in popularity.

Client-Side Imagemaps

An alternative to imagemap CGIs was introduced by the Microsoft Explorer Web browser and has since been picked up by the current Netscape browser and others. Rather than depend on the Web server to translate a client's click on a map graphic into a URL, the server can include the information about what portions of the graphic correspond to particular URLs in the page's HTML code and rely upon the client to do the translation internally, eliminating the trip to the server (and the subsequent delay) to find out which URL to go to. Figure 7.2 illustrates the difference between client-side and server-side imagemaps.

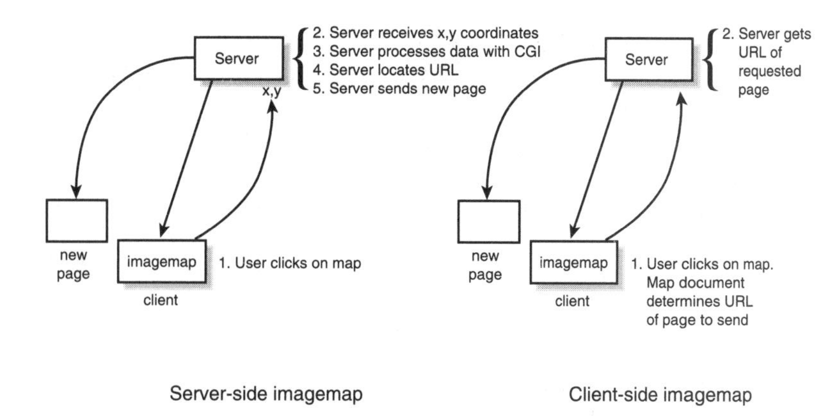

Figure 7.2 *Client-side versus server-side imagemaps.*

In the meantime, you'll need some applications like the following to implement your own imagemap CGIs.

MapServe

Contact: http://www.spub.ksu.edu/other/machttp_tools/mapserve/

Cost: About $20.00, shareware

MacHTTP-compatible: Yes

MapServe is probably the most popular imagemap CGI for the Mac, and is written in C to be as fast as possible. One special feature is its own logging output, so you can track which parts of your imagemaps are being clicked the most (or least!).

Mac-ImageMap

Contact: http://weyl.zib-berlin.de/imagemap/Mac-ImageMap.html

Cost: Free for noncommercial use

MacHTTP-compatible: Yes

Mac-ImageMap is very similar to MapServe, albeit without the logging features. Some people have reported problems with

MapServe causing odd crashes on their servers—if this happens to you, you might want to try Mac-ImageMap as an alternative.

WebMap

Contact: http://www.city.net/cnx/software/webmap.html

Cost: $25.00

MacHTTP-compatible: N/A

WebMap is the best program I've found for creating the circles, rectangles, and other "hotspots" on your images and writing out the map files most imagemap CGIs need to operate. Note that this application isn't actually a CGI, but it is an extremely useful tool to use with any imagemap CGI.

Dynamic HTML

Dynamic HTML is a catchall term that refers to any process for returning different responses to the same URL. The simplest form of dynamic HTML allows the insertion of information into a document at the time the page is returned to the client, typically with information like the current time, the client's IP address or domain name, the number of previous visitors to a particular page, or the name of the browser being used by the client.

This is mostly used to add a little "personal touch" to a page, but really isn't particularly functional. These CGIs work by inserting some of the information passed to them by the server about the client into the document being returned.

Another use for dynamic HTML is for macros, short "placeholders" in HTML documents that can be expanded at the time the page is requested into HTML code. This is usually used to assist in page creation and site maintenance, as a single file can hold the HTML code for a standard footer for a large number of pages. When the pages are requested, the application responsible for replacing the macro with the text it refers to does so, enabling large collections of documents with common elements to be edited or updated by changing a single file.

Because the alternative is often to open and edit every file individually, this kind of functionality can save a great deal of time and effort. In the non-Mac world, this kind of functionality is often referred to as "server-side includes."

At the other end of the spectrum, dynamic documents can contain fairly sophisticated scripts that display different information or formats for different browsers or visitors. A private Web site can be "layered" on to a public one this way by returning different HTML code to people accessing the site from a local network than to clients visiting the site from the rest of the Internet.

Because all dynamic documents require processing of the original document before it can be returned to the client, some implementations can also "preload" the dynamic pages' source text into RAM to maximize response time. Even if a page doesn't require processing, including it in cache of such a CGI can improve the lag time between clicking a link and having the page begin to display on the client's screen.

Here are a couple of the CGIs available for implementing dynamic HTML on your own pages.

NetCloak

Contact: http://www.maxum.com/NetCloak/

Cost: About $200.00

MacHTTP-compatible: Version available

NetCloak is probably the single most popular commercial CGI for Mac servers. It provides over 30 new tags you can insert into your HTML documents to add macros, display different text to different clients, request passwords, and hundreds of other functions. It is capable of caching pages as well, and is often fast enough that visitors to your site won't even realize a CGI is serving their pages!

MacHTPL

Contact: http://www.ice.com/

Cost: Freeware

MacHTTP-compatible: Yes

MacHTPL is a port of a UNIX CGI system for sophisticated pre-processing of HTML pages. It's a bit difficult to get used to, but provides a rich set of flexible commands that allows you to build scripts into your HTML pages that determine what actually is sent to clients. It is very similar in functionality to NetCloak, in that files with HTPL code in them are actually processed like scripts to generate a final page of HTML for serving to clients. If you have some experience with programming, you may find that the HTPL scripting language gives you more flexibility than NetCloak does, although NetCloak's performance is likely to be superior for most sites.

Chat Forums/Discussion Groups

In the world of Web servers, the idea of discussion groups is more closely related to how Usenet newsgroups work than to live, interactive forums such as those used by the online services. Typically, pages are maintained that collect postings to a particular "topic" at the site, allowing clients to read other postings by clicking links and to add submissions of their own via a form interface.

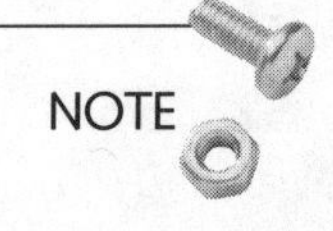

NOTE

> Duplicating traditional "chat" services with a scrolling list of current postings in single window is certainly possible with a Web server, but would take a toll on your server's resources, as each "viewer" must keep a TCP/IP connection open on your server so that each new message can be copied to all the participating clients. Because Open Transport will remove the 64-connection limit on MacOS servers, traditional chat services are likely to be available for MacOS Web servers in the near future, although you'll still need a relatively fast machine and Internet connection to run.

The interface to Web-based forums can be based upon static files that are updated or rewritten by a CGI that accepts submissions, or they can exist as entries in a database that builds each HTML page from its current records when a request is received. Either approach works fairly well, although the latter is usually a bit more flexible.

Here are a few applications I recommend for implementing discussion groups on your server.

GenesisJive

Contact: http://www.webgenesis.com/

Cost: About $300.00

MacHTTP-compatible: No

GenesisJive is built upon a database engine, which makes it both fast and sophisticated. It can manage large numbers of concurrent "forums" and even include graphics in the displays!

WebCrossing

Contact: http://webx.lundeen.com/

Cost: About $400.00

MacHTTP-compatible: No

WebCrossing is probably the most sophisticated (and most expensive) of the chat CGI solutions. It provides extensive username/password control of access to discussion groups, and offers highly customized formatting of the HTML pages used in the discussion groups.

Interaction/IP

Contact: http://www.ifi.uio.no/~terjen/interaction/

Cost: Free! (for now)

MacHTTP-compatible: Yes

Interaction/IP is more of a general CGI for managing concurrent users or "sessions" than it is designed specifically for chat services, but it can be used for that purpose very effectively. You can add other services to it that are based on tracking visitors through your site, such as "shopping basket" catalogs.

NetForms

Contact: http://www.maxum.com/NetForms/

Cost: About $200.00

MacHTTP-compatible: Yes

NetForms is a generalized forms-processing engine that not only can be used to implement discussion groups, but can also email form information to the address of your choice, set up message boards, and generally handle any task that requires converting form-based information into HTML pages on your site.

Email Gateways

An email gateway is a CGI that takes the information entered in a form, sends it to a designated email address, and returns an HTML page to the people submitting the form, thanking them for their input or whatever else.

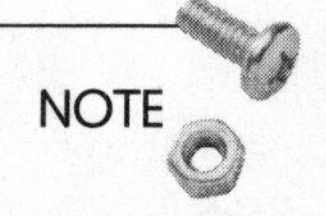

All of the email gateway CGIs mentioned here work exclusively with Internet-standard email systems and require that a SMTP (Simple Mail Transfer Protocol) server be available for forwarding email.

A common application for email gateway CGIs is in receiving comments from visitors or requests for further information. Rather than relying on the client to send email, you can use a CGI to allow clients to fill out a form on one of your Web pages, and then simply click the form button to transmit the information to you. Of course, you could also use a database to collect information from forms or even just write the information out to a file on your disk, but many people find email to be the most convenient method of collecting information, especially when managing a site for several different clients.

Flexmail

Contact: http://www.netdreams.com/net.dreams/software/flexmail/

Cost: About $20.00

MacHTTP-compatible: Yes

Flexmail provides a lot of features for customizing the response pages visitors receive after submitting forms and sending the form contents. You can even specify different email addresses for each form!

NetForms

Contact: http://www.maxum.com/NetForms/

Cost: About $200.00

MacHTTP-compatible: Yes

Sure, NetForms does a lot more than email form information, but it's nice to have a stable, commercial CGI running even if you only use its email capabilities.

File Indexing and Searching

Sites that need to serve a large number of text documents, such as a university's policy documents or a collection of tech support reports, rapidly find that attempting to organize all of their material into links and directories rapidly becomes unmanageable for both the site administrators and Web clients, who have to navigate through many links to find what they need. A better solution is to use a text indexer, which allows visitors to search the text of your document collections for words relevant to them, with varying degrees of sophistication.

Note that text indexers are most effective when the documents they search are available as HTML, so that users can click links returned from their search to immediately view the pages returned. As Acrobat technology evolves, however, look for the capability to allow searching and viewing of PDF documents as well as simple text.

What follows is the current applications I recommend for indexing and searching large document collections.

AppleSearch CGI

Contact: http://kamaaina.apple.com/

Cost: Free

MacHTTP-compatible: Yes

If you've already purchased AppleSearch ($1300–$1400) for other purposes, this CGI provides a way for you to link your AppleSearch technology to your Web site. It's very easy to set up, but not especially flexible, fast, or reliable. I'm including it only as a way for folks with large existing investments in AppleSearch technology to bring those resources onto their Web sites immediately. I would highly recommend pursuing one of the other options if at all possible.

MacSite Searcher

Contact: http://www.blueworld.com/macsite/searcher.html

Cost: About $300.00

MacHTTP-compatible: No

MacSite Searcher is a hybrid application that combines the Frontier scripting system with a FileMaker Pro database to provide very rapid text indexing and searching. It also sports a very slick user interface, and can be completely configured using a Web browser.

Database Connections

As the information served on the Web becomes more complex, and as the needs of Web sites to deliver information customized to a visitor's individual needs becomes more critical, databases are becoming increasingly common as means to organize, process, and deliver information to clients over the Web. Moreover, many organizations just beginning to publish online find themselves looking for convenient ways to provide information already stored in databases to visitors. These CGIs can assist you in making existing information accessible via the Web.

Tango

Contact: http://www.everyware.com/

Cost: About $300.00

MacHTTP-compatible: Yes

Tango is almost an application in itself, and offers a huge variety of tools to create HTML interfaces to ODBC-compliant databases (including the Butler database made by the manufacturers of Tango) without any programming at all.

Web FM

Contact: http://www.macweb.com/webfm/

Cost: About $100.00

MacHTTP-compatible: No

Although I'm normally pretty resistant to AppleScript CGIs, Web FM is very well done and has worked well for many sites. If you need to add access to a FileMaker Pro database to your site, Web FM will provide the means to do so.

You should already be able to work effectively with FileMaker Pro to use Web FM, as it doesn't isolate you from the database to nearly the same degree that Tango does.

Troubleshooting CGIs

Even with commercial CGI applications, you will occasionally experience problems with your CGIs that seem difficult to track down. Because Apple Events are somewhat difficult to "see" while they pass back and forth, working out the source of errors is especially difficult. What follows are some common problems and likely solutions.

Server Reports "Timeout" Errors

This usually means that the Web server is sending the proper Apple Event to the CGI, but that the CGI isn't returning a response before the event times out. Either the CGI is being asked to accomplish something that takes a very long time, or it is not handling the request correctly. You should check the URL you are sending to the CGI very carefully—paying special attention to the arguments being sent along with the main URL—until you are certain it is correct and meets the requirements of the CGI as described in the CGI's usage instructions. If you are sending a request to the CGI via an HTML form, also review your HTML code for possible errors.

If you are certain that the URL and HTML code are correct, try to establish if only certain browsers or clients experience problems—many odd CGI responses can be traced to particular browsers or proxy server configurations.

CGI or Server Crashes Unpredictably When Busy

This symptom can have a lot of disparate causes, but if the crashes occur only when the CGI is being accessed by more than one simultaneous client, it usually means the CGI doesn't support multiple simultaneous connections. You'll need to replace the CGI with one that does, or change the CGI's file suffix so that it is treated as a synchronous CGI by your Web server.

CGI Responses Are Sent Back to the Wrong Client

Whoops! This is commonly seen in poorly written AppleScripts, which can "cross wires" when attempting to handle multiple events at once. See the previous problem for the solution...

Server Seems to "Hang" Temporarily When a CGI Is Called

This is most likely due to calling a CGI synchronously. Check your suffix mappings to ensure that your CGI's filename matches a mapping for an asynchronous CGI and not a synchronous one.

Finally, the single most useful action you can take to cope with mysterious CGI problems is to tell other people about it! Contact the author of the CGI and post a description to a mailing list or newsgroup read by other Mac Web site administrators. Chances are that the problem has been fixed already, and you just need to upgrade to the latest version.

CGIs versus Built-Ins

As I mentioned at the beginning of this chapter, WebSTAR is the only Mac Web server application with what I consider to be robust and useful CGI support. Rather than compete with WebSTAR in this area, the makers of most other Mac HTTP servers argue that because a majority of Web sites need only a few common CGI functions, why not build those functions directly into the Web server?

There are both advantages and disadvantages to this approach. The major disadvantage is in a loss of flexibility—if you want to add a new CGI function to a server that doesn't support external CGIs, you're probably out of luck unless you can convince the makers of your server to add the functionality you want to their product. The main advantage, of course, is that you don't need to worry about finding and managing a bunch of (usually) single-purpose CGIs, each of which offers yet another potential source of crashes or other problems for your site.

If you feel capable of narrowly defining the needs of your site, and one of the non-WebSTAR server applications provides all the functionality you anticipate needing, your life is likely to be simpler by finding one of those offerings that meets your needs. If your plans for your site are still somewhat vague, however, you may want to stick with WebSTAR until you can establish how much CGI functionality your site will require.

Summary

This chapter has introduced you to the basic concepts and ideas behind using CGIs, but you may want to develop your own CGIs, add more sophisticated CGI functions than those described here, or just learn more of the technical details of how CGIs operate. Chapter 8 discusses all of these topics and more, so as soon as you're ready—grab your server and turn the page!

CHAPTER 8

Advanced Techniques

As you begin to discover the power of the Web to change the way you communicate with others, you'll quickly find that many of the more sophisticated uses of your server demand more skills than simply managing the server software itself. Whether you are planning to integrate a database into your site, begin serving pages customized for the individuals requesting them, or develop novel CGIs to meet more esoteric needs, this chapter introduces you to the means to your ends.

Rolling Your Own

Many people who never dreamed of learning to program a Macintosh are starting to find that the needs of their Web site demand such skills. Whether existing CGIs are simply insufficient for your needs or you just want to experiment with the technology, you'll find that there is a plethora of options available to you.

The next section discusses pros and cons for all of the popular languages for developing CGIs on the Macintosh. Rest assured that you have many more options than do site administrators on any other platform—no matter what your level of programming experience or desire to learn, there is an environment to meet your needs.

Programming/Scripting Environments

There is a subtle distinction between scripting and programming. Although both allow writing procedures to process information, a scripting language is designed to provide an abstracted view of the MacOS, provides many tools for controlling the Finder and other applications, and generally uses a simpler syntax and format than a programming language.

Scripting systems are easier to learn and use than programming languages, and offer nearly the same functionality with a lot less work.

Both AppleScript and Frontier (described later in this chapter) are scripting systems for the MacOS that execute small programs (scripts) that you can easily revise as individual entities. In a sense, scripting systems provide an application (the scripting system) that you can customize by writing procedures that the application will run for you. This relieves you from having to cope with the many details of working directly with the MacOS and allows you to concentrate just on the actions specific to your scripts.

Programming languages allow you to access the MacOS directly and require that a complete application be designed and compiled (converted from text into a machine-readable form) as a single entity. They also allow you to take advantage of new or specialized features of the MacOS that might be impossible to access with a scripting system until the maker of the scripting system decides to include functions to access those features in their applications.

Generally, scripting systems are easier to learn and use than programming languages, and offer nearly the same functionality with a lot less work. The downside is that you lose the flexibility of writing your own applications and you are dependent on the scripting systems' manufacturers to provide the tools you need to realize your designs.

I've listed the most common CGI development environments on the Mac along with discussions of their features and suitability for creating CGIs. Most of the languages mentioned here have "shells," sample CGIs that you can modify for your own purposes, included on the CD in the **Software, Programmming** folder.

AppleScript

In the early days of Mac-based Web serving, AppleScript was the environment of choice for aspiring CGI developers. It was easy to learn and use, and many tutorials and example scripts were available online by the early pioneers in this area.

One advantage of AppleScript is that it is installed on just about everybody's Mac, so that you can try or distribute different scripts without concern about whether a particular application is installed already. Even now, many Web sites depend on AppleScript to accomplish a variety of tasks.

Unfortunately, as Mac-based Web sites began to be placed into more critical applications and the performance of Mac-based Web servers increased, AppleScript quickly hit the limits of its capabilities as a CGI development language.

The primary problems are twofold:

- AppleScript copes very badly with multiple simultaneous requests from a Web server. This is because incoming Apple Events are processed by AppleScript in a "last-in, first-out" manner, so that if a second Apple Event is sent to a running script that is already in the midst of handling a CGI request, the script will stop handling the first request and immediately begin handling the second, only returning to the first after the second has completed.

- If many events arrive at a script quickly, the first few requests will often time out before the script finishes handling the later requests. An unfortunate result of this behavior is that, unless the AppleScript programmer is extremely skillful, responses are sometimes returned to the wrong client when multiple requests are made at once. If you are attempting to collect credit card numbers or perform any other type of confidential transaction with your script, these "crossing wires" in the responses can be a major problem.

For the previous reasons as well as problems with speed, I highly recommend avoiding AppleScript for any CGI applications. The only situation in which you might find them acceptable is when you are sure that only one person will be using the CGI at any given time (a script that sends Apple Events to control your Web server is a good example, because presumably only one administrator has access to it) and when speed is not of any particular concern.

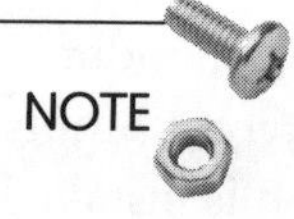

AppleScript is great for automating administrative tasks, but inappropriate for serious CGI development. If you are unfamiliar with both AppleScript and Frontier (see the next section), your investment in time to learn CGI development will be much better spent with Frontier.

The CD does contain AppleScript CGI *shells*—example scripts that you can customize for your own use—as well as shareware and commercial CGIs based on AppleScript that you can try on your own system if you wish. I encourage you to experiment with AppleScript if you desire to, but please do so forewarned of its limitations.

Frontier

Frontier is the most powerful and efficient tool available for developing CGIs without learning a fundamental programming language such as C or Pascal. It provides a rich set of commands and functions for writing scripts and is rapidly displacing AppleScript as the most popular CGI development tool. Frontier was originally a rather pricey commercial product, but has since been released as a free version alternately called Aretha and Frontier (or The Scripting System Formerly Known as Frontier, by Prince fans). It's still a bit unclear whether future versions of Frontier will also be freeware (a PowerPC-native version is in beta as I write this, for example), but the "word on the street" is that such will continue to be the case.

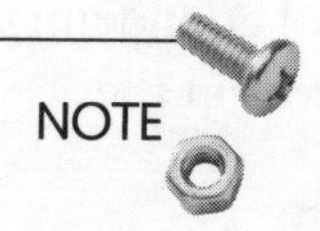

You can download the latest release of Aretha/Frontier from Dave Winer's Aretha page at `http://www.hotwired.com/staff/userland/aretha/`.

In keeping with creator Dave Winer's heritage in developing outliner software for the Mac, Frontier is organized as a hierarchical database, much like an outline, with scripts, commands, and data all organized as tables within tables called an "object database."

Although Frontier's structure can be a little difficult to follow when first encountered, it is a powerful conceptual tool that you will learn to appreciate over time. The scripting language used by Frontier is vaguely C-like, but provides a much more complete set of commands (called "verbs" in Frontier) and functions than does AppleScript. Frontier supports *multithreaded processing*—multiple independent scripts or instances of a single script that run simultaneously—so receiving multiple CGI requests at once presents no problem.

Even though Frontier (or Aretha) is still in an extremely dynamic state, with updates being released on a weekly or even daily basis, you will find several Frontier sample scripts along with the current release of Frontier on the CD (look in the **Software, Programming** folder). Be sure and stop by Dave's home page (`http://www.hotwired.com/staff/userland/`) for the latest update of Frontier and to find information on the many other Web projects he has going.

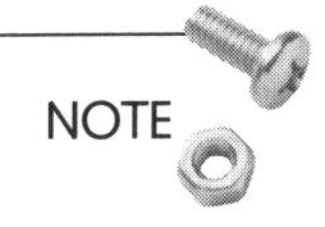

One publication with an in-depth treatment of Frontier scripting is Tom Trinko's *Applied Mac Scripting*, which is available at `Amazon.com` (`http://www.amazon.com/`), frankly the best bookstore on the Web I've come across.

I cannot emphasize strongly enough the value of learning to use Frontier on your site, both for administrative and Web-serving tasks. The investment in time to learn AppleScript may be slightly less, but the return on your investment will be many times greater with Frontier.

Traditional Programming Languages

C, Pascal, and Fortran are "real" programming languages—the same languages used to write applications such as WebSTAR. Fortunately, much of the complexity normally associated with programming on the MacOS originates in the user interface, and CGIs generally don't need any but the most primitive user interface elements, especially if you're developing software for only your own use. This simplifies your programming task enormously, even if you are coming to the Mac from another environment, such as UNIX.

Upcoming versions of WebSTAR will offer support for "plug-ins," which are compiled procedures that WebSTAR can use in place of CGIs by calling the plug-ins directly from WebSTAR, much like scripts can be added to Frontier.

The advantage of plug-ins is that they add CGI functions without the overhead of Apple Events and running separate applications on the Mac. Plug-ins are therefore the most efficient way to add high-performance CGI functions to a WebSTAR server. If you want to create your own plug-ins, however, you have to use a programming language such as C. Please check the current documentation for WebSTAR at http://www.starnine.com/ for more details on writing plug-ins.

C is by far the most popular programming language for the Mac, and most of the source code available for you to reuse is written in C or C++, which is a "superset" of the C language. If you are just starting to program, C is likely to be the best place to invest your time. I recommend using the CodeWarrior programming environment (http://www.metrowerks.com/) along with a good book on programming the Mac in C, such as the *Programming Starter Kit for Macintosh* by Hayden Books (ISBN: 1-56830-174-X) or one of the CodeWarrior-specific books available from the CodeWarrior Web site.

Several different C shells (Responder and CGI Framework) are available on the CD for you to work with in developing your own CGIs. All provide the basic CGI functions, leaving you with the job of filling in the code for the specific tasks you need your CGI to perform. Be sure also to check the **HTML** folder, also on the CD, for more resources.

In general, Grant Neufeld's shells are considered to bo the best written overall, and I recommend choosing his work as a starting point for your own applications.

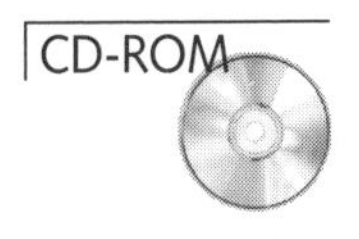

If you already work with Pascal or Fortran, you can use either language to create CGIs. Unfortunately, I am not aware of any CGI shells available for Pascal programmers. An example shell written in Fortran is, however, included in the **Software, Programming** folder on the CD.

4D/NetLink

Although 4D is neither a scripting nor programming environment under the strict meanings of those descriptions, I've included mention of it here because it offers a unique capability among Mac databases—with the NetLink external, it can act as a CGI without any intermediary applications to handle Apple Events from your Web server. 4D can therefore be considered a CGI development environment in its own right, as you can create any CGI function you desire directly in 4D, including the capability to control other applications via Apple Events.

This removes the necessity for an intermediary CGI (which all other databases require) and allows you to take advantage of 4D's built-in threading and powerful internal procedural language to build a framework on which you can hang a multitude of CGI functions within one package, much like Frontier.

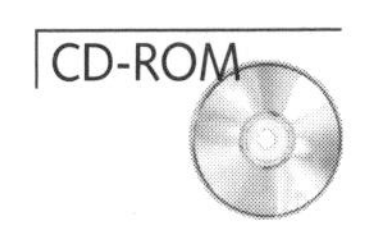

You can find out more about using 4D/Netlink as a CGI by experimenting with the demo database provided on the CD (in the **Software, Programming** folder) or by visiting the Web site of the makers of NetLink, Foresight Technology, at http://www.fsti.com/.

Other CGI Development Environments

Although the previous methods are by far the most popular and effective means of creating your own CGIs, the following languages have also been used successfully as CGI development tools. Whether you have a particular need to use one of them on your own site, or just want to experiment with different options, a brief description of each is included.

MacPerl

At first glance, MacPerl would seem to be an almost ideal language for developing CGIs—most CGIs on UNIX machines are written in Perl, and Perl is specifically designed for processing and manipulating text, which is 90 percent of the work for most CGIs. However, MacPerl suffers from similar problems as AppleScript, namely that it cannot handle multiple requests simultaneously. Furthermore, differences between the UNIX and MacOS operating systems prevent most UNIX-based Perl scripts from being used on the Mac without a great deal of work rewriting the code.

I don't recommend using MacPerl to write CGIs, but a development shell is included on the CD for your own review, and you can find pointers to documentation on MacPerl at http://err.ethz.ch/members/neeri/macintosh/perl.html.

Forth

Forth is yet another "real" programming language, but is very rarely used except in research or educational settings. If you already have some experience with Forth, you may want to peruse the Forth CGI shell included on the CD, but I consider it more of a curiosity than an active environment. The Forth programming environment and additional documentation can be found at http://chemlab.pc.maricopa.edu/pocket.html.

Prograph

Prograph is unique among Mac programming languages in that it is entirely visual—rather than write out procedures in a text format, you "build" procedures using iconic tools and functions. It does provide complete access to the MacOS, and is gradually increasing in popularity.

Of all the nonstandard languages in this section, I would consider Prograph to be the most likely competition for C or Frontier, and recommend you investigate the shell on the CD to get a better idea of whether its approach to programming is attractive to your style of thinking. A fully functional version of the Prograph Classic (http://www.pictorius.com/pi/products/classic.html) programming environment is included as well for your review.

CGI Development Reference

The following section provides a reference for CGI development in any language or setting. Keep in mind that the following may be handled differently by different scripting or programming environments—you will need to refer to the documentation for your language and CGI shell of choice for specifics before using the following information in your CGIs.

The process of handling a CGI request is always the same:

1. The Web server sends an Apple Event to the CGI containing a list of parameters specific to the particular request.
2. The CGI parses out the information of interest from the Apple Event and decodes any URL-encoded data provided by the client.
3. The CGI performs whatever custom processing of the request it is designed to do.
4. The CGI constructs a valid HTTP response, and sends it back to the Web server via an Apple Event.
5. The server then passes the CGI-supplied response back to the client and closes the TCP connection.

All the CGI shells provided on the CD take care of parts 1, 2, and 5 of the CGI sequence described here for you. Your job is to know what the different parameters provided mean so that you can process the request correctly and construct a valid HTTP response for returning to the server.

What Goes In

The parameters provided by the Web server to your CGI will vary somewhat depending on the server application and the type of request made by the client.

The following list contains descriptions of all the parameters currently sent by MacOS Web servers to CGIs. All of them work with

MacHTTP, WebSTAR, or InterServer Publisher unless otherwise indicated in the description.

The format for each entry is (<id>)<name>: <description>, where <id> is the case-sensitive four-letter code used by the Apple Event to designate the parameter, the <name> is the common name for the parameter, often seen in CGI shells, and the <description> is just that. Note that the order in which these parameters appear in a given Apple Event may vary from one server to another or even one event to another, so you should not as a rule depend on them appearing in any particular order.

CGI Parameters

- (meth)method: Generally, either GET or POST, used mainly in form-handling CGIs to determine whether to look in the search_args (for GET) or post_args (for POST) parameters for form data. The HTTP standard also supports a PUT method for posting files to a server, but this is not implemented on any Mac servers to date because POST can work just as well for the same purpose.

- (addr)client_address: If the server is performing DNS lookups, this parameter contains the DNS hostname for the client's machine or proxy server. If DNS lookups are not on, it contains the IP address of the client or proxy server sending the request.

- (frmu)from_user: Some browsers include an identifying bit of information about the client here, such as the email address. Most of the time, however, it is empty.

- (user)username: If HTTP basic authentication was requested previously (see the Response header section), this parameter contains the username submitted by the client.

- (pass)password: In the same context as the username, this parameter contains the password submitted by the client.

- (svnm)server_name: The name of the server that is sending the CGI request, normally the hostname for the server machine.

- (svpt)server_port: The TCP port the server is listening on, usually 80.

- (scnm)script_name: The URL path sent by the client, decoded and stripped of any path arguments or search arguments.

- (refr)referer: Many browsers send the URL of the last page visited before sending the current request: In that case this parameter contains the complete URL (including path and search arguments) of the page that linked to the current request's URL. This is often useful for determining whether a link came from one of your own pages or an outside site, and for determining the origin of malformed URLs.

- (Agnt)user_agent: Almost all browsers send identifying information about themselves with their requests, but many also allow the client to modify it arbitrarily, so you should be careful to write CGIs that can handle anything that appears here. If the clients sent their request by way of a proxy server, the proxy server will usually append identifying information about itself to the referer parameter.

  This parameter is primarily used to return different responses to clients using different browsers, such as Netscape-specific HTML to Netscape users, and more generic HTML to other clients.

- (ctyp)content_type: The MIME type of the data sent as a POST argument, if applicable. This is almost always www/x-form-urlencoded.

- (Kcip)client_ip: Always contains the IP address of the client or its proxy server, regardless of whether the server is performing DNS lookups.

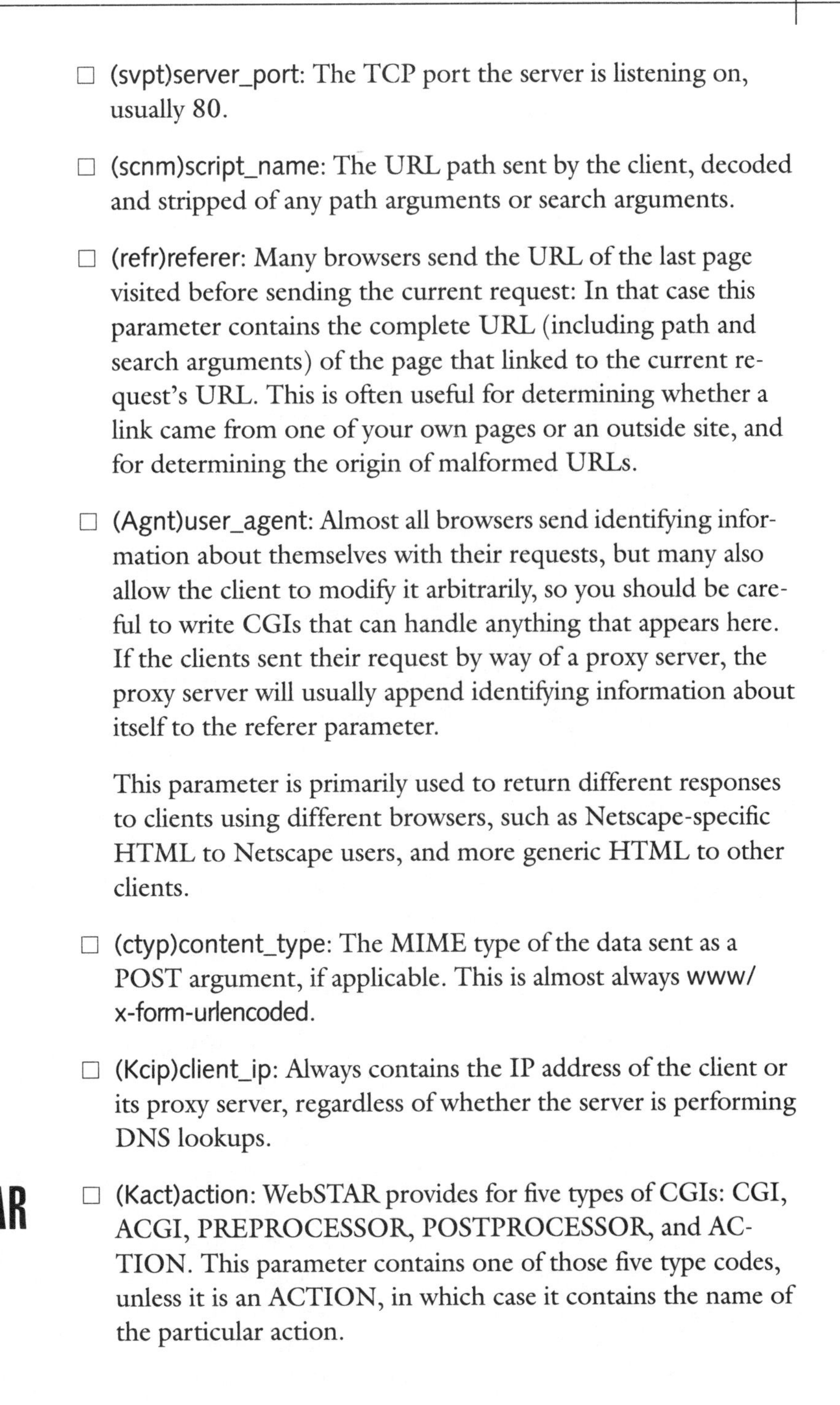

- (Kact)action: WebSTAR provides for five types of CGIs: CGI, ACGI, PREPROCESSOR, POSTPROCESSOR, and ACTION. This parameter contains one of those five type codes, unless it is an ACTION, in which case it contains the name of the particular action.

Actions are a means provided by WebSTAR to redirect URL requests to a particular CGI without forcing the client to actually specify the path to the CGI in the URL. This is accomplished by specifying in WebSTAR that certain file suffixes are always to be handled by a particular CGI, regardless of whether the filename specified actually exists. This is often used with CGIs like NetCloak (see Chapter 6) to allow all *.html file requests to be processed by the CGI rather than WebSTAR. It also allows the use of "virtual filenames," so that you can send commands to a CGI using the full URL path. This works because the URL path is ignored by WebSTAR, which only looks at the suffix, but can be parsed by the CGI and given whatever meaning you like.

PREPROCESSOR is another special method of accessing CGIs only available from WebSTAR. If you specify a particular CGI as a preprocessor, every request that WebSTAR receives is sent to the CGI similarly to the way WebSTAR deals with ACTION CGIs. The difference is that while an ACTION CGI is required to return an HTTP response just like a normal CGI, a PREPROCESSOR CGI has the option of returning nothing (an empty '----' Apple Event parameter) to WebSTAR. WebSTAR will then proceed to process the request normally, even to the extent of calling another CGI to handle the request if that is indicated. If the PREPROCESSOR CGI returns any information at all, however, WebSTAR will send that response back to the client just as with a normal CGI transaction.

CGI and ACGI indicate that the CGI application is being called synchronously and asynchronously, respectively.

POSTPROCESSOR CGIs are sort of anti-PREPROCESSORS—they are sent a full CGI request for every request, but a POSTPROCESSOR is sent the request only after WebSTAR is done handling it normally. Because WebSTAR has already completed the HTTP transaction with the client, a POSTPROCESSOR CGI must not return any data at all to WebSTAR; its purpose is solely to collect information about incoming requests for custom logging or statistical analysis.

You can find out more about all of these special WebSTAR CGI interfaces by consulting the WebSTAR documentation.

WEBSTAR

- (Kapt)action_path: If the CGI was called by WebSTAR as an ACTION, the path to the CGI application on the user's hard disk is placed here. Otherwise, it just contains a duplicate of the script_name parameter.

WEBSTAR

- (Kfrq)full_request: The entire HTTP request received by WebSTAR, exactly as submitted by the client, without any POST data. This is used primarily to extract information from HTTP headers sent by the client that are not part of the HTTP standard.

  Netscape 2.0 and later, for example, adds a "Host:" header that identifies the hostname used in the requested URL, but this information is not in any of the standard parameters described previously. To retrieve its value (or any other custom header), you'll need to search the `full_request` parameter for the header in question (in this case, the string "Host:") then grab all the data following the header to the next <CRLF> line delimiter.

  The data between the header and the end of the line can then be parsed or otherwise dealt with as you wish. This allows your server to differentiate between requests using different aliases of your server's hostname, which can be used to serve "virtual domain names" as discussed in Chapter 11.

WEBSTAR

- (Kcid)connection_id: A unique integer ID number that WebSTAR understands to refer to a particular client if multiple connections are being handled simultaneously.

- (post)post_args: This parameter contains any information submitted by the client via the POST method, normally information collected via an HTML form. It is not decoded by the server, so your CGI is responsible for parsing it into its individual variable/value pairs and decoding the information before you can use it in your CGI.

- (kfor)http_search_args: If search arguments were present (after a "?"), they are placed here. Your CGI is responsible for decoding these arguments after it receives them.
- (----)path_args: No that's not a misprint—the four-letter designator for the "direct parameter" to an Apple Event is four dashes. If path arguments are present, they can be found here.

What Goes Out

When constructing an HTTP response to return to the client, you must follow the HTTP standards, which, fortunately, are pretty simple. On the Mac, the entire response is placed as text in the direct parameter (code "----") of the Apple Event to be returned to the server. This response consists of a series of HTTP-defined header lines and the data (HTML text or picture information, for example) to be returned, if applicable. You read about these elements in detail in the next sections.

Elements of the HTTP Response

The two essential parts of your response are the HTTP headers, some of which are optional, ending in two <CRLF> character combinations in a row (basically, an empty line), and the data you are returning, if any. Let's examine each part in turn.

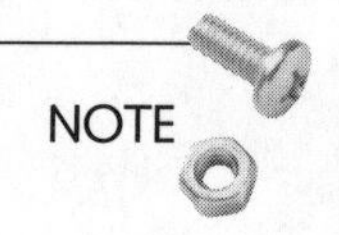

NOTE

It's standard for the second line of an HTTP response to be the following:

```
Server: <server name><CRLF>
```

where `<server name>` is a string identifying your server software's name, such as "MacHTTP." It is completely optional, however, and is almost always ignored by the client's software. I'll leave it out of the examples in this section for brevity's sake, but you can feel free to include it if you wish.

Normal Response

The standard HTTP response is as follows:

```
HTTP/1.0 200 OK<CRLF>
MIME-version: 1.0<CRLF>
Content-type: text/html<CRLF>
<CRLF>
<DATA>
```

Let's look at each line in turn:

```
HTTP/1.0 200 OK<CRLF>
```

The only variation in the first line of HTTP responses is in the response code (`200`) and some text following the response code that makes it easier for humans to read HTTP responses if they wish to. The text is technically both optional and undefined, so you could include anything you like after the response code, but I'll use the common descriptions in these examples. `200` is the response code meaning that information is being returned to the client and that the client's software should look in the `<DATA>` portion of the response for that information.

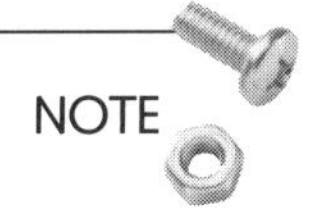

NOTE

> A complete list of the official HTTP response codes can be found at `http://www.w3.org/hypertext/WWW/Protocols/HTTP/HTRESP.html`. Most of the codes found there are not used in current practice, but they may become more important in the future, so I would suggest you glance through the list at least once.

```
MIME-version: 1.0<CRLF>
Content-type: text/html<CRLF>
```

Whenever you return information to the clients to be saved on their disk, displayed, or passed to a helper application for processing, you must include the two header lines shown previously so that the client knows what to do with the information you're sending.

The MIME-version line is standard and should always be the same, but the Content-type will vary depending on what you are returning to the client. The string following the Content-type: header must be a valid MIME type, as described in Chapter 6. For HTML pages, the text/html MIME type is appropriate, for GIF images you would use the MIME type image/gif, and so on.

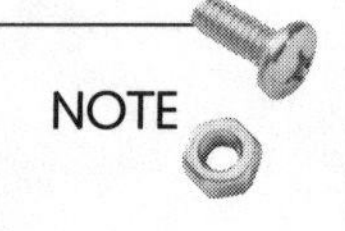

> At the end of the headers, you must include an extra <CRLF> string so the client knows you're done with the headers and will read any data that follows as information according to the MIME type you specified previously.

Once you've completed adding the headers to the response, you can simply append whatever other information you want to send to the client after the final <CRLF>. In this case, you would simply insert the HTML code where the <DATA> tag occurs.

Two other common HTTP responses are Redirection and Authorization responses. They are described next.

Redirection Response

The format of a redirection response is

```
HTTP/1.0 302 Found<CRLF>
Location: http://www.ncsa.com/<CRLF>
URI: http://www.ncsa.com/<CRLF>
<CRLF>
```

The redirection response code is normally `302 Found`.

Note that:

- There is no <DATA> to be appended to a redirection, because all the client needs to know is what URL you are asking it to retrieve.
- The complete URL must be specified.

- You can include path or search arguments in the URL, just as if you placed them in an HTML anchor.
- Although the current standard specifies only that the URI: line must be included, many older browsers still depend on the obsolete Location: header, so it's good practice to include both in your response. (Recall that URI stands for Uniform Resource Identifier, another name for the URL.)

Authorization Response

The format of an authorization response is

```
HTTP/1.0 401 Unauthorized<CRLF>
WWW-Authenticate: Basic realm="<REALM>"<CRLF>
MIME-version: 1.0<CRLF>
Content-type: text/html<CRLF>
<CRLF>
<DATA>
```

An authorization response causes the client's software to ask the client for a username and password to access the originally requested URL. On most systems, this is done via a dialog box. The client has the option of either canceling the request, in which case the <DATA> portion of the response will be displayed to the client, or sending back a username and password with a duplicate of the original URL request, which appear in the user and pass parameters, respectively, of the Apple Event for the second request.

The <REALM> portion of the WWW-Authenticate: header is a string of characters indicating a name for the group or server authentication is being asked for. This name is displayed to the clients when they are asked for the username and password by their software programs.

Database Connectivity

Whether you use a Web server application with a built-in database (see Chapter 5) or add a database via CGIs to your Web site, the power of database management systems to organize information and write custom procedures makes them the most efficient way of expanding the capabilities and functions of your site. Often, a single database can replace several separate CGI applications by duplicating the functionality of each separate CGI within one application, increasing your site's speed and decreasing the opportunities for software problems or incompatibilities to arise.

Databases can be used to create entire Web sites or subsections of Web sites at the time the URLs are requested, allowing custom pages to be created for each visitor. The possibilities are endless, and I urge you to begin thinking about databases less as simple searching and sorting engines and more as generic CGI environments that allow you to manage large amounts of information with ease and add new CGI-like capabilities to your site within a single development environment.

As a site increases in size and complexity, databases also offer the means to organize your site and manage changes more easily than can be done with a collection of individual files. You can even use a database "off-line" to manage your site and add procedures to export HTML files for uploading to your Web server if running a CGI on your server Mac is not an option.

The battles between adherents to various database systems can often be as vehement and protracted as those between the supporters of different operating systems (or religions, for that matter). Although virtually any database system can be used with a Web server given enough time and programming skill, four systems in particular are widely used and described in detail in this chapter.

Characteristics of a Good Database CGI

Here are some items to look for when choosing a database backend for a Web server:

- Speed

  For just a few hundred records and simple searches for single items like names, dates, prices, and so on, you don't notice a significant speed difference among any of the databases described here. For very large data sets, 4D probably offers the fastest solution, but Butler and FileMaker are not far behind. FoxPro is blazingly fast, but very difficult to use with a Web server when compared with the other options.

- Feature matching

  Know what you need before you go shopping for a database. Your database system may easily be the most expensive piece of software running on your server, both in terms of dollars and the amount of time you'll need to spend learning and using it. How many records will your database need to handle efficiently? What specific features, like full-text indexing and searching, will you need? If you need to upgrade your site to a server array (see Chapter 5), will your database be able to work in a client/server configuration? Will you need your database to access other databases or information servers on your LAN? These are the kinds of questions you should be asking yourself before even looking at the possibilities for your server.

- Extensibility

  Sometimes the most powerful applications require features that are not part of a standard database package. Even if you cannot imagine a feature you might want that is not already provided, changing database systems can be an expensive endeavor, and your investment is best protected by the knowledge that you can expand your system to meet your needs if necessary.

  Both 4D and FileMaker are the most extensible applications presented next—4D through compiled "plug-ins" that add commands to its internal language, and FileMaker through its strong support of controlling other applications through Apple Events. For example, a number of extensions to 4D are available that allow you to add direct TCP/IP functions like FTP or email to your database (this is the basis for the NetWings and Web Server 4D applications discussed in Chapter 5). You could also use the Apple Event support in

FileMaker Pro to control other applications such as Eudora or Fetch to accomplish the same ends.

- Past experience

  Don't overlook the value of your current knowledge when deciding on a database system. If you or your company has worked exclusively with FileMaker Pro for years, the additional functionality of a database like 4D may not balance the learning time and conversion processes necessary to bring your existing data into a new system and learn how to interface that system with your Web server.

Butler

Butler is, to my knowledge, the only true SQL-compatible database available for the Macintosh. SQL (Standard Query Language, pronounced "see-quel") is the lingua franca of databases on most other platforms, so Butler offers a familiar environment for database developers coming to the Mac from other operating systems. Because Butler works as a server application, you cannot simply sit in front of it and manipulate the database.

Most user-interface functions require the use of a database client or "front-end" application to provide the layouts, menus, scripts, and other niceties that enable a user to directly interact with a database. The advantage of this kind of server system is that all data-intensive operations like searching and sorting can be performed on the server, whereas user-specific operations like formatting the results of a search into HTML can be done by the client, efficiently splitting the work between the relevant machines.

For Web serving, this means that you can set up multiple Web servers, each running its own CGI "client," that can simultaneously access a central database server when responding to queries. This configuration guarantees that all your servers are using the same data, easing the process of creating server arrays as described in the "Upgrading Your Site" section of Chapter 5. Butler normally likes to be on its own Mac, although it can run on the same machine as your Web server if necessary, with some degradation in performance.

Tango provides tools for the rapid creation of custom CGI systems that interact with Butler or any other ODBC-compliant database system.

The real advantage of Butler lies in the CGI bundled with it by Everyware—Tango. Tango provides tools for the rapid creation of custom CGI systems that interact with Butler or any other ODBC-compliant database system. Tango can help you create Web pages for database searches, recording form submissions, calling AppleScripts in response to arbitrary URLs, and half a dozen other features, rapidly and easily.

4D/NetLink

4th Dimension offers a unique advantage for CGI developers—it is the only database CGI development system that does not require an intermediary CGI to accept CGI requests and send back responses to a Web server. Because 4D is also cross-platform, NetLink is being developed to work in a Windows environment as well as the MacOS. Why do you care about that? Because it will provide the only serious cross-platform environment for developing CGIs, allowing you to market or use CGIs you develop in 4D to either Windows NT or MacOS users simply by recompiling the database for the other platform.

Even if you don't plan to market the CGIs you develop in 4D, this is a nice tidbit of information to pass along to clients or bosses who might be wary of committing to the Mac as a platform for Web serving. With 4D, you can develop a site on the Mac and still have the option of moving to Windows NT if necessary with minimal effort.

Unfortunately, although a complete demo with source code of a 4D/NetLink CGI is in **Software, Programming** folder on the CD, you cannot run the demo without a copy of 4D. 4D can be purchased from most Mac mail-order firms, normally for about $500–$600. You can stop by http://www.acius.com/ (see Figure 8.1) for more information on 4D products, or check the HTML pages for this chapter for additional URLs.

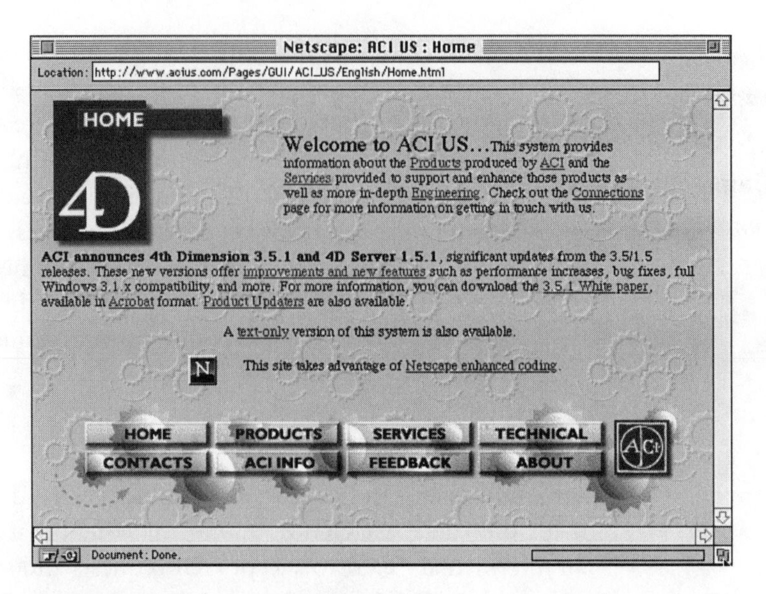

Figure 8.1 *ACI's products page tells you about the latest versions of 4th Dimension and 4D Server.*

FileMaker Pro

FileMaker has always been known as the easiest Mac database to develop applications with and version 3.0, which added basic relational capabilities, only makes it better. Its internal Apple Event support is rich, making it ideal for controlling other applications such as MacAuthorize (see the next section on online commerce) or an email program, and it is unique in its capability to automatically index each word of text fields, allowing rapid searching by keyword of documents or other long text fields entered into the database.

FileMaker does, however, lack the extensibility and speed of more expensive databases such as 4D. Searching speeds tend to be about the same for 4D, Butler, and FileMaker on small data sets, but, except for indexed text searches, 4D and Butler will outperform FileMaker on complex searches or on large data sets of over fifty thousand records in a single file.

FoxPro

FoxPro has one advantage over all other Mac database applications—it always wins the speed test for returning results.

FoxPro has one advantage over all other Mac database applications—it always wins the speed test for returning results. Searches in FoxPro, especially for long or complex queries that need to look through several tables of information to find results, are unbeatably fast. However, the advantages of this wonderful speed are offset by a very steep learning curve, a DOS-like interface, and almost no support for receiving Apple Events from a CGI or any other application.

The most common way to interact with FoxPro from another application is to have an intermediary CGI send FoxPro a command to execute a program using parameters supplied by the CGI. Because FoxPro cannot return the results directly to the CGI via an Apple Event, the best workaround is to have the database create a temporary file that the CGI can then read and delete, returning the contents to the client.

NOTE

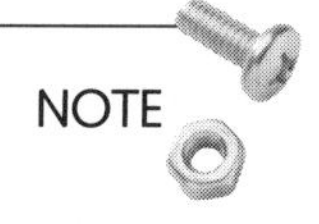

> You can also use the Clipboard to pass information back to the CGI, but I don't recommend that approach because of problems with multiple results being returned simultaneously.

Online Commerce

One of the hottest growth areas on the Internet is in commercial sites that actually sell items over the Web, whether the products are services, physical items, or information. Millions of dollars are already changing hands, and the amount of and variations in online commerce are expected to grow substantially in the coming years.

Although it's certainly possible to simply collect order information via HTML forms and process the orders off-line, the efficiencies of online commerce can't be fully realized until the process of transferring funds from the customer to yourself is automated as well. There are a variety of schemes in different stages of maturity available to assist you in doing so; the most popular ones are covered next.

MacAuthorize

MacAuthorize, from Tellan Software (http://www.tellan.com/), is the only means I am aware of to handle credit card authorizations and related transactions from a Mac (see Figure 8.2). You'll need a Mac with a phone line and modem attached that can be used to dial the bank with which you have a merchant account to perform card authorizations.

Figure 8.2 *Tellan Software's MacAuthorize site.*

MacAuthorize is a full-featured credit card transaction manager, able to handle manual or automated (via Apple Events) single and batch transactions. You can authorize credit cards, submit charges and refunds, or even perform check guarantee transactions from a single program.

MacAuthorize is also available in a network version that allows multiple Macs to process card transactions simultaneously and, perhaps more significantly for online commerce, keeps the modem connection to your card processor open indefinitely, allowing authorizations to take place in just a few seconds rather than the 10–20 seconds required if the modem needs to dial out for each new transaction.

Working out all the details necessary to accept credit cards, however, can be a hassle, especially if your sole purpose in obtaining authorization to process credit card orders is to facilitate online transactions. Many banks and other major card issuers are reluctant to deal directly with small startup companies, and will refer you to card processors who act as a kind of wholesaler for credit card account transactions.

Tellan Software has a list of such service providers at their Web site, and is the best place to start if you are looking for a card services provider in your area who is familiar with MacAuthorize. Be sure to shop around, as startup requirements and processing fees can vary widely from provider to provider.

First Virtual

First Virtual Holdings, Inc. (http://www.fv.com/) has developed a process that allows Internet buyers and sellers to sell information via credit cards without ever transmitting the actual credit card account numbers over the Internet—see Figure 8.3.

Customers open a First Virtual account by entering their credit card numbers into First Virtual's databases over the telephone, and then receive account names that they can give to First Virtual-enabled merchants to purchase information. The seller sends the account names and amount of the purchases to First Virtual, which then charges the customers' credit cards (after verifying the purchases with the customers) and credits the seller's checking account with the moneys received, minus a small percentage for processing the transaction.

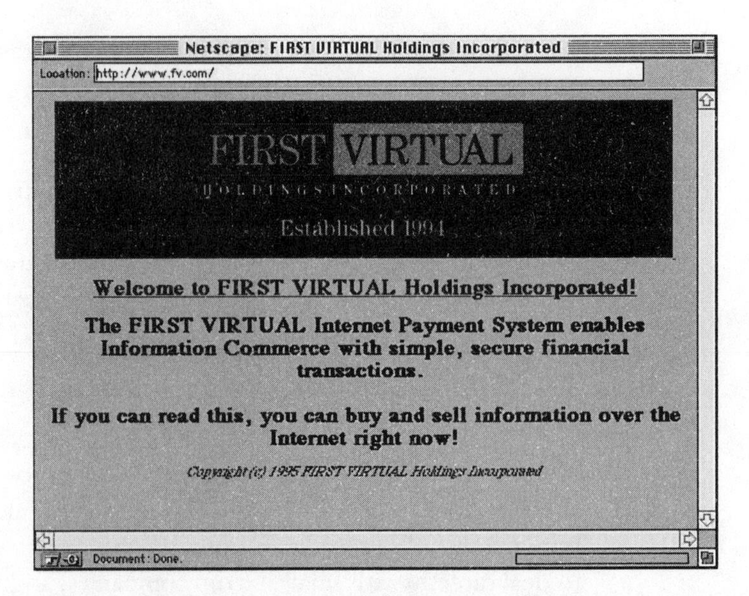

Figure 8.3 *Buy and sell information over the Internet with First Virtual Holdings, Inc.*

You may have noticed that I was careful to mention the purchase of information, specifically, in the preceding discussion. This is because the First Virtual system cannot be used to sell tangible goods—only information, such as software or a newsletter, is acceptable. This is an important limitation for retail sites on the Web, and you should check the First Virtual Web site for more details and exceptions to the "information-only" rule.

Transactions with First Virtual can be performed via a TCP/IP connection similar to Telnet or via email, so the simplest solution for working with the First Virtual system is an email gateway such as NetForms to send orders for processing (see Chapter 7 for a discussion of the NetForms CGI). The better solution is a CGI specifically designed to work with the First Virtual system—which is the subject of the next section!

WEBSTAR

WebSTAR Commerce Toolkit

The Commerce Toolkit from StarNine Technologies, the distributors of WebSTAR, is a CGI that contains all the functionality needed to add both MacAuthorize and First Virtual transactions to your

Web site. Details on the Commerce Toolkit were not available at the time this book was written, but it will certainly have been released by the time you read this and you can find out about its current status at the StarNine Web site, http://www.starnine.com/.

Web Commerce Solution

Although this product (from Pacific Coast Software, http://www.pacific-coast.com/) offers a complete Web publishing package in a database engine, it also builds in the ability to conduct commerce through MacAuthorize and other means, similarly to the StarNine solution. If you need to publish a catalog or create a complete ordering system for your products anyway, the Web Commerce Solution may be more cost-effective than the StarNine system.

Other Transaction Methods

A number of novel schemes have been developed over the past two years to enable secure Web-based transactions. Most depend upon technology similar to that underlying SSL encryption to allow the generation of strings of digits that represent money, much as though you could purchase items by sending the serial number from a dollar bill rather than the bill itself.

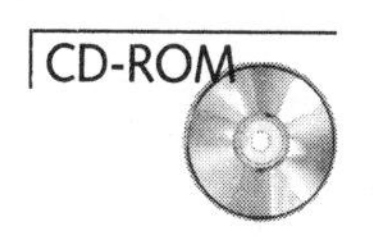

None of these schemes is quite mature yet, so I don't describe them in detail as it is unclear which will survive or become widespread in the future. You can find links to most of the major alternatives in this area on the HTML pages for this chapter on the CD. The most likely candidate for widespread adoption is the S-HTTP (Secure HyperText Transfer Protocol) method, which you can read about at http://www.commerce.net/information/standards/drafts/draft-ietf-wts-shttp-00.txt.

Encryption and Credit Cards

The WebSTAR Security Toolkit, which enables SSL-encrypted Web transactions for your site (see Chapters 5 and 10 for more information on SSL and the Security Toolkit), allows you to move sensitive information such as credit card numbers over the Internet, essentially without danger of anyone intercepting the information for unauthorized use. The value of doing so is still somewhat debatable—Netscape, as the maker of the first SSL-capable browser, has certainly done a good job of encouraging clients to be concerned about the safety of their personal information and generally raising the level of concern about security on the Internet. However, many sites without any encryption report strong sales, with some even offering to cover the losses of any customers whose card numbers are used fraudulently due to interception en route.

Two major issues will influence your decision about whether to offer encrypted transactions at your site:

- ☐ Will customers demand such protection to feel comfortable placing their orders?

  This question is the hardest to answer—many sites report strong sales without encryption, whereas others say their customers demand the protection, whether real or perceived, offered by encryption. Many browsers still cannot handle SSL-encrypted transactions at all, so to some extent the question is moot for those individuals. Whether encryption becomes *de rigueur* for commercial Web sites will likely depend more upon overall consumer perceptions of the need for protected transactions than on the actual likelihood of fraud.

- ☐ To what extent will you be at risk for sensitive information used fraudulently as a result of its transmission to you over the Internet?

  Perhaps even more relevant to site administrators is this question of liability. If someone intercepts credit card numbers being sent to your site and uses those numbers to make unauthorized purchases, are you responsible for those charges? This is still a gray area, but is a real concern as you can be sure that the card issuers are going to attempt to place responsibility anywhere they possibly can to reduce their own losses.

Remember that the most important security problem arises when the credit card data is off the Web and in a database or other file on your own system. You will very likely be held liable if credit card account information in your possession is stolen by an employee or anyone else and used fraudulently.

Overall, the risks of passing information over the Internet are probably extremely small. You will no doubt face a much greater risk from employees or others with physical access to sensitive information than you do from card bandits on the Internet. Online risks do exist, however, and you need to judge both the current mood of the marketplace and your own willingness to take a chance, however small, on potential problems when deciding whether to add encryption to your site.

Summary

Most serious development of Web sites on the Mac (and even a few not-so-serious ones) require the application of advanced features like custom CGI development or database integration. These types of skills will be increasingly in demand in the coming years and any investment you make in self-education now is likely to be very productive in the long term, even if your immediate needs don't require it.

Chapter 9 discusses issues of charting statistics and usage at your site.

Part III

Site Administration

CHAPTER 9

Serving by the Numbers: Statistics and Usage

Web sites are an odd combination of openness and secrets—a server that sits quietly under a desk or in a closet can hold the attention of thousands of people a day without any indication of its activity except the faint clicking of a hard drive. Yet your server's activity logs hide rich patterns of usage, descriptions of your clients, and the keys to understanding what aspects of your site are meeting the goals you've set for them.

This chapter is about extracting the secrets from your server logs. You'll look at why your server's statistics are worth examining, tools to extract and analyze them, and some advanced methods for tracking clients.

Why Do You Want to Know?

Many commercial sites measure their profits in terms of their site's usage. For these types of sites, whether they relate their visitor numbers to advertising rates, track user demographics to direct marketing efforts, or simply want to gauge the effectiveness and scope of their online presence, accurate statistics are critical to their operation.

For non-commercial sites, however, the effort involved to track and analyze your site's usage may not seem worthwhile. Private sites that serve a pre-defined clientele might follow the same line of reasoning—namely, why bother with it? Isn't just knowing roughly how busy a site has been in the last day or week enough?

The answer is no, and here's why.

Improving Service

Stasis is death on the Web. To keep attracting new and repeat visitors, continue to analyze and improve your site.

Every Web site is "under construction" to one degree or another. Stasis is death on the Web. To keep attracting new and repeat visitors to your site, you must analyze what parts of your site are effective—or not—at meeting your goals. If your logs reveal that 50 percent of the first-time visitors to your site are visiting your home page and moving on, perhaps you need a new home page! And if you discover that most of the people who only visit once use browsers that don't support vital features of your site like tables, perhaps you should remove the tables or at least provide a table-free version of your pages for your more limited clients.

Reporting

No Web site is free. Even non-commercial sites belonging to an academic department or a community organization are supported in terms of staff time, bandwidth, or purchases by someone who will eventually want to know whether your site has provided a value to the organization's overall mission. Describing the content of your site and quoting a simple "hit" count (see the next section) is not nearly as impressive as listing numbers of unique and repeat visitors, reporting usage of your site by content area, and tracking changes in usage as your site was modified or upgraded. This chapter addresses all these areas and more.

Site Management

Everybody underestimates the time required to maintain a Web site, and it's just as easy to underestimate the information required as well. If, for example, another server has a link to your site that is incorrect, how will you know it? And how will you track down the source so the incorrect link fixed?

So what *do* you want to know? Now is the time to refer to your site plan (see Chapter 1) and recall what you need to extract from your site to gauge its success at meeting your goals. As you read through this chapter, think about how the tools described here can help you extract that information and consider what value other types of statistics might have for you as well.

Lies, Damn Lies, and Hit Counts

The most basic (and most commonly used) measure of your site's usage is the *hit*, a single URL request handled by your server.

Unfortunately, hits are almost meaningless when attempting to understand what actually happens on your site in terms of unique clients, repeat visitors, and the like. As a raw number (that is, "My site receives 10,000 hits a day now…"), hits are useful primarily to help establish the amount of work your server is doing, as each hit does represent a single Web transaction handled by your server. Even that context has its limits, however, because the distribution of hits among different URLs can drastically alter the actual load your server experiences.

Hit counts are misleading because they can both overestimate and underestimate the number of people visiting your site. If you have a home page with 10 small graphics on it, and one client downloads the page and all the images, that's eleven hits recorded for one page and one client. If the next clients have image loading turned off on their browser, they might ignore the graphics completely and register just one hit on your server per client. So, if a site claims to receive 10,000 hits per day on its home page, what does that really mean?

If you want to score your usage more accurately, ignore requests for graphics in your hit count. The remaining counts more accurately reflect the actual number of pages served to clients.

If you want to score your usage more accurately, ignore requests for graphics in your hit count (I'll explain how to do this later in this chapter). The "page counts" that remain will more accurately reflect the actual number of pages served to clients. Now you have a lower figure on the number of people who have seen your pages, but the actual number might be much higher. Why higher? One word—*caching*.

Caching is the computer term for holding local, temporary copies of information that can be used more rapidly or efficiently than original copies. Two types of caching affect your server statistics, and neither are very good news for a dedicated log-cruncher—client caching and proxy server caching.

Client Caching

Web browsers with caching capabilities, such as Netscape, maintain copies of recently accessed pages and images both on the user's local disk and in RAM. This saves both time and bandwidth, because the browser can display the locally cached copy of a page or graphic rather than download the same information over the Internet every time the user returns to the same URL. Unfortunately, it also creates problems for tracking your site usage.

Most client software is intelligent enough to check occasionally to see whether the cached copy is current, before deciding whether to display it or retrieve a new copy. These kinds of requests use a special HTTP method called CONDITIONAL-GET (see Chapter 8 for details) that show up in your server logs as zero-length data transfers if the file in question has not changed since the client last requested it. Nevertheless, client caching can have a severe impact on your statistics by hiding repeat visitors or, at the very least, reducing their apparent interest as recorded in your logs.

Caching Proxy Servers

A proxy server is a "gateway" Web server that acts as a conduit for URL requests from the clients it serves. A client using a proxy server sends all URL requests to the proxy, which then sends the request to your server, retrieves the response, and forwards a copy back to the original client.

This is bad enough, as each client using the proxy server appears under the same IP address (the proxy server's address) in your logs, reducing the apparent number of unique visitors to your site. Many proxy servers, however, also have *caching capabilities*, meaning that they keep a copy of your pages and graphics locally and, when your

URL is requested again, serve the local copy back to the client without contacting your site. Because of this caching mechanism, proxy servers are often used by online services, such as America Online, and other organizations that provide Internet access to large numbers of people and want to reduce the amount of data that flows over their Internet connection.

Proxy servers do update their local copies periodically by ignoring their cache and making a new request to your server when a URL is re-requested by a client, but you have no way to predict how often this occurs.

The upshot is that proxy servers, while conserving your bandwidth, severely limit your ability to detect how often and in what ways your site is being used. As an extreme case, consider that one hit on your home page by an America Online subscriber could represent millions of subsequent accesses by other subscribers if the AOL proxy servers are not updating their local copies of your pages regularly!

Unfortunately, estimating the number of people hidden from your logs by the various caching mechanisms is problematic at best. If you can accept the argument that proxy-hidden requests increase proportionally with the general traffic at your site, you can conservatively add another 10 to 20 percent to your access counts to estimate the total viewers of your pages.

Unfortunately, there is still no agreement on how the nature of Web transactions could change to enable more accurate user tracking—nor is there any agreement on whether it even *should* change. In the meantime, page counts are still the simplest way to measure traffic, with the understanding that they cannot record the actions of many users who might be re-examining your pages without returning to your server.

Collecting Information

Now that you know why you should examine statistics about your server and some of the obstacles you will face, let's take a look at how you can gather the information you need.

You Are the 5,629th Reader of This Page

The simplest form of statistic collection registers the number of times a URL has been requested from your server. This information is often displayed on a home page as a counter graphic, as shown in Figure 9.1.

Figure 9.1 *A typical page counter graphic.*

Adding page counters requires the use of a CGI to insert the current image URL or HTML code into your pages. You can find out more about adding page counter CGIs to your site in Chapter 7, "CGI Applications and Usage."

As an alternative, a number of Web sites are now offering the capability to track your page counts without installing a CGI. A small graphic, whose URL points back to the page counting service, is inserted on your page, like the one in Figure 9.2 from the Internet Audit Bureau (http://www.internet-audit.com/).

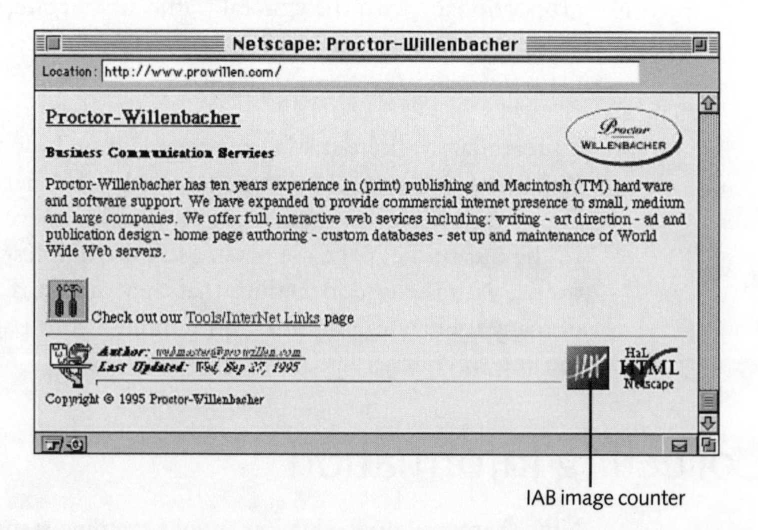

Figure 9.2 *A page displaying the Internet Audit Bureau (IAB) graphic.*

If you maintain multiple Web sites on a single server, these services can be a great way to provide your clients basic information about the traffic on their pages without separating their particular information from your main server log. An example of the activity reports provided by the IAB is shown in Figure 9.3.

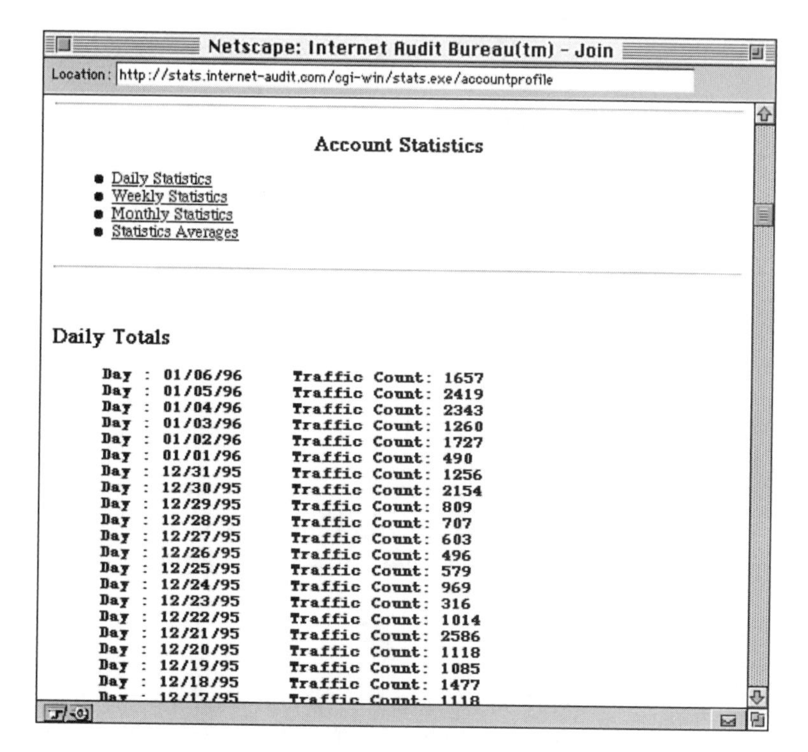

Figure 9.3 *A typical IAB site activity report.*

The downside is that if the graphic isn't requested by the client, such as when they are browsing your site with image loading turned off, the visit won't be counted by the remote service. Some services cope with this by including text in the HTML image tags to display when the graphic is not loaded. This technique is demonstrated in Figure 9.4, which is the same page shown in Figure 9.2.

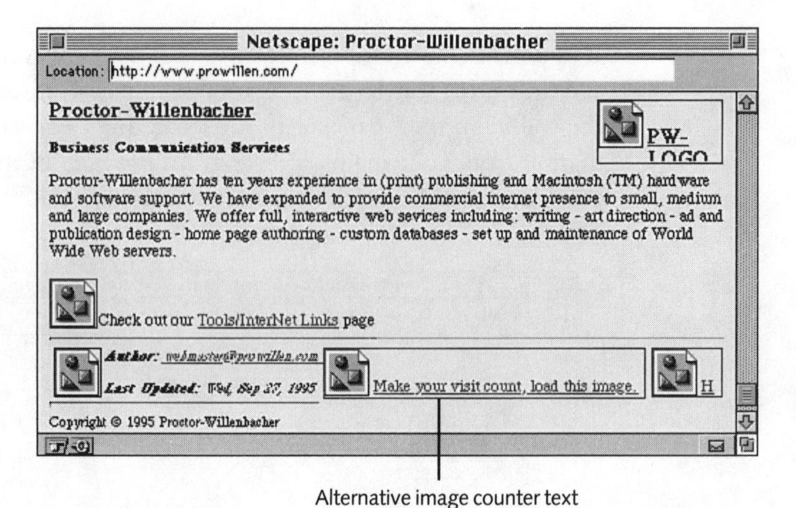

Figure 9.4 *Figure 9.2 viewed without image loading on.*

Server Logging

Each HTTP server discussed in this book collects and reports statistics slightly differently. Unlike the UNIX and Windows NT world, there is not a commonly accepted format for logging server activities.

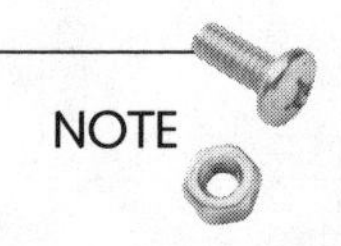
NOTE

> HTTP servers in the UNIX and Windows environments usually create server logs in a format known as the *Common Log Format*. There are literally dozens of log analysis tools available on these platforms for analyzing log statistics written in this common format. On MacOS HTTP servers, only *httpd4Mac* uses this format. Its logs can be transferred to another platform and analyzed with the same tools commonly used with UNIX and Windows NT Web server logs.

All the Macintosh HTTP servers record information about their activities, but each does so in its own, idiosyncratic way. I'll describe each of them, but you should keep in mind that newer versions of these servers might be released after the book's CD was created. You should make a point of checking the latest versions for changes before making any decisions based on the information reported here.

Web Server 4D

Web Server 4D provides the most extensive set of built-in statistical reporting tools of any of the Macintosh Web servers. Here are a few of the summaries it maintains:

- New and repeat visitors for the site and per page
- Types of browsers used and percentage of visits by each type
- Session tracking of visitors—the URLs visited by a particular client (IP address), in the order visited
- List of URLs that contains links to your pages (Referrers)

Web Server 4D's strength in summaries, however, is the equal of its lack of information about individual requests. Although you can export all the information contained in the summaries to text files, much of the detailed per-transaction information available from WebSTAR or NetWings is missing from Web Server 4D.

If the built-in summary information meets your needs (and it *is* quite extensive), you probably won't miss the other kinds of information. If your reporting needs are more complex, however, the non-development version of Web Server 4D may not be adequate. Figure 9.5 shows 4D in action.

Of course, unlike the other 4D-based Web server, NetWings, Web Server 4D is available as source code, which enables you to customize the database to obtain and manage statistics of any sort. This requires the purchase of the *4th Dimension* development environment (which could cost 500 to 1500 dollars, depending on your needs) and the ability to learn 4D's internal language. Check out Chapter 7, "CGI Applications and Usage," for more information on programming 4D.

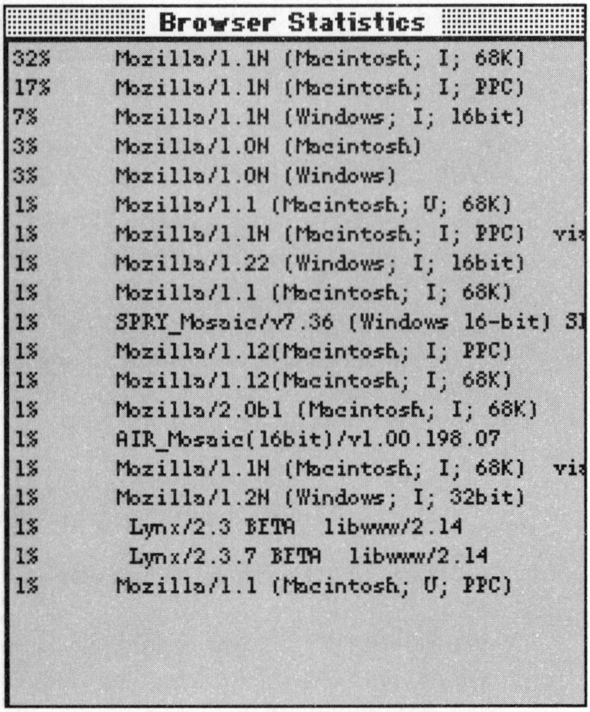

Browser Statistics

32%	Mozilla/1.1N (Macintosh; I; 68K)
17%	Mozilla/1.1N (Macintosh; I; PPC)
7%	Mozilla/1.1N (Windows; I; 16bit)
3%	Mozilla/1.0N (Macintosh)
3%	Mozilla/1.0N (Windows)
1%	Mozilla/1.1 (Macintosh; U; 68K)
1%	Mozilla/1.1N (Macintosh; I; PPC) vi
1%	Mozilla/1.22 (Windows; I; 16bit)
1%	Mozilla/1.1 (Macintosh; I; 68K)
1%	SPRY_Mosaic/v7.36 (Windows 16-bit) SI
1%	Mozilla/1.12(Macintosh; I; PPC)
1%	Mozilla/1.12(Macintosh; I; 68K)
1%	Mozilla/2.0b1 (Macintosh; I; 68K)
1%	AIR_Mosaic(16bit)/v1.00.198.07
1%	Mozilla/1.1N (Macintosh; I; 68K) vi
1%	Mozilla/1.2N (Windows; I; 32bit)
1%	Lynx/2.3 BETA libwww/2.14
1%	Lynx/2.3.7 BETA libwww/2.14
1%	Mozilla/1.1 (Macintosh; U; PPC)

Figure 9.5 *The Browser statistics window from Web Server 4D.*

NetWings

NetWings keeps track of all transaction information in a single record for each transaction. Figure 9.6 shows a record for a single URL request.

Because NetWings is based on a 4th Dimension database, all the searching and reporting tools available in 4D can be applied to the NetWings logs and the information exported. Although NetWings does not contain the extensive summary functions of Web Server 4D, it is the equal of WebSTAR in its capability to record information about each Web transaction (it even adds a couple items, such as POST arguments) and superior to WebSTAR in its capability to manage information without the assistance of other applications.

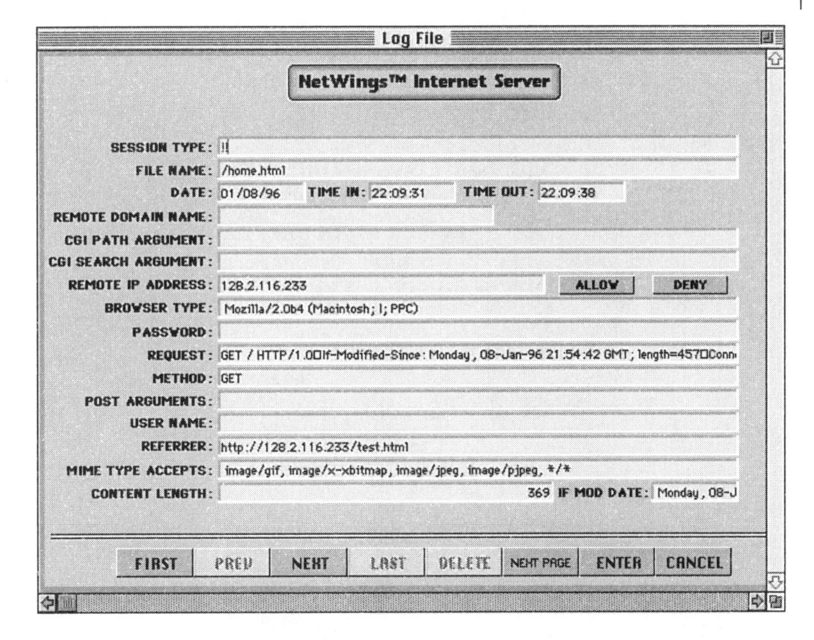

Figure 9.6 *A single NetWings Web transaction record.*

InterServer Publisher

InterServer's logs have two problems that make them almost unusable for automated analysis: they mix information from each of the InterServer Internet services (FTP, Gopher, and HTTP transactions), and they include messages other than actual transactions, such as reports of internal errors or changes that must be removed before importing the log into an analysis program or database.

InterServer Publisher is adequate for the most basic statistical summaries of your site's activities. You might be able to use a page counter service (described later in this chapter) effectively with InterServer, if that type of information is enough for you.

WebSTAR

WebSTAR creates highly customized logs, which you define according to the types of reports you need. Some of the options that can be recorded are

- Date and Time of transaction
- Result (OK, Error, Busy, and so on)

- ☐ IP address or domain name of client
- ☐ URL requested
- ☐ Number of bytes sent to client
- ☐ Username of a username/password authentication
- ☐ Path arguments, if any
- ☐ Referring URL, if any
- ☐ Search arguments, if any (note: not POST arguments)
- ☐ Method used by request (GET, POST, and so on)
- ☐ Browser description, if supplied by client
- ☐ Total transfer time in ticks (1/60 second)

You'll need to use the WebSTAR Admin application (included with WebSTAR in the **Servers** folder on the CD) to change the log format. Please see the WebSTAR documentation on the CD for more information on using WebSTAR Admin. In keeping with the minimalist design of WebSTAR, analyzing WebSTAR logs (other than by simply looking through them) requires another application to import and process the data—see Figure 9.7.

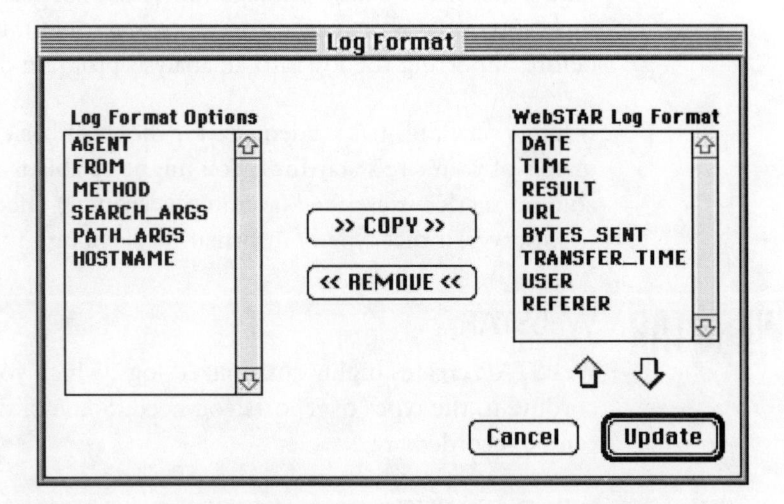

Figure 9.7 *The WebSTAR Admin server log configuration dialog.*

Analyzing Logs

Even if you use an HTTP server that performs some statistical summaries internally, such as Web Server 4D or NetWings, you still might want to export that information to a log file, either to construct custom summaries or to format the data for a report. If you use WebSTAR or httpd4Mac on your site, you need to process the server logs to view any summaries at all. Either way, log analysis methods are a vital part of most site administrators' toolkits.

Log Analysis Software

Frankly, there's not much out there. The choices are pretty slim. If you use WebSTAR, you can use *ServerStat* to analyze the log. If you use httpd4Mac, you can use *WWWStat4Mac*. Otherwise, you'll have to analyze the logs yourself with a database or spreadsheet program (see next section).

WEBSTAR

ServerStat

ServerStat (http://www.kitchen-sink.com/) is the only log analyzer that works effectively with WebSTAR logs, and WebSTAR (or its shareware cousin, MacHTTP) is the only server with which it can effectively work. Seems like a match made in heaven.

ServerStat's interface takes a bit of getting used to, but is fairly straightforward in practice. It doesn't create fancy graphs or tables, but does create a nicely organized summary, in text or HTML, of your site statistics and can report on every kind of information WebSTAR logs produce. Figure 9.8 shows a sample of a ServerStat report. It's quite similar in format to most popular UNIX packages.

The *ServerStat Lite* version (in the **Software, Miscellaneous** folder on the accompanying CD) has limited functionality, but it should give you enough of a taste of its capabilities to decide whether you want to purchase the full commercial version.

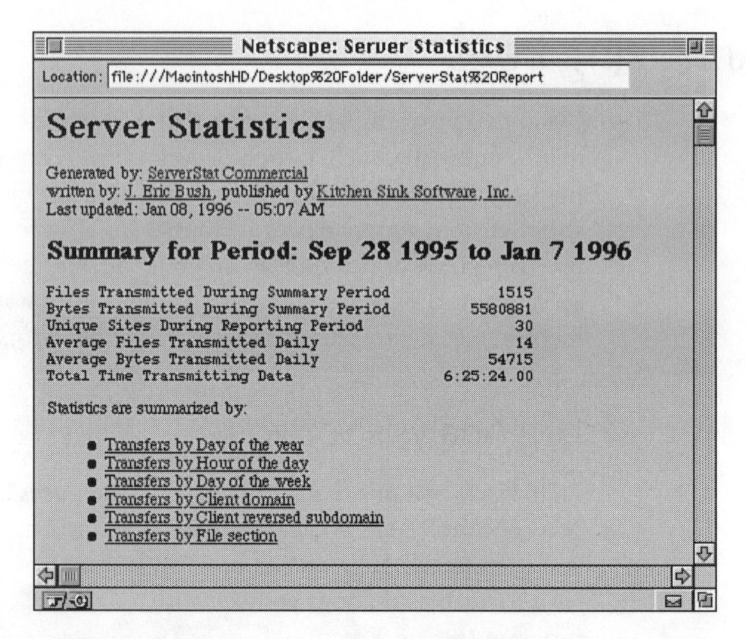

Figure 9.8 *The top of a typical ServerStat report.*

ServerStat Lite is shareware—if you continue to use it, send your license fee to Kitchen Sink Software, the makers of ServerStat and ServerStat Lite. For more details, check the files on the CD that accompany ServerStat Lite.

WWWStat4Mac

WWWStat4Mac (http://sodium.ch.man.ac.uk/pages/wwwstat4mac.html) is a non-commercial server log analyzer that occupies a rather unique position on the Mac. Because it requires server logs to be in Common Log Format, the only Mac server it can work with is httpd4Mac, which would seem to limit its usefulness. But that same requirement renders it the only Mac-based log analyzer that can interpret logs from UNIX or Windows NT servers. So, if you need to look at logs from other server platforms on a Mac, this is your only alternative to writing an analyzer yourself.

NOTE

> Much of the data that WebSTAR and other Mac servers log is not available from Common Log Format files, such as the referrer or browser items, so output from WWWStat4Mac is limited in comparison to that from ServerStat.

Figure 9.9 shows a WWWStat4Mac sample reporting page.

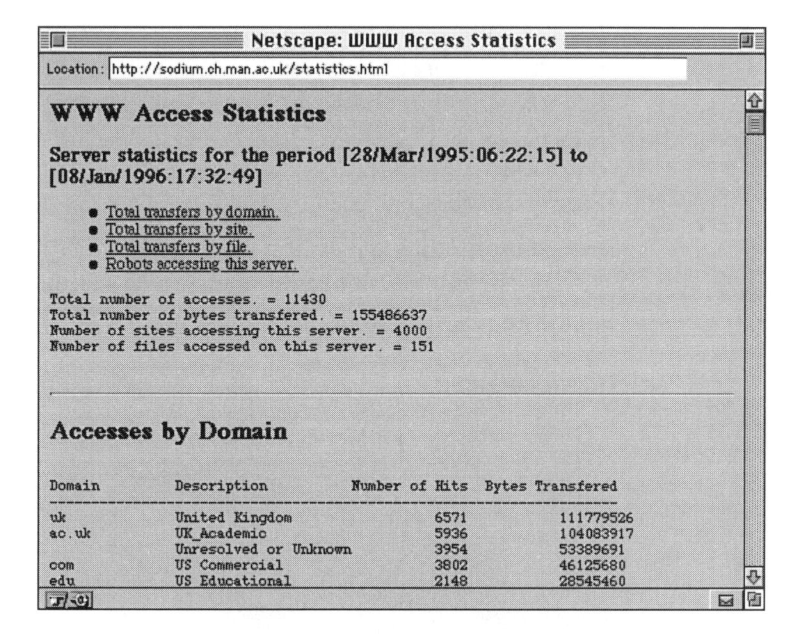

Figure 9.9 *WWWStat4Mac sample reporting page.*

And that's it! If neither ServerStat nor WWWStat4Mac meet your needs, you'll have to use one of the methods presented in the next section to manage your server data. The following solutions require more work to use than does a pre-built application such as ServerStat, but you also gain the ability to customize your reports to address your needs more precisely.

Databases

The ideal place to manage your log data in the long term is in a database, where you can organize and create custom reports. This approach offers the most flexibility, but usually requires some expertise in your database's internal scripting language. Any standard Macintosh database (4D, FileMaker, Butler, FoxPro) should do an adequate job of managing the information, so choose the one that you work with best.

Spreadsheets

If you're already an expert at managing information and generating reports with spreadsheet applications such as Excel—the Swiss Army Knife of numbers—feel free to use it to manage your server statistics as well. All server logs can easily be imported into a spreadsheet application and processed further using formulas, commands, and macros. Because Excel is scriptable, it can also be controlled by another application like FileMaker Pro, 4D, or even Frontier or AppleScript to reorganize and summarize server data, create graphs, and store moderate amounts of information.

Figure 9.10 shows a WebSTAR log imported into Microsoft Excel.

WebSTAR.log

	1	2	3	4	5	6	7
1	Date	Time	Result	Client IP address	Path	Bytes Sent	Time Taken
2	9/28/95	15:45:09	OK	199.234.151.131	:default.html	52	134
3	9/28/95	15:46:22	OK	199.234.151.131	:default.html	0	1343
4	9/28/95	15:48:08	OK	199.234.151.131	:default.html	1239	107
5	9/28/95	15:49:18	OK	199.234.151.131	:default.html	0	72
6	9/28/95	15:49:27	OK	199.234.151.131	:images:answer	115	116
7	9/28/95	15:49:45	OK	199.234.151.131	:default.html	0	75
8	9/28/95	15:49:59	OK	199.234.151.131	:images:answer	115	251
9	9/28/95	15:51:04	OK	199.234.151.131	:default.html	0	83
10	9/28/95	15:51:11	OK	199.234.151.131	:default.html	0	68
11	9/28/95	15:51:17	OK	199.234.151.131	:images:answer	115	89
12	9/28/95	16:03:36	OK	199.234.151.131	:default.html	0	63
13	9/28/95	16:16:33	OK	199.234.151.131	:default.html	0	119
14	9/28/95	16:16:35	OK	199.234.151.131	:images:answer	115	67
15	9/28/95	16:17:40	OK	199.234.151.131	:default.html	0	71
16	9/28/95	16:17:42	OK	199.234.151.131	:images:answer	115	42
17	9/28/95	16:17:52	OK	199.234.151.131	:default.html	0	67
18	9/28/95	16:18:01	OK	199.234.151.131	:default.html	0	75
19	9/28/95	16:18:04	OK	199.234.151.131	:images:answer	115	65
20	9/28/95	16:18:09	OK	199.234.151.131	:default.html	0	57
21	9/28/95	16:18:11	OK	199.234.151.131	:images:answer	115	53
22	9/28/95	16:21:01	OK	199.234.151.131	:default.html	0	84

Figure 9.10 *A sample WebSTAR log after being imported into Microsoft Excel.*

If your site is even slightly busy, you should import and summarize your logs daily, as the amount of raw data your site generates can rapidly outstrip the capabilities of most spreadsheet applications.

NOTE

This section is much smaller than it should be. If we were reviewing statistical tools for UNIX servers, I could list a dozen decent solutions (and many times that number of inadequate ones). Macintosh tools always tend to be fewer but better than their off-platform peers, and ServerStat is a wonderful and effective tool, but I always feel better when I have a choice.

Will the next developer please stand up?

Advanced Usage Tracking

Recording server statistics other than the standard values usually requires some scripting or programming to capture the data. The sections that follow list some possibilities.

Session Statistics

A common technique groups a client's actions to trace that individual's progress through your site and to discover what links visitors are most likely to choose after viewing your home page for the first time. These group records are referred to as *sessions* (you might also see the term *clickstreams* used to refer to sessions).

Sessions can be connected into *persistent sessions*, which connect client actions over many individual sessions, so that you can track how often users return and how their access patterns change.

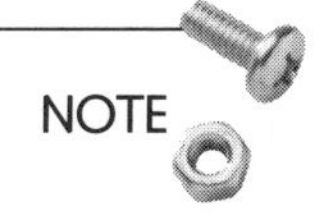
NOTE

Persistent sessions have another use as well—if you can identify clients with their previous behaviors, you can change the content of the information they see based on their histories at your site or other information you have captured about those particular users. This is usually done by inserting short identifying strings (tokens) into your URLs and serving your pages out of a database or CGI application. See the following section on tokens for more information.

Many CGIs and other systems that purport to track sessions (persistently or not) use the IP address of the client as the session identifier. Web Server 4D, for example, uses IP addresses to track new and repeat visitors for individual URLs and the overall site, as can ServerStat when processing a WebSTAR/MacHTTP log. However, IP addresses are subject to all of the same limitations as are hit counts. Under the IP address method, for example, if three different people using the same proxy server are requesting pages from your site, they all appear to be the same individual. On the other hand, most clients using dialup Internet access receive a different IP address every time they connect to the Internet, making them appear as new visitors every time their IP address changes.

You need a method, not dependent upon a client's particular browser or type of Internet connection, which unambiguously identifies individuals interacting with your site. Fortunately, three methods are available to accomplish this—all discussed next.

User Registration/Authentication

The simplest method of recording sessions is to require visitors to use passwords and usernames to access your pages. When the client enters a valid username/password combination, that information is sent with every subsequent URL request until the client leaves your site or ends the current Web browsing session. *Wired* magazine's online site, *HotWired* (http://www.hotwired.com/) is a good example of this approach.

After the username information is recorded in your server logs, how you use and analyze it is up to you. Most server logs will record usernames, so you can use its standard reporting to extract for analysis the record of hits from a particular client. Authentication has the advantages of being simple to implement, easy to process (all information is recorded automatically in the server logs), and able to record visitor information over persistent sessions. Many people, however, feel that the process of registering visitors and the necessity (for clients) of potentially having to remember dozens of different usernames and passwords for various sites is cumbersome.

Although it's true that an authentication system places more demands on the client than simply clicking links, you can add a great deal of value both to the visitor's experience and your own statistics by registering users. It's up to you to design a site that can convince a client that the content "behind the password" is worth the trouble.

Tokens

Tokens are character strings inserted into URLs to control the content of pages delivered to clients and to record a visitor's actions during a single session on your Web site.

Tokens change the URLs of your document's links to include a code that is specific to one client. Every time a new URL is requested by that client, the HTML pages are scanned for URLs and the appropriate client code inserted.

Tokens, however, require advanced CGIs that process every request for an HTML page from your site and that maintain the individual users ID. You can find more information about implementing token-based sessions in Chapter 8, "Advanced Techniques."

Cookies

Cookies (no apparent reason for the name) are a proposed browser feature from Netscape that currently only work with Netscape's products, but might see broader use in the future. They enable Web servers to force browsers to store information sent to the client by your server or CGI and to return that information whenever a URL is requested from the same server.

Cookies add name and value pairs to the headers of the server's response to a client request, just as you would add any other sort of HTTP header information (see Chapter 8, "Advanced Techniques," for more information on HTTP headers). The primary advantage is that they put the burden of storing session information on the client rather than the server, and enable the server to retrieve the information when needed.

Because cookies are still in an experimental stage, I won't delve into them any further here, but you can examine the original cookie proposal at (http://home.netscape.com/newsref/std/cookie_spec.html).

Marketing Information

Publicizing your URL can be an expensive proposition, whether your expenses are limited in terms of money or just your own time. Understanding the effectiveness of different approaches is vital to efficiently promoting your site—but if you are using multiple methods to market your site, how can you track which are worthwhile and which are wasting your resources?

The simplest approach is to use aliases to your home page that count the number of visitors a particular ad or directory has directed to your site. Suppose you advertise your site in three different locations and want to compare the results from each. For each marketing effort you want to track, simply create aliases to your home page with different names, throw them into the same folder as your home page, and use the corresponding URL for each ad. You easily can compare the number of visitors that arrive through each promotion by examining the access counts for the different URLs in your server log.

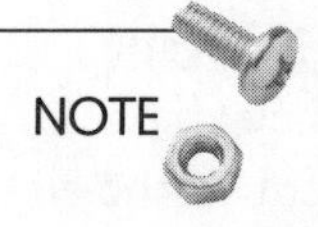

NOTE

> You probably don't want to make the different names too obvious—the URL for your ad on Lycos, for example, probably shouldn't be lycos.html. I suggest using codes that look reasonable (if a bit odd) to the client, such as home1.html, and that enable you to extract the information you need. Just keep track of which names correspond to which marketing effort, and you'll be fine.

Summary

Statistical analysis for Mac HTTP servers has a long way to go to catch up with the tools available for Windows and UNIX servers, but the opportunity for enterprising application and CGI writers is wide open.

In the next chapter, you'll look at how to control potential security threats to your server and some options for conducting encrypted transactions over the Web.

CHAPTER 10

Security

If this were a book about UNIX Web servers, I'd probably be referring you now to yet another book written entirely to address the problem of security, or even recommending that you hire a UNIX security professional to advise you on creating and maintaining a secure Web server. Fortunately, we're building a Web server on a Macintosh, so all you'll have to do is read this chapter.

One of the biggest headaches in the UNIX world of providing Internet services, including Web services, is the problem of security for your data and your site as a whole. Luckily for you, most of the ways that traditional UNIX systems can be compromised from other computers are not available on Macintoshes, and your server is fairly secure right out of the box. If you followed the guidelines I explained in Chapter 5, "Choosing a Server," you already have a server that is immune to most types of unauthorized access.

In this chapter, I share a little background information about why Macintosh servers are inherently more secure against outside attack than other systems, and also point out those areas that should still be a concern for you, such as physical security. Your own site may not require extreme levels of protection against unauthorized access to your data, but every Web server administrator should at least be aware of potential problems and know how to cope with them if they arise.

Figure 10.1 illustrates some common security problems for Macintosh Web sites.

Figure 10.1 *Common security problems for Macintosh Web sites.*

Background

All UNIX systems use what are termed "multi-user" operating systems. In this scheme, someone attempting to use the machine (either in front of it or from a remote location via a terminal interface such as a Telnet program) is authorized to access different areas of the file system or to execute certain commands according to the privileges assigned to particular username/password combinations. Even if you had physical access to a UNIX box, it would be extremely difficult, if not impossible, for the average user to compromise security without the correct password and username information.

However, this very feature provides the mechanism for unauthorized access by experts. If unauthorized people are able to find a way to change the privileges assigned to their own login information or discover the "privileged" passwords, they can obtain whatever access they want and wreak havoc on the target machine from any Internet-connected computer in the world.

Single-User System

By contrast, a single-user operating system, such as the Macintosh or DOS operating systems, does not differentiate among users. Anyone sitting in front of the physical machine is assumed to have privilege to do anything, assuming that the desired information or application is not physically encrypted. Anyone not directly using the computer is severely limited in affecting changes or obtaining information, as long as network access (via file sharing or other services) is restricted or password-protected. Note that any password-protected access is only as secure as the password, so it's important to keep that information secure as well.

Security Trade-Off

There is a trade-off in terms of security on a Macintosh—on one hand, nobody can assume full "privileges" and control of your system without physically being in front of the machine, which stifles most traditional methods of "hacking" into computers remotely, but on the other hand, anyone in direct contact with your Mac is given a free hand regardless of actual identity.

Because there is no "generic" remote interface to the MacOS, a Macintosh out of the box with just a Web server installed is highly secure from Internet-based intrusions with a minimum of fuss.

Because there is no "generic" remote interface to the MacOS, such as telnet provides for UNIX boxes, a Macintosh out of the box with just a Web server installed is highly secure from Internet-based intrusions with a minimum of fuss. Of course, you can always disable that security by adding additional software or services, but you'll need to go through some contortions to compromise your Mac's security, whereas on a UNIX system you'd have to go through a lot more contortions just to maintain security.

Physical Security

No matter what lengths you go to protect your site from security breaches via the Internet, all will be for naught if you cannot maintain physical security for your server. The Macintosh platform is highly secure against attacks performed over TCP/IP networks like the Internet, but is just as highly vulnerable to a user with physical access. Because there is no concept of users with different privileges, even novice Macintosh users can access and modify anything on your server if provided the opportunity to use the machine directly.

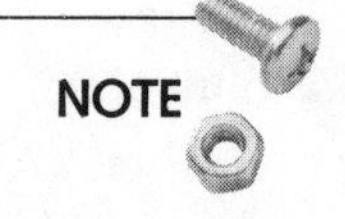

> If you keep sensitive information on your server in an environment where unauthorized people might conceivably be able to use your Mac, you should go to great lengths to control access to the machine. If you use a screen-sharing program such as Timbuktu to control and administrate your server (see Chapter 13, "Walkaway Serving"), you can place your server virtually anywhere with a power plug and an Ethernet cable and still control it effectively. Of course, you're just moving the security problem from the server to the machine you are controlling it from, but presumably you'll have more direct control over access to your personal machine and Timbuktu passwords.

There are programs available that purport to prevent unauthorized usage—you've probably seen them used in computer store displays. They are usually restricted to rendering a screen-saver type of image and won't allow access to the Finder or other programs until a password is entered on-screen. I do not recommend using or depending on such software for two reasons:

- First, it is extremely difficult to effectively secure a Macintosh against a determined intruder. Someone with knowledge of how the operating system works can usually bypass any type of security that requires a password to control the machine if given enough time in front of the Mac in question.
- Second, these programs will cause a performance drag on your server and may not interact well with other administrative software, such as screen-sharing programs.

Another approach to prevent others from accessing sensitive data is to encrypt information on the server so that the data is not usable without the proper password or key. This approach is adequate for securing data that you want to record but have no need to make available directly through your server. If you collect credit card numbers, for example, you may want to record each transaction to a file on disk that can be protected automatically by a commercial encryption program and decrypted later at your convenience.

> Be extremely cautious when working with credit card numbers accepted over the Web. The less time that information spends in an unencrypted form or on your Web server, the better. If that information is stolen and used for fraudulent purposes, you can still be held liable for the unauthorized usage even if you had no involvement in the misuse. In fact, don't be cautious—be afraid. Be very afraid.

Even that method, however, still leaves room for a lot of potentially problematic access to your site—an intruder can change the content of your unencrypted files to deliver pornographic or otherwise unwanted information to clients, or even delete your site altogether. The only reliable way to secure your Mac against this kind of abuse is to physically secure it in a locked room or place a security cage around it. Your site doesn't need a keyboard or monitor to continue running, so feel free to remove the cables when you're not around and lock the server in a cage or closet.

If you have placed your server at an ISP's premises or other location where you cannot monitor who has access to it, making sure that your server is placed in a security cage or other location with limited access can be an effective deterrent to would-be hackers.

Network Security

There are three types of network access that can cause problems for your site. The first is AppleTalk, which was discussed in the section on setting up your server in Chapter 5. The second is TCP/IP access to your server. This access is a problem only if you place sensitive information in the root directory of your Web server or if you offer services to clients that open up paths for possible abuse, such as allowing users to upload files to your site. The third problem is inherent in the Web itself—the ability of others to view the messages passing between your clients and you. We'll take a look here at some of the common problems and ways to address them.

Access Control

Whenever you've attempted to go to a URL that caused a dialog box to pop up on-screen asking you for a username and password, you've experienced the most common version of access control on the Web. A "protected" URL will not return information to the client until the proper username and password have been passed to the server for the path in question. Additionally, most servers can screen access to their pages by domain name or IP address, denying access to clients whose IP addresses do not fall within an approved range.

One such example of a protected URL requesting a password is *Wired* magazine's online site, *HotWired* (http://www.hotwired.com), shown in Figure 10.2.

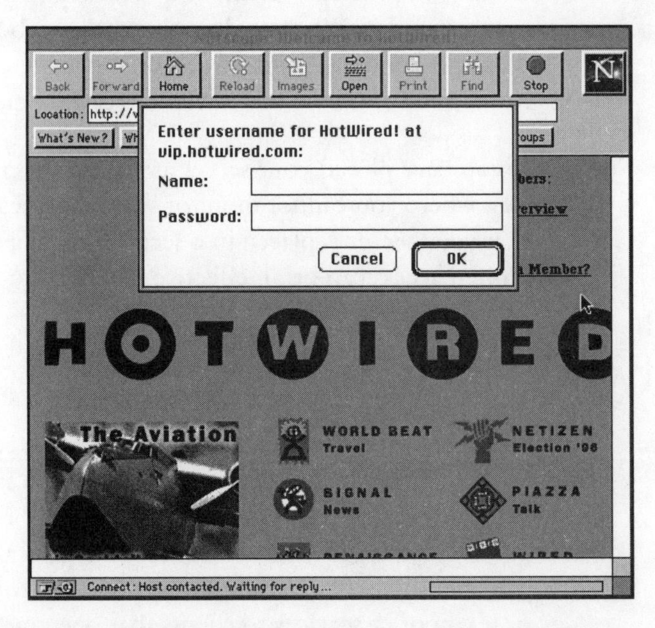

Figure 10.2 *To access HotWired's members section, you must have a valid username and password.*

When a request is received by a server for a URL that is subject to authorization, the request is checked to see whether a valid username and password have been included in the request. If not, the server (or a CGI that handles security functions on your site) returns a message to the client's browser that causes it to ask the user for the login information. This request is usually accompanied by some HTML that is displayed on the browser if the client decides not to continue trying to connect to the server, such as a registration form for new users of a subscription-based server.

Every Web server handles the configuration of usernames and passwords slightly differently, and you should consult the documentation that came with your server software to determine exactly how to implement passwords on your server.

Typically, you can specify a string of characters that, if found in the path to the file being requested by the client, causes a password check to be done. This method is commonly known as "realm-based" authorization, with the realm being defined as all URLs containing the protected string of characters.

Realm-based security, as opposed to protecting a specific file, is useful because it enables you to protect great swaths of your site with one entry and prevents visitors from accessing any files within a folder with a protected name.

URL Abuse

One of the great qualities of the Web is the equality of URLs—a URL on your page to a CGI on your site is no different from the client's point of view to the same URL on another site's page. If you construct a useful CGI that has generic applications (such as a forms-to-email gateway), you may find others utilizing your capabilities in their own pages, thereby using your resources to support their operations.

The same warning can be applied to images on your site—because an image on a page is represented by a URL, the same URL can be used in other pages without your knowledge or permission. This may not be a concern for you, but if it is, or if you find "unauthorized" use of your resources beginning to be a drag on your own efficiency, you should be aware of the possibility and have a method for detecting and controlling this kind of "URL abuse."

There are two methods to detect URL abuse: context and arguments.

URL Arguments

Suppose that you have a CGI that accepts, as an argument, an email address and message and then forwards that message to the email address specified. Many form-to-email gateway CGIs work this way, with the intended email address listed as a hidden field in the form used to send the message. Unfortunately, anyone on the Web who understands HTML can read the source of your page and re-create the form with a different email address that benefits them instead of you.

For example, assume that your CGI looks for a field in your form called "recipient," that is written as a hidden variable, such as:

```
<INPUT TYPE="hidden" NAME="recipient"
VALUE="me@mydomain.com">
```

In order for malcontents to use your CGI for themselves, they would need simply to copy your form to their own site and replace the previous HTML with:

```
<INPUT TYPE="hidden" NAME="recipient"
VALUE="someone@baddomain.com">
```

The simplest way to thwart this kind of abuse is to remove the hidden email address from your HTML. If you always mail your messages to one particular address, you should configure your CGI that way to prevent other addresses from being used. Alternatively, you might be able to set up the CGI to maintain a list of approved addresses, so that every request to send email is checked against that list and if a match is not found to the approved list, you can return an error message to the sender.

Context of the URL

The second method you can use is context. The context of a CGI request or image URL can be thought of as the page that the form or link that contains your URL is contained in. If the context is your own page, all is well. If the context is another page, you might want to detect that and not execute your CGI for that request. Unfortunately, the use of caching clients and proxy servers can present a problem for this approach because your CGI can be called from a page that was requested in the distant past and recalled from cache, thereby preventing your server from knowing whether the CGI was called from your own page.

The recommended approach to this problem is to set up your CGIs so that only authorized arguments can be included and to monitor your log for potential abuses of both CGI and image URLs. Most servers will allow you to log the URLs of pages that link to your CGI's URL (see the section on "referers" in Chapter 8).

If you find such abuses occurring, the most productive approach is likely to be to contact the authors or administrators responsible for the offending page or pages and to ask them to desist from including URLs to your CGI from their site, or to include a note in the CGI's responses about the source of the CGI so that your site gets credit for the activity.

Blowing the Whistle

To report a potential problem when your only information about the offender is the IP address or the domain name used to access your server, the simplest method is to send email to the "postmaster" of the domain in question. Suppose that you notice a problem with an address in the domain gulp.com. The first step you should take is to send email to the addresses postmaster@gulp.com and root@gulp.com. For the vast majority of sites, these addresses are sent to the administrator of the domain.

If you still don't have any luck in making contact, use the *whois* service explained in Chapter 3, "Me and My (Internet) Shadow," to locate the administrative contact for gulp.com. Because the whois listings include normal mailing addresses and phone numbers, you shouldn't have any trouble locating an administrator.

Other Internet Services

The one activity that is most likely to lead to inadvertent security problems is the addition of other Internet services like FTP to your Web server. Each new service requires careful consideration of how the new capabilities it grants to clients can adversely affect the security of your site.

Because CGIs have the capability to perform any action that a user or normal application can perform, unauthorized CGI execution has an unlimited potential to cause problems for you.

Most problems occur through file uploading—the ability of users to deposit files or applications on your server's disks. If users can place a script or CGI application in an area accessible to your server, they can cause the script or application to run by sending the URL that refers to your site. Because CGIs have the capability to perform any action that a user or normal application can perform, unauthorized CGI execution has an unlimited potential to cause problems for you.

WARNING

I strongly recommend that you do not allow clients to upload files to your server's disk without you reviewing what is being sent before it is installed. If your site's needs require you to offer file upload privileges to clients, at least be aware of the possible problems and take steps to monitor what is being deposited at your site, such as reviewing your FTP server's logs daily for suspicious entries.

Denial of Service Attacks

Denial of service describes any kind of intentional attack on your server that prevents it from doing its job normally. This can range from simply swamping your available connections so that your server appears to be extremely slow to actually causing system or application failures that take down your server completely. Obviously, someone conducting this kind of attack has a malicious intent, and in point of fact, it is extremely rare.

Nevertheless, you should be aware of how to detect and cope with these kinds of malicious activities so that you can prevent anyone from causing long-term damage to your operations.

If you detect an inordinate number of hits on your site from a particular IP address or domain that you suspect to have ill intent, you can configure your server to deny access to clients from that domain or IP address. This approach can still allow a dedicated attacker to overwhelm MacTCP and your server because each incoming request from the attacker is still processed, however quickly, by your server. Additionally, if the attacker is smart enough to use multiple IP addresses to reach your server (you can pretty much assume this will be the case), you may lock out legitimate users along with the malicious clients.

Once you detect any sort of attack you can reasonably label as malicious, you should immediately contact the person or persons that administrate the domain that is the source of the trouble. If the domain contact is not available or is not responsive (it might even be the same person that is attacking you), you should work your way up the line to the access provider, and so on, until you find someone willing to investigate the situation. Virtually all domain administrators and ISPs are sensitive to the misuse of their facilities and will deny service to individuals or organizations who are acting inappropriately if you can help them identify the user and the problem.

Firewalls

A *firewall* is a kind of router (see Chapter 3 for more information on routers) that watches the IP messages being passed through it and controls which messages are allowed through. Typically, a firewall can be set up to allow or deny passage to messages based on the IP addresses of the source or destination of the message, on the TCP/IP port number being used, or even on the direction of the message, so that it can allow outgoing but not incoming messages, for example.

In large organizations that maintain private TCP/IP networks, Web servers are often placed "outside the firewall" for security reasons. This allows the firewall to continue denying access to TCP/IP networks inside the organization's private network, yet allows full public access to the server. In this scenario, of course, your Web server should not have any sensitive data on it!

Another common use for firewalls is to filter messages that meet certain criteria, so that you can control which types of messages are allowed into a firewalled network.

Suppose that you are running two Web servers on the same Mac—one for external visitors that runs on port 80 and one reserved for internal usage that runs on port 8080 (this is explained in Chapter 2). You can use the domain name filtering built into your Web server to prevent clients outside your internal domain from accessing the private server, but the more secure approach is to use a firewall to only allow TCP/IP connections from the outside world that are addressed to your server's IP address and specifically meant for port 80. Your second server won't even be known to the outside world.

Currently (early 1996), there are no firewalls available to run on the MacOS. Firewall service is normally conducted by a dedicated router or a UNIX machine that uses software to perform routing and firewall services. If you need a firewall, even if you consider yourself a UNIX expert, you should retain the services of a consultant to assist in configuring your firewall properly. It is quite easy to set up your UNIX system or a router so that you think it is secure, yet is not.

If your organization or Internet Service Provider makes firewall services available to you under its administration, you should approach it with a clear idea of what services you need so that it can set up the firewall properly to meet your demands.

SSL and Secure Transactions

If you read Chapter 3, you already know that IP messages are commonly broadcast to every computer connected to a local network, even if the messages are not meant for all the computers that see the data. Even if such "broadcasting" were not the case, all your messages that cross the Internet also cross through an unpredictable number of routers maintained by others that could potentially be used to interfere with or monitor your own messages.

This fact makes it possible for others to configure their computers or even the routers themselves to read and record packets of information that traverse the network. Because you already know how many networks and routers a message traveling the Internet can cross, you can see that the possibilities for unauthorized access to your messages are substantial.

Packet Sniffers

A computer that is listening or watching messages that are not addressed specifically to that machine are known as "packet sniffers," among other names. A person using such a program could conceivably read all the sensitive information transported between the client and your server, including passwords, credit card numbers, and other information you probably don't want the world to get its hands on. Theoretically, a person could even receive packets meant for your server or for your client, change their contents, and pass them on to their intended recipient without anyone being the wiser.

Fortunately, the sheer volume of IP-based data that gets passed through most routers and that travels along most networks is so huge that screening the information for the tiny portion that would be valuable rapidly becomes an exercise in futility because the odds of finding useful information in the torrent of packets are so slim. However, as electronic commerce becomes more common, the potential rewards for such hacking will increase and make this kind of activity more worthwhile.

Protecting Your Data

There are two ways to protect the data that passes between client and server from unauthorized snooping or modifications—either the data itself can be encrypted (such as an attached file or the credit card number portion of a message) or the connection as a whole can be encrypted so that all the data that passes across the network is protected.

If you are transferring files to known users from your server, you can utilize an encryption program like MacPGP (available from http://bs.mit.edu:8001/pgp-form.html) to encrypt the data before sending it. This method has the advantage of keeping the original data secure on your server until it reaches the client, but can be a hassle to administer and maintain.

You can find out more information about PGP encryption on the Mac at http://web.mit.edu/network/pgp.html.

The second method is to utilize a secure server like the WebSTAR Security Toolkit (currently the only secure server available on the Macintosh) to encrypt the connection itself, so that you can maintain your data or pages in a normal fashion on your own server, yet be assured that the client has received the data without modifications or unauthorized "snooping" on the information while it was in transit.

Although a number of schemes and methods have been proposed to provide encryption of TCP/IP connections, the only method currently in widespread use is called *Secure Sockets Layer* (SSL), and it has been popularized by its inclusion in Netscape's browsers. The downside to this approach is two-fold. First, you are not securing sensitive data on your own disks, so anyone with access to your machine can still read it. Second, secure SSL servers can handle only secure Web transactions, so you must run another server application if you want to be able to serve data both securely and non-securely.

I want to emphasize the point that SSL and other "secure" servers are only secure in the sense that they prevent other people from pretending to be your server, and they prevent people from "listening" to the messages that pass between your server and a client over an encrypted connection. This can certainly be valuable, and it is becoming increasingly popular for sites that regularly work with sensitive information, such as credit card numbers, over the Web.

But these types of connection-based security do nothing to protect the data already on your server from unauthorized access, either by physical means or over your AppleTalk network, which is the focus of this chapter. So if you're interested in using a secure server, refer to Chapter 5 and read the discussion there on using one, but keep in mind that the security of the data residing at your site is still vulnerable to unauthorized access unless you take other steps to *physically* protect it.

Summary

Now that you've secured your server, you can take a look at some miscellaneous administrative issues you may face in the coming months.

CHAPTER 11

Advanced Server Management

This chapter is devoted to miscellaneous issues and concerns that show up repeatedly in postings to newsgroups and mailing lists and don't quite fall into any of the other chapters very well. Everybody should find something of use here, although not all of it may be relevant to your immediate situation.

Integrating Other Internet Services

Sometimes a Web server just isn't enough. Many sites need to offer a broader range of Internet services than just HTTP services, and the most popular services to add are email and FTP capabilities. The following sections discuss the most popular ways of doing so.

Email Services

Email is probably the single most popular Internet service around, and having your own server grants you a lot of flexibility in managing your presence on the Internet. You can use it to set up mailing lists (listservs), create systems to automatically reply to requests for information (mailbots), and project a professional image on the Internet. The following products help to make that happen.

Using Different Macs for Different Server Types

Although you can run other Internet services such as email from the same Mac as your Web server, the ideal situation is to place each type of server (FTP, email, Web) on a different machine to isolate the services. Often, sites will start out by running different Internet server applications on one machine, and then gradually move them onto separate machines when the traffic on their sites grows enough that the different applications are slowing each other down significantly.

The trouble comes when sites forget to assign different hostnames to each service. If you start out with the hostnames mydomain.com for email, www.mydomain.com for Web services, and ftp.mydomain.com for FTP services, you'll be in good shape, because you can assign a new IP address to the appropriate domain name when moving server applications to different machines. If, however, you have people Webbing into www.mydomain.com and also FTPing into www.mydomain.com, you can't move the FTP server to another machine without telling everyone that the hostname in the URL has changed. Big problem.

The solution is to make sure that the URLs you publicize for each Internet server application use different hostnames so that you can move the server applications to different machines as needed.

One more tidbit—the DNS system maintains separate entries for mail servers versus other Internet services. If you want both your Web server URLs and email accounts to use your primary domain name (such as http://mydomain.com/ and myaccount@mydomain.com) and you need to move your email server elsewhere, ask whomever provides your DNS services to change the "MX" entry for your site to point to the IP address of the machine where you want your email messages sent, and you'll be fine.

AIMS

AIMS (Apple Internet Mail Server—http://www.solutions.apple.com/AIMS/default.html) is a complete email server application that allows you to create user accounts, forward email among different accounts, and send email to the rest of the Internet. It's very easy to use and most importantly for a free application, reliable, although it is no longer being actively developed or supported.

AIMS was purchased in 1995 from its original author by Apple Computer, and distributed as freeware. However, it's not currently being developed or supported (to my knowledge) by Apple, so its future remains somewhat cloudy. AIMS is also not suitable for very heavy use, so you wouldn't want to run an ISP's user accounts on it (unless it was a particularly unsuccessful ISP) but it is perfectly able to manage loads up to several thousand message transfers per day. If you urgently need a heavy-duty mail server regardless of the platform, I (reluctantly) recommend Netscape's Mail Server, which runs on both UNIX and Windows NT systems. The most common mail server in the UNIX world, sendmail, is a horrible administrative nightmare, but Netscape's product is a breeze to manage, especially if you're new to the non-MacOS world.

Figure 11.1 shows the opening screen and Preferences settings of AIMS.

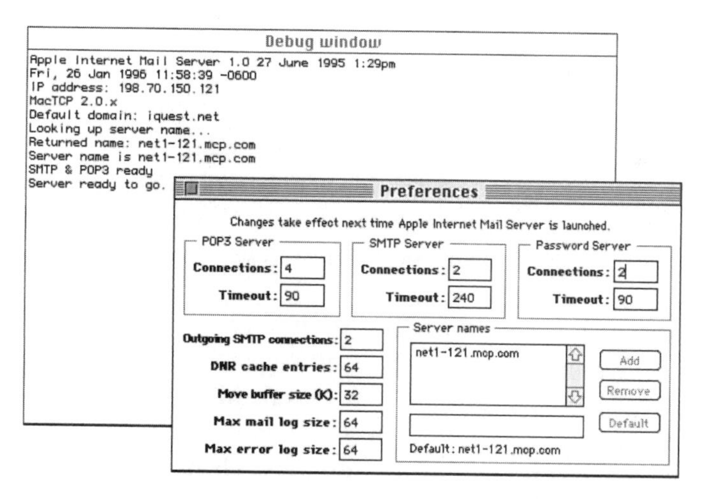

Figure 11.1 *Opening screen for AIMS.*

ListStar

ListStar (http://www.starnine.com/liststar/) is actually a group of products ranging from about $200 to $500 that interacts with various email systems to process incoming mail according to user-defined rules. It allows the creation of mailing lists and mailbots (automatically generated replies to incoming email messages), can receive Apple events from a CGI to send email from your server, and can launch AppleScripts in response to incoming mail. You cannot use it, however, to set up accounts for people to log into with an email client such as Eudora to pick up mail.

NetWings

The Web server NetWings (see Chapter 5 for a description—you can find it in the **Servers** folder on your CD) also offers a full-featured email server similar to AIMS, with some additional features like mailing list management thrown in. The same caveats about heavy usage that I mentioned in the AIMS section also apply to NetWings, with the disadvantage that you cannot place your email server on a separate machine than your Web server when using NetWings, because both services coexist in a single application.

FTP

People add FTP servers to their sites for a variety of reasons, most commonly for uploading HTML pages or other documents to the server. It's also true that some browsers (notably Netscape's browser) still have trouble with downloading files via HTTP, and you may not want to tie up your Web server with long file transfers that slow down its capability to serve normal pages to your clients.

The total number of simultaneous connections you allow for your Web server and FTP server (with each simultaneous FTP client counting as two connections) should not exceed 50 if you are using MacTCP on your server.

Whatever your reasons, rest assured that an FTP and Web server can coexist quite peacefully on the same Mac. There are a couple of caveats: FTP connections keep two TCP/IP connections open per client, so you need to be especially aware of the 64-connection limit in MacTCP when adding FTP services. I would recommend that the total number of simultaneous connections you allow for your Web server and FTP server (with each simultaneous FTP client counting as two connections) not exceed 50 if you are using MacTCP on your server.

Adding an FTP server also opens up your site to any number of potential security problems. Be sure to double-check everything you do when setting access permissions for an FTP server—it's quite easy to accidentally make the entire contents of your hard disk available for downloading, or to create an opportunity for others to upload scripts or CGIs that take control of your server, either to cause damage or obtain unauthorized information.

The next sections discuss a few FTP servers that I found to easily integrate with a Web site.

FTPShare

FTPShare is a full-featured commercial FTP server from About Software, Inc. (http://www.ascus.com/), which works as a system extension. It is much easier to configure and use than FTPd, its shareware cousin, and doesn't require File Sharing to be activated (see next section).

FTPd

FTPd is the most popular FTP server on the Mac, and can also act as a Web server, much like InterServer Publisher. FTPd uses File Sharing to control access to your disk and configure users, so you can set the same permissions for your FTP clients as for people using AppleTalk services to access your disk directly. This is both convenient and a pain, as File Sharing will slow down your server somewhat, and FTPd won't operate unless File Sharing is on. Some combinations of access permissions are simply impossible to implement under FTPd, although that may change in future releases.

On the other hand, it only costs $10 to register a copy, which makes it one of the greatest shareware values around. You can find out more about FTPd by referring to its entry in Chapter 5.

InterServer Publisher

You can't add FTP services to your Web server much more easily than by using an integrated application that includes an FTP server out of the box. The same warnings I gave you earlier about watching the total number of connections you're allowing under MacTCP still apply to an integrated server. InterServer's security options for controlling FTP access are more limited than that of either FTPd or FTPShare, but may meet your needs. Please refer to InterServer's entry in Chapter 5 for contact and pricing information.

Hosting Multiple Web Sites

If you're planning to provide Web site hosting services for multiple clients, you'll be coping with issues unknown to most other site administrators. Because the MacOS wasn't designed, as UNIX was, to operate in a multi-user environment, you'll need to use a little creativity to handle hosting services effectively. It *is* possible, though!

Client Management

Two issues always seem to come up when attempting to host sites for disparate clients—file uploads and reporting log statistics.

Most clients want to manage their own sites, adding and editing their HTML files without your intervention. Typically, this means providing FTP services on your server for your clients, but giving clients the capability to upload files to your Web site raises some serious issues.

Security

The foremost issue is security—if your clients can add whatever they want to your site, they can add CGIs just as easily as HTML pages, and CGIs can easily be written to completely take control of your server or interfere with your site's normal operation. Some site hosting services simply don't allow clients to modify their directories directly—every file upload must be reviewed by the server administrator before it is placed in a directory accessible to outside clients. The issue really comes down to one of trust, and you'll need to balance your confidence in your clients against the potential for problems to determine your best course of action.

Logging Information

Clients also seem to be consistently curious about who is viewing their pages and how often. The traditional method of accomplishing this was to use a script or text processing program to separate your server's main log file into a bunch of little log files, one for each client with individual page accesses. A more elegant solution is to use the commercial version of ServerStat (see Chapter 9), which allows you to "chain" different settings files together to run consecutively.

Because you can configure each settings file to construct reports for each client's particular URLs and then write out the resulting summary files to different directories, it's a great way to keep everyone happy with a minimum of work on your part.

Serving Multiple Domains

Please note this well: The MacOS has no facility for allowing two different hostnames that refer to the same machine (like http://www.site1.com/ and http://www.site2.com/) to return different default home pages to clients using the different URLs. No Web server available for the Mac has the capability to discern which hostname your clients are using, because they all resolve to the IP address of your server.

The MacOS has no facility for allowing two different hostnames that refer to the same machine to return different default home pages to clients using URLs containing the hostnames alone.

You can set up separate folders for each site you are hosting on your server, but you need a way to direct clients to the appropriate folder for the hostname they are requesting. This is one of the disadvantages of using the Macintosh as a Web server, because most UNIX servers can handle multiple domains quite easily.

Although it was hoped that the release of Open Transport would solve this problem, it is very unlikely that Open Transport or any other upcoming events will provide a decent solution in the immediate future.

The simplest response is to provide a default home page for your server that lists all the sites you are hosting, with links to the appropriate URLs for each site's home pages. Unfortunately, many clients are resistant to the idea of paying for the domain name without enabling visitors requesting the domain to go directly to the home pages.

Fortunately, a solution has been provided by Open Door Networks, Inc. (http://www.opendoor.com/homedoor/), using a system extension called HomeDoor. Figure 11.2 shows the home page.

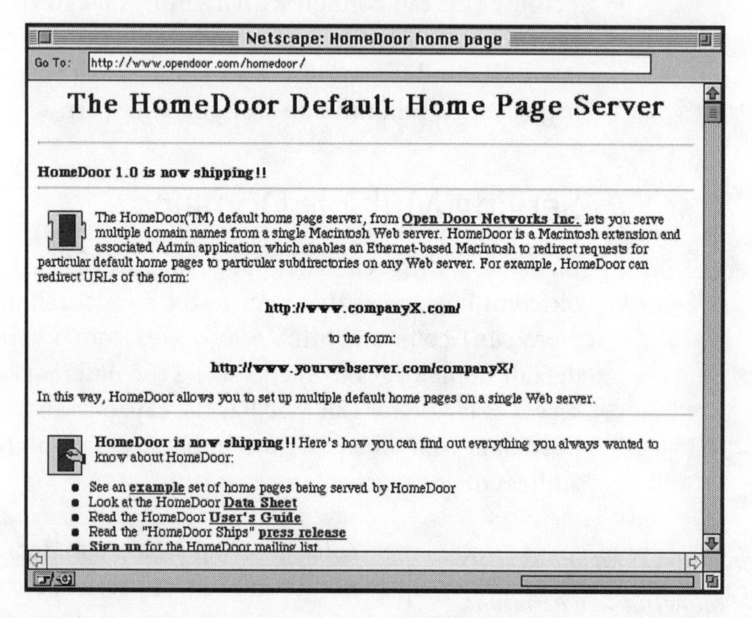

Figure 11.2 *Open Door Networks, Inc.'s home page for HomeDoor.*

HomeDoor works by listening for incoming HTTP requests and redirecting them to the appropriate directory for their domain name. So if a client types http://www.mydomain.com/ as a URL, the request is intercepted by HomeDoor before it ever reaches your Web server and a HTTP redirection response is sent back to the client's browser, which promptly retrieves the proper URL http://www.mydomain.com/mydomain/, exactly where you want the client to go. The URL for virtual domains still needs to be extended into that domain's directory, but URL redirection is handled automatically by the client's browser and it is likely that the client will not even notice the change in the URL.

To use HomeDoor, you'll need an Ethernet-based Mac, a series of contiguous IP addresses, one for each domain you want to serve up to a maximum of 256 (including the Web server's own IP address), and a few hundred dollars to spend on the extension, but that will get you the only reliable method of serving virtual domains that I am aware of. Note that OpenDoor will work equally well when installed on the same Mac as your Web server application or on a different Mac on the same LAN.

Heading for Hostsville

Recent versions of Netscape are adding the domain name of the URL being requested to its HTTP requests, so that a server or CGI that knew to look for this information can determine which hostname is being requested and return different responses for different hostnames.

This is an ideal solution, but utilizing it currently requires either a custom CGI or a modified Web server application, and its utility is restricted to clients using browsers that send the hostname information. If you develop your own CGI functions and would like to take advantage of this information, you'll need to use WebSTAR as your server application and locate a line beginning with "Host:" in the full_request (Kfrq) parameter of the CGI Apple Event sent from the server. If the information exists, it will appear as follows in the Kfrq parameter:

```
<other headers>
Host: www.site1.com <CRLF>
<other headers>
```

Once you determine the hostname being requested, you can either deliver the appropriate response page directly to the client or return a redirection response to send the client to the appropriate directory, for instance, http://www.site1.com/site1/. Please review Chapter 8 for more details on constructing your own CGIs.

Of course, the big disadvantage of HomeDoor is that it can't get around the basic problem with virtual domains on the Mac—namely that all the virtual sites' URLs still have that extra folder name stuck in the beginning of the path.

I, Robot!

If your server is accessible to the Internet, you'll eventually start noticing requests for a file called "robots.txt" appearing in your logs. These requests are generated by automated site indexing services such as Lycos (http://www.lycos.com/) or InfoSeek (http://www.infoseek.com/), which maintain arrays of machines that do nothing but download Web pages from the Internet and index their contents—the programs that actually go about downloading URLs are called "robots" (among other things) and they will, by default, attempt to locate and download every page on your site.

According to standard Internet practices, well-behaved robots are supposed to ask for the URL http://www.myserver.com/robots.txt before beginning to download your pages. The purpose of this file is to allow you, the site administrator, to stop or limit the robot's activities on your server, and if it is not found, the robot is to assume by default that your entire site is available for indexing.

To use the robots.txt file, simply create a text file and place it in the top level of your Web site's root directory. You can indicate which portions of your site you do not want to have indexed by adding the paths of the folders or files you want to be excluded to the file.

The complete specification is available at http://info.webcrawler.com/mak/projects/robots/norobots.html, but I've written a few examples here to clarify usage:

- To protect one top-level folder hierarchy (in this case, a folder called myfolder) at your site from indexing, type the following lines in your robots.txt file:

```
User-agent: *
Disallow: /myfolder/
```

- To restrict access to multiple folders, simply add more Disallow lines to the file. The following text stops indexing of two different folders:

```
User-agent: *
Disallow: /myfolder/
Disallow: /myotherfolder/
```

- To refuse all robots permission to index any of your site, include the following two lines in your robots.txt file:

```
User-agent: *
Disallow: /
```

Of course, there's no guarantee that a given robot is "well-behaved" enough to pay attention to your instructions, but most common robots will request and abide by the robots.txt instructions when attempting to index your Web server's pages.

Summary

If you've absorbed this chapter completely, you can camp out on most Mac Web-related newsgroups or mailing lists and take the title of Web guru in three rounds. Or you can keep going and learn in the next chapter how to "audit" your site for potential problems and ensure that all of its parts are working together harmoniously.

CHAPTER 12

Not Another Audit!

At least you'll be the examiner this time.

Every time you change a page, a link, a bit of HTML on your site, or when you upgrade the system software, install a new disk driver, or add a CGI to your site, you're also potentially adding an error or the potential for new problems to your server.

This chapter explores some of the more common sources of problems in your site's content, and then discusses how to test your server's and CGI's capabilities to withstand a heavy level of traffic.

This chapter contains an underlying assumption that your Web server is used exclusively for serving—that is, you don't let your neighbor's kids play CD-ROM games on it, and you may not even switch on the monitor unless you're doing site maintenance.

Links and Pages

The best way I know of to ensure that your site does not contain any errors in its HTML and links is to use a Web site management program that prevents you from creating problems when first designing or editing your pages. The alternative—hunting down and fixing problems after you've already updated your site—can be time-consuming out of all proportion to the time required to create the problem in the first place.

Unfortunately, there are no such programs available for the Macintosh while this book is being written. By the time you read this, however, Adobe (http://www.adobe.com/) should have released SiteMill, which purports to accomplish exactly this kind of preflight checking. Hopefully, other vendors will follow suit and release comparable software in the coming year. In the meantime, if SiteMill or its competition is unavailable or too expensive for your budget, I'll show you a few tricks of the trade to get your site in order and end all those sarcastic complaints from your clients about how your links or CGIs aren't working today.

There are three main areas of concern in your pages themselves—the HTML code, the URLs or links in your pages, and the actual content of your site. You read about all three in the next sections.

HTML

Verifying the accuracy and correctness of your HTML is absolutely vital for ensuring that your clients see your site in the way that you intend it to be seen. Nothing looks more unprofessional than a bit of a URL being rendered as text because a client's browser might not be as forgiving of your badly formed HTML code as the browser you used to test with during development.

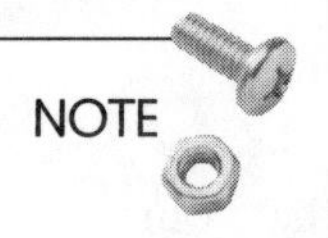

I briefly discussed the use of HTML editors in Chapter 6, "Serving from Storage," and their use goes a long way toward preventing errors in your pages. None of them is perfect, however, so you'll eventually need to run your pages through a program that checks your HTML against the standards and notifies you if something is out of place, missing, or otherwise incorrect.

Please don't discount the value of having your HTML verified for correctness—if you want your pages to be accessible to a majority of the new browsers being released, as well as to the armies of older versions that will still be used for a long time to come, you need to conform to the standards.

HTML "correctness" is independent of its actual contents. Using HTML tags interpretable only by Netscape, for example, is your choice, but using unmatched quote characters, nesting HTML tags incorrectly, or otherwise not conforming to the syntax of HTML (*syntax*, meaning the structure, as opposed to *diction*, meaning the content) is a dangerous occupation.

There are a number of HTML verification services available on the Web, but I've chosen one of the few that seem to be the most up-to-date and useful.

WebTechs HTML Validation Service

WebTechs (see Figure 12.1) is the Big Gun in HTML validation—you might have seen the little icon before that checked pages are entitled to display. Formerly offered by HALsoft (http://www.halsoft.com/html/), this service should be a regular stop for any HTML writer. One very nice aspect of the WebTechs service is that you can use the radio buttons shown in Figure 12.1 to choose the HTML standard you want your pages to be checked against—the further to the left you go, the more likely your pages are to be viewable by older or unusual browsers. "Mozilla," by the way, refers to the current state of the extended HTML tags Netscape Navigator uses in its released versions, so if you are willing to restrict your clients to using current versions of Netscape's browsers to view your site, choose the Mozilla option. Note that some other browsers, such as Microsoft's Explorer (http://www.msn.com/), also recognize many of the "Mozilla" HTML tags.

Further down on the page shown in Figure 12.1 (below the bottom of the window) is a box where you can type in a little snippet of HTML you'd like to be checked on its own rather than assigning a URL to check. This is very helpful when working with new HTML tags or a complicated table you'd like to have verified for correctness.

Whether you point an HTML validator at a URL or type tags directly, the checks performed will identify malformed HTML, either by highlighting the incorrect sections or by listing excerpts that it finds problematic. Each service reports errors slightly differently, so be sure to read the instructions and FAQs at each site before submitting your own code for review.

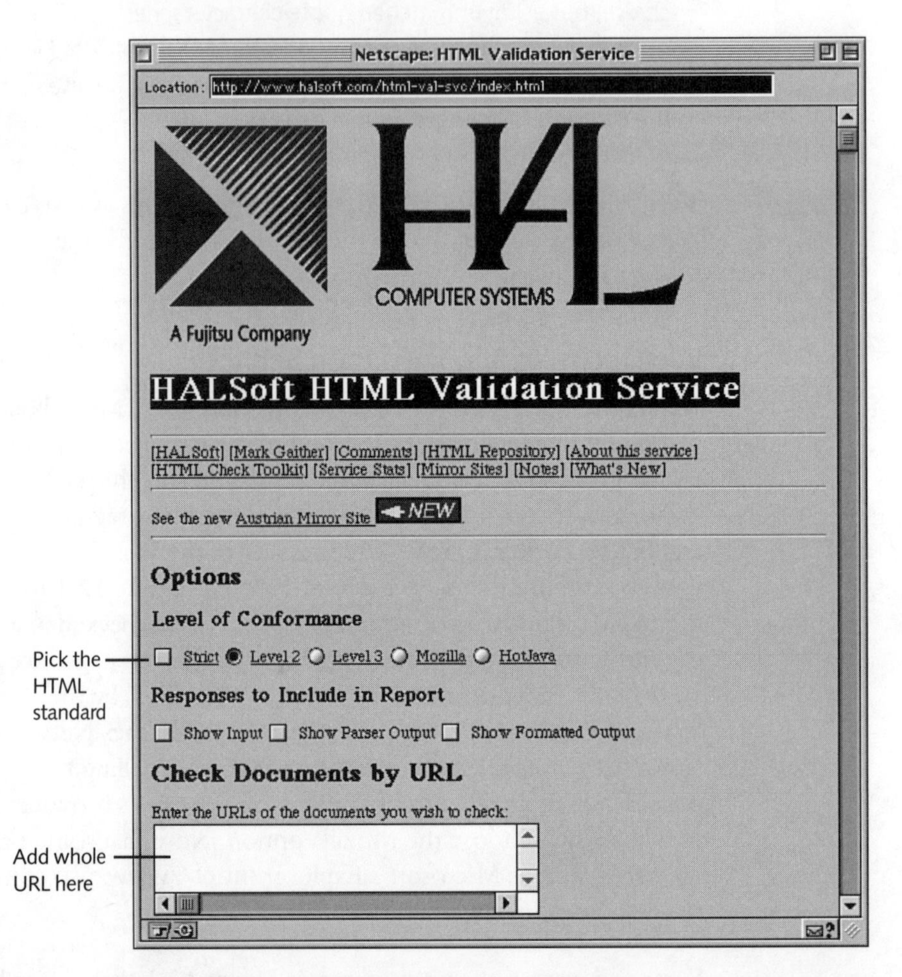

Figure 12.1 *WebTechs HTML Validation home page*—http://www.webtechs.com/html-val-svc/.

If you'd like to try other services, take a look at http://WWW.Stars.com/Vlib/Providers/Validation.html and explore the options!

Internal Links

Internal links are the URLs that connect your own pages to other pages on the same server. Often, they will be written in HTML in a relative form, such as /images/logo.gif. The client is responsible for translating the relative form into a full-fledged URL by appending it to your server's domain name and current location in your directories, if applicable.

Internal links are also the most common place where errors in your HTML references can creep in when you're not watching. Even if they are correct when you write them, moving files between folders or even using aliases can render them invalid.

Suppose, for example, that you have a page within a folder called joe inside a folder called users. That page might contain a relative link to another page in the same folder such as /users/joe/secondpage.html. If you move the joe folder into another folder, all the links that included /users/ in the URL will fail. If, alternatively, you had used the relative URL secondpage.html in the URL, you could move the joe folder anywhere you like and still have the secondpage.html link resolve correctly from the original page.

Any decent HTML tutorial or book describes how relative URLs should be written and used—they are very helpful for building self-contained Web sites that can be moved to different servers en masse without changing the link URLs. Be careful with them, though—moving part of your site without verifying the new relative references is a recipe for disaster.

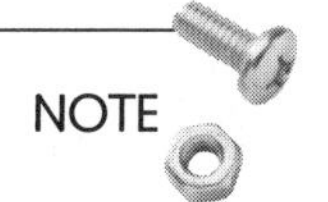
NOTE

One way to detect bad links takes advantage of the fact that most servers will allow you to specify an "error" page that will be served to clients by default if they request a non-existent URL from your server. Your error page should contain links to main areas or indexes of your site, so that clients can quickly recover from a bad URL, as well as provide the means (forms, email) for the client to inform the Webmaster (you) that the client had a problem.

External Links

External links are URLs in your pages that connect the client to sites outside your own server. Technically, they could also be to a server of your own, as long as the hostname is different from the one used to retrieve the page where the link being used was written.

Fortunately, you cannot misuse relative URLs in your external links, because by definition, an external link must contain a full URL that specifies the address of the other server and the full path-name of the URL.

External links can, however, still point to nonexistent pages or pages that move or change in such a way as to no longer be appropriate. Catching such errors requires either that you review all your links yourself (See the section entitled "Content" later in this chapter) or that you use an automated program to check your links for accuracy. I would recommend checking your external links at least weekly to keep up with changes.

Link Checkers

Ideally, there would be a simple program available that you could point at your site and get a list of all the URLs that return error messages when retrieved, together with the URLs of the pages they appear on. As I write this, there are no such programs available for the Macintosh, although you should be sure to check the Web site for this book for any late-breaking news.

There are three possibilities for performing automated link checking today: Each has its own potential advantages and disadvantages, and you should try each before deciding on the method you want to use on your own site.

David Habermann's AppleScript Link Checker

David Habermann's Link Checker (see Figure 12.2) is actually a collection of AppleScripts that works together to verify the URLs contained in a given site's pages. It's not a bad piece of software on the whole, and is fairly comprehensive in its reports. It does require a lot of RAM, especially if you have a large site, and I've had a lot of problems with crashes and other difficulties when it was running. It's worth looking into (you can try it for free) but may not be suitable for many sites. Pay careful attention to the Read Me files with usage instructions, and make sure you have the AppleScript extension (it is installed with System 7.5) active before using Link Checker.

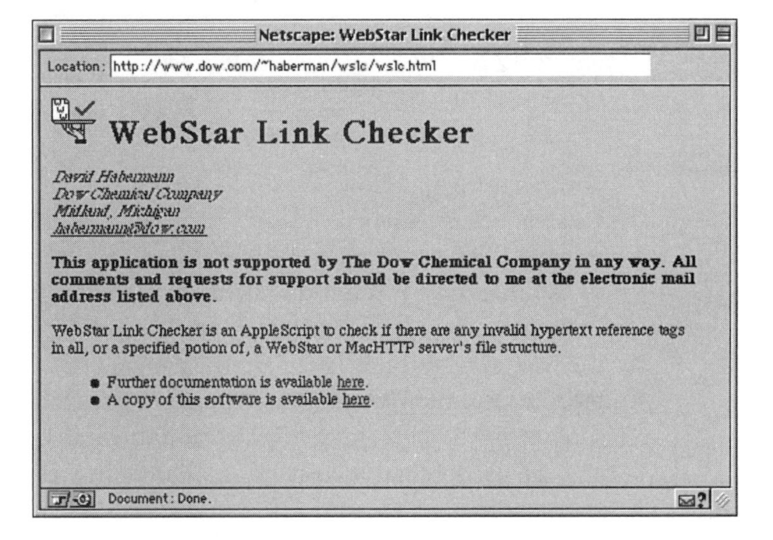

Figure 12.2 *Link Checker home page*—http://www.dow.com/~haberman/wslc/wslc.html.

WebTools Service

This site (see Figure 12.3) is actually quite cool—you submit a URL, and the service checks all of the links appearing in that URL and emails you the results.

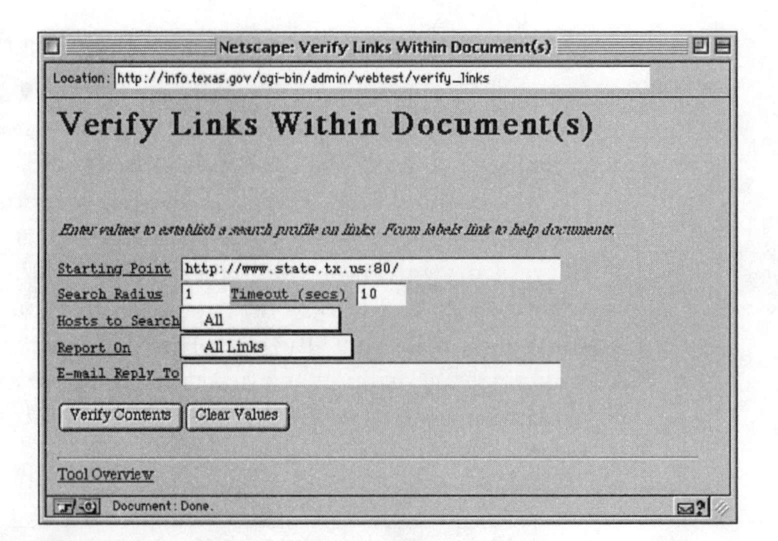

Figure 12.3 *WebTools verification form*—http://info.texas.gov/cgi-bin/admin/webtest/verify_links.

You can set it to follow your links deep into your site (use the "search radius parameter to set the number of links away from the starting URL you want to have checked), and it even checks links to external sites. I'm not discussing it at length because it could easily have disappeared or offer a completely different interface by the time you read this (such are the dangers of writing about a fluid medium like the Web in a static medium like this book), but be sure to try the URL in the figure caption—if it's available, it can be a useful service, and it costs no more than the time to fill out a short form.

WebWhacker

WebWhacker is a commercial product that is primarily used to download self-referencing copies of Web sites, including pages and graphics, to the user's hard disk. This is very useful for presentations and other situations where you might want to surf through a site without an active Internet connection.

Initially, I was very excited about using WebWhacker for link checking—not only do you receive a list of all the URLs with bad references from your site, it would also download a copy of your site to your local disk. Unfortunately, although WebWhacker tells you what URLs return errors, it won't tell you on what page from your site the URL was read from. So you know that something is wrong, but don't know where to go to fix it. Sigh.

You should take a look at the current version to see whether parents of URLs are available now—it would be a neat tool for auditing a site were it not for the one lacking function, which they claim to be adding even as I type this line. Check out the WebWhacker info page at http://www.ffg.com/wwmac1.html.

Content

The one part of site reviewing that will likely not be automated for quite some time, if ever, is verifying that the pages and images being linked to by your URLs refer to the correct page or image. An automated link checker can tell you when a URL points to a reference that does not exist, but it cannot confirm that the link points to the correct resource, or that the data being returned is in fact what you intended it to be.

You can keep track of your external links by using one of the services or tools that notify you when the contents of a URL change (see previous sections in this chapter)—you might spend a lot of time reviewing pages from other sites with only cosmetic changes, but at least you will be able to rest easy knowing that your references to those sites are still correct.

For your internal links, however, there is no substitute for actually reviewing the site personally, by clicking every URL and trying every imagemap and form. The difficulty, especially for large, dispersed sites, is making sure every link has in fact been reviewed—it's always that link from your copyright statement in tiny print that seems to have an error.

The simplest method to ensure that you don't miss anything is to use Netscape or some other Web browser that keeps track of what URLs you've visited in the past. I use Netscape as an example of how to do this:

1. First, choose General Preferences from the Options menu in Netscape. The Preferences window will open and the Appearance section will be displayed, as shown in Figure 12.4.

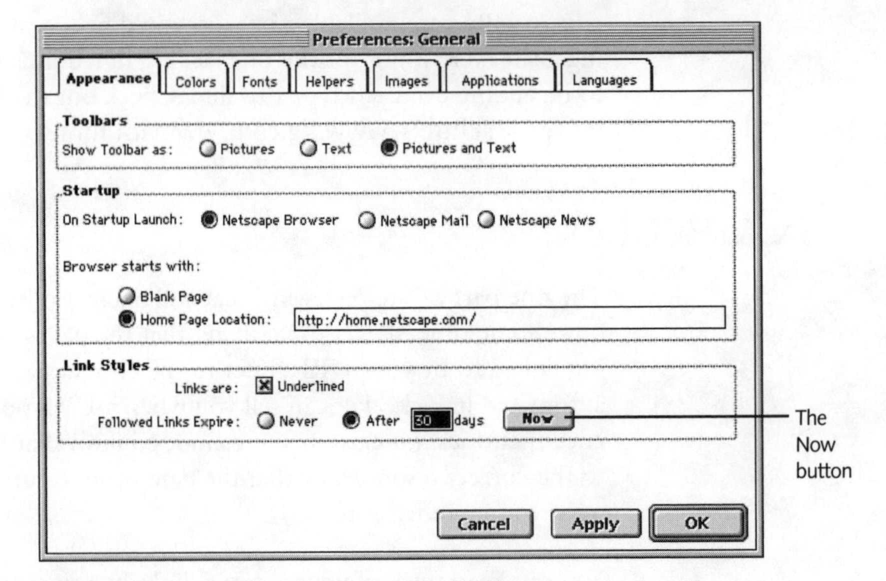

Figure 12.4 *Netscape's Appearance preferences settings.*

2. Click the "Now" button indicated in Figure 12.4 to clear Netscape's memory of your previous URLs.

3. You'll also need to provide yourself with some indication of where you have been in your site so you don't review pages more than once and don't miss any links on your site.

   To do so, click the "Colors" tab near the top left of the Preferences window—the display should appear similarly to the one shown in Figure 12.5.

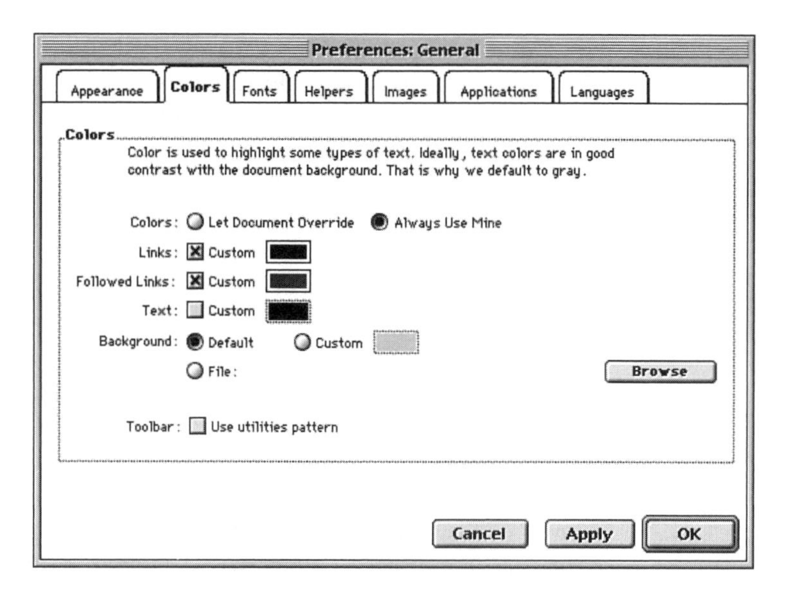

Figure 12.5 *Netscape's Colors preferences settings.*

4. You'll need to make sure three options are set correctly here: that the radio button for "Always Use Mine" is checked, and that the options for "Links" and "Followed Links" are set correctly. Both "Links" settings should have the "Custom" checkbox selected, and the colored boxes to their right should display strikingly different colors, so that you can differentiate reviewed from unreviewed links by glancing at your Web pages.

5. To change the colors used, click the colored box in question once—you'll be presented with Apple's standard color picker window to choose a new color to use.

6. Once you're done, click OK on the dialog box and quit Netscape. You really shouldn't need to quit Netscape, but there have been many reports of new preferences settings not "taking hold" until a restart, so be safe and do so.

7. Now that you have Netscape restarted, go to the home page for your Web site—all the links will appear in the "unfollowed link" color you saw earlier. Review the page, and when you're satisfied it is as you expected it to be, click one of the unreviewed URLs, which you can now identify by color.

8. Continue reviewing and clicking until you get to one of your pages that has no unfollowed links on it. Once you get to this "bottom" page, use the "go back" button on Netscape to return to the page one level up in your site's hierarchy.

9. Repeat this process of moving as far as you can into your site and then backing up a page at a time, never leaving a page with unfollowed links behind you when you back up. Eventually, you'll end up back on your home page, with all the links indicated as followed.

There—a no-brainer way to make sure that you visit every page on your Web site.

Because you're visiting every page on your site anyway, this might be a good time to pull out a pencil and paper and diagram your site, drawing lines to connect pages together to indicate links, to help you visualize its structure.

> This method works only for pages that can be reached through your top-level URL, or home page. If your site has multiple "home pages" that don't refer to each other in any way, you'll need to keep track of all of them so you can check each linking hierarchy individually.
>
> One easy method is to maintain a home page just for your own use that contains the URLs of all the other "top-level" pages on your site. Simply use this page as your testing home page, and the previous method will work fine.
>
> Note that this method will not work for imagemaps—you'll need to be careful to try every possible area of your imagemap to ensure that it is also referring clients to the correct pages or other resources on your site.

An effective way to ensure the correctness of the HTML, links, and content of your site is to establish a regular routine of reviewing and verification using whatever tools you find most appropriate whenever you make substantial changes to your site. If other people than yourself contribute material for serving, it becomes doubly important that someone take responsibility for ensuring that new or changed material hasn't dragged a new problem along with it.

Once you're satisfied that your site works as expected, you'll need to check that your server can handle unexpected situations such as a sudden increase in traffic without suffering a MacCrash.

Let's take a look at that kind of auditing next.

Server Response

The responsiveness of your server can be summarized in two questions. Does it answer every request it receives? How quickly is that response returned to the client?

These are the kinds of questions this next section will help you to answer.

Testing Response Speed

Obtaining an accurate measurement of your server's responsiveness (the time required to completely handle an incoming client's request) is problematic at best. Even after ignoring aspects of your site that remain constant, such as your server's CPU speed and the size of the page or image being considered, the time required for any given request can vary enormously. Here are some of the variables that can affect your response time:

- ☐ Network congestion
- ☐ Number of clients' requests being handled at once
- ☐ Speed of a given client's Internet connection
- ☐ The mix of speeds for all current clients
- ☐ The speed of your Mac's CPU
- ☐ The number of CGIs or other software on your Mac that can take CPU time away from the Web server application

Any or all of these elements can affect the time your server requires to respond to a given request, and the times you see in your server logs for serving one particular file can vary tremendously. Look back through Chapter 9, "Statistics and Usage," for more information on how to collect this data from your logs, but be aware that you should always look at averages or other numbers that measure overall performance before reaching a conclusion about your server's capabilities.

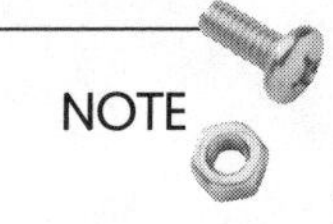

NOTE

> One note—and I'll mention it again in the next section on stress testing—the single most important element in your server's response time is often the maximum number of simultaneous connections you are allowing clients to make. If you want to know why, check out Chapter 14, "My Other Ferrari Is a Mac."

Stress Testing

Stress testing is the process of pushing your server until it fails to determine its capacity to handle clients and the reliability of the software running on it. A poorly designed CGI that works great for one request per minute, for example, may cause a system crash when two or more requests are made at a time.

To stress your server, you'll use a tool rather appropriately called Pounder (ftp://ftp.comvista.com/pub/net/www/WebPounder.sit.bin).

Pounder

Pounder (see Figure 12.6) is not a commercial piece of software—in fact, it is barely a working piece of software that Chuck Shotton, the author of WebSTAR, provided as-is to the Mac Web server community. But it doesn't crash much and does the job, so we'll take advantage of it here. All Pounder does is repeatedly try to retrieve a list of URLs from your server, opening up to 20 simultaneous connections while doing so.

To download Pounder, FTP to ftp://ftp.prowillen.com/stewart/pound.hqx and follow the instructions there.

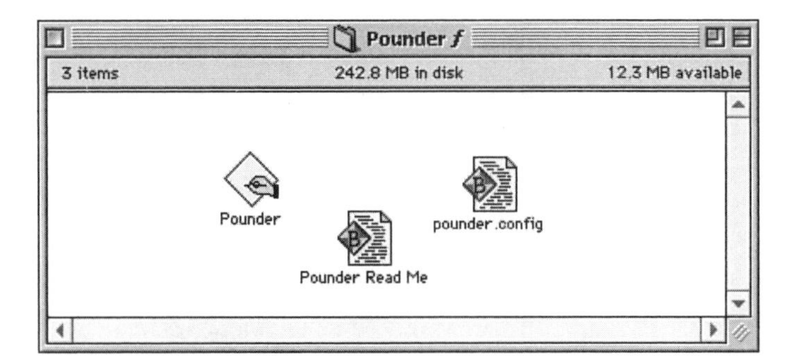

Figure 12.6 *The Pounder application and files.*

Ideally, it should be run from a very fast client, such as another Mac on the same Ethernet as your server. If that's not possible, be aware that the client's connection to the Internet can be as much of a constraint on your testing results as the server's own capability to return information. I don't recommend setting Pounder to open more than 10 simultaneous connections if you're using a dialup line (28.8K speed or less)—the best solution in that case is to get a friend to run another copy of Pounder against your site at the same time you are doing so.

Configuring Pounder

Configuring Pounder requires editing a text file called "pounder.config" (see Figure 12.7) that resides in the same folder as the Pounder application.

The configuration information consists of three lines, followed by a list of the URLs you want to check:

- The first line is the IP address of your server, as shown in Figure 12.7. Do not use the domain name, such as myserver.com, because Pounder won't be able to translate it into an IP address. You can obtain the IP address for your server from the MacTCP control panel.

- The second line is the maximum number of seconds you want Pounder to wait between connection attempts. I recommend setting this to 10 seconds, but you may want to increase it to 20 or 30 if you are running Pounder over a dialup connection.

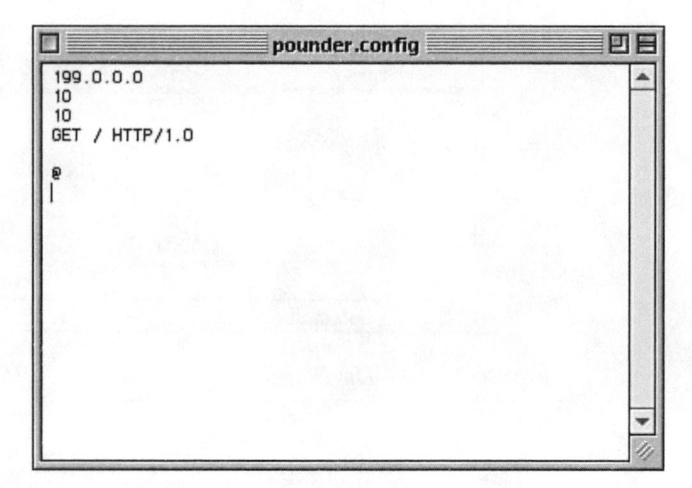

Figure 12.7 *Pounder configuration file contents.*

- ☐ The third line is the maximum number of simultaneous connections Pounder can open, which must be between 1 and 20. If you want to open more than 20 connections at a time (which you should do if your server is set for more than 20 simultaneous clients), you'll need, again, to run Pounder on a different Mac. I don't recommend using multiple copies on one machine at the same time.

The rest of the configuration file is a list of the URLs that you want Pounder to request from your server. They can be images, text, or anything else that you can refer to in a URL.

NOTE

> If the URL you are testing is a page that contains inline images, you should include the images' URLs in your Pounder configuration as well for the sake of accuracy, because most clients will request the image files automatically when they view your HTML page.

Each request is formed as the word <GET> (use uppercase), followed by a space and the URL path (shown here as a placeholder for the real thing), followed by another space, the phrase "HTTP/ 1.0," and two carriage returns. Finally, add a "@" character and another carriage return. The following codes show the request form:

```
GET <url_path_here> "HTTP/1.0"

@
```

You can continue adding URLs in the same format one after the other in the configuration file as much as you like—Pounder will request all of them from your server repeatedly until you tell it to stop.

To determine what path you should insert in the URL request (the path is the part between the GET and the HTTP), follow these steps:

1. Look at your browser's window when you are at the page in question, as shown in Figure 12.8.

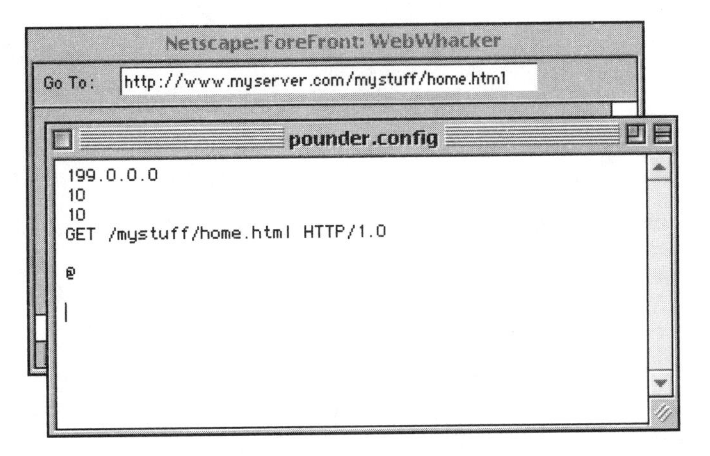

Figure 12.8 *Check the URL of the page in question.*

2. Select and copy all of the URL that appears after the host-name, including the first "/" character. Paste this into the Pounder configuration file as shown in the examples, and repeat as shown until you have all the URLs you want to "pound" listed in the file.
3. Save the amended configuration file to the same folder as Pounder—making sure that you haven't changed its name from "pounder.config"—and you're ready to start Pounder.

Using Pounder

When you launch Pounder, you will see a very ugly screen, much like the one shown in Figure 12.9.

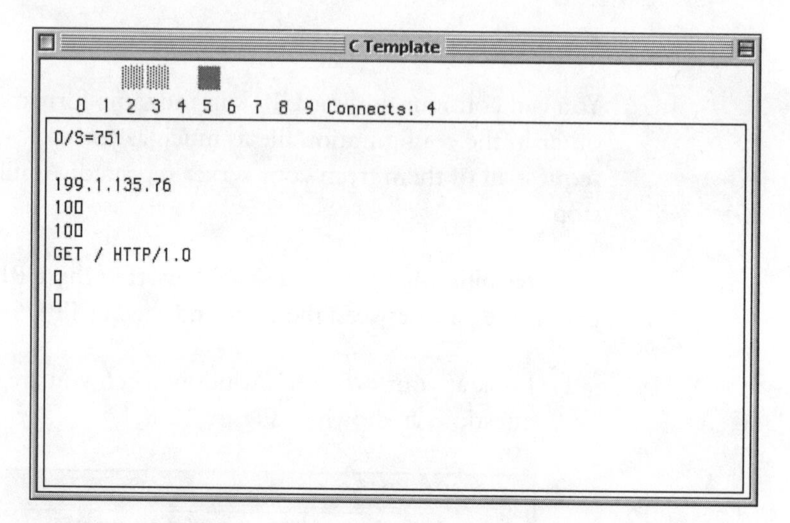

Figure 12.9 *Pounder's main window.*

The boxes at the top will start appearing and disappearing as Pounder opens and closes connections. You'll also see error messages appear on Pounder's screen—don't worry too much about what they say, but keep track of roughly how many there are. You can let Pounder run as long as you like, and then either choose Quit from the File menu or press Command-Q to end the session. You may have to wait a few seconds for Pounder to finish its active connections before it quits.

The configuration file supplied at the aforementioned URL and used in Figure 12.9 is set to retrieve your site's default home page (the "/" path), allow up to 10 seconds between requests, and open up to 10 simultaneous connections to the server. All you need to do is replace the fake IP address with that of your own server and run Pounder to get started.

You should also try using your normal Web browser to access your site while Pounder is running against it to get a feel for the effect of a heavy load on your server. Try starting Pounder with just a few connections, and increase the number of connections by five at a time until the response from your server becomes too slow to be tolerable. Reduce the number of connections allowed by five, and use that number to set the maximum connections setting on your server to avoid overloading your resources.

CGIs Response

The first test of your CGIs is for you or a friend to use them as much as possible. If the CGI receives information via forms on your pages, try filling out the form in every wrong way you can imagine. Leave fields empty, fill them in wrong, try and fill them in as much as possible, use strange characters like question marks and dollar signs—do everything you don't expect anyone else to do, and make sure that the response from your server is appropriate.

You can also use Pounder to test how your CGIs perform under stress, even if the CGI is accessed via a form. As I discussed in Chapter 7, "CGI Applications and Usage," client requests can be submitted under different HTTP methods, such as GET or POST. When using the POST method (as most forms do), the information from the form is appended to the request rather than added to the URL itself.

You can configure Pounder to simulate form submissions by copying the data from a real form submission (See Chapter 7 again for more details) and replacing the GET method requests used before with the POST request. An example is shown in Figure 12.10.

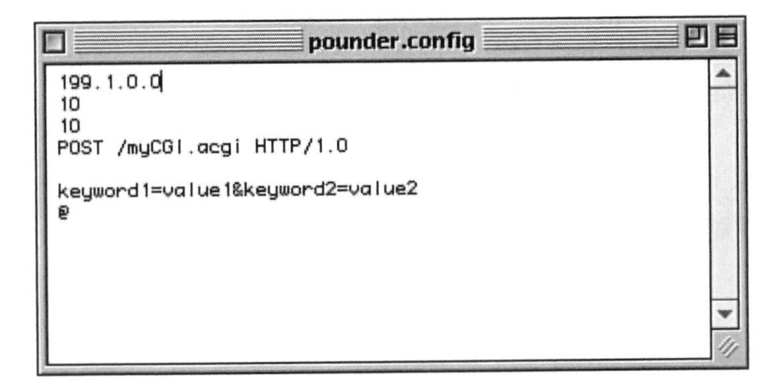

Figure 12.10 *A Pounder configuration for a POST method request.*

A properly written CGI will not crash, no matter how many requests are thrown at it. If you experience a crash, contact the author of the CGI and explain the situation in which the CGI failed so that they can attempt to fix the problem. Note that testing performance under heavy stress is different from testing your CGI's capability to handle unexpected information in requests sent to it. You should verify that the information in your POST data is correct before using it to test CGI performance as described.

You should also test the CGI's response time with your Web browser while Pounder is running, just as you did with the normal URLs previously. If the CGI becomes very slow, the server may stop waiting for it and return an error message to the client even though the CGI is still working on the request.

Evaluating Your Results

Now we can take a closer look at the two questions with which we began this section: "Is the server responding?" and "Is the response time tolerable?"

The first should always be true as long as you haven't experienced any crashes. If you do have trouble with applications crashing or quitting, you should immediately deal with them by isolating and removing the source of the problem using the methods in Appendix A. Normally, this means removing or changing CGIs you have installed.

The second question is a judgment call—your server may respond to every request even when you have 30 modem users connected to it, but half your clients may abort the connection halfway through because they are tired of waiting for your extremely bogged down server to deliver its response to them. Generally, a fast server that is occasionally busy leaves a better impression than a server that is always available but always slow—but that's a subjective opinion. Your priorities will determine what is best for your site.

Summary

What a lot of work! And all just to avoid a few broken links.

On the other hand, if you've ever tried to follow a link that seemed to lead exactly where you wanted to go and received an error message, you'll understand the importance of maintaining a server that is consistently dependable.

Performance is a more tricky issue—after all, links and HTML formatting either work or they don't—and your priorities in providing speedy and reliable service to the Internet will determine the amount of effort you invest in stress testing your server and exploring its capacity. Many site administrators are unwilling to tolerate even the occasional crash or client complaint, and a properly audited and maintained server should be able to run for months without even a hiccup of trouble.

Ultimately, though, most of us want to present the best possible face to the world while spending as little time as possible actually maintaining our servers. After all, every moment spent on maintenance is a moment not spent creating real content for your site.

That will be the subject of the next chapter—how to walk away from your server in confidence that it will continue to do its job without supervision.

CHAPTER 13

Walkaway Serving

After a prolonged bout with full-time Web serving, you might start wondering if that guy behind you with the pager strapped to his belt is a doctor, drug dealer, or… Webmaster.

This chapter is about setting up *walkaway servers*, Web sites that maintain themselves without your constant intervention. You'll still need the pager if you want to keep track of your site's activity, but at least you won't need to get up at three in the morning to reboot your Mac.

As a corollary to the walkaway concept, I'll also discuss some of the tools available to make remote administration of Web servers via the Internet as simple and reliable as sitting directly in front of the machine, plus a few tips and tricks to create the illusion that you are constantly slaving away over your server while you take that well-deserved Tahitian vacation.

Walkaway servers are Web sites that maintain themselves without your constant intervention.

First, though, I'm going to focus on how to set up your Web site so that it can cope with problems (and avoid them) on its own.

Designing a Server-Monitoring System

It's entirely possible to set up a simple Web site that serves only static pages and images, maybe even using a couple CGIs, that will stay up for weeks or months without hiccuping once. But when you start throwing in database operations, more complex CGIs, conflicting software upgrades, extensive continuing site development, and maybe a couple other TCP/IP services like email or FTP into the mix, you might find yourself babysitting your server as though it were a hyperactive five year old.

One of the first steps toward building a reliable Web site is, therefore, setting up a monitoring system that ensures your server is both accessible to the Internet and functioning. A properly designed system will respond appropriately to different situations without your intervention and keep you informed of the overall status of the server.

Parts of a Server-Monitoring System

To design your own system, you need to decide what aspects of your server's functioning are most important to you and how you want the system to respond when a problem is discovered. This section looks at your options, explores the tools available to help you implement your own system, and describes some sample systems that you can use in your own operations.

There are three elements necessary to any self-sustaining server:

- A monitoring system
- An alert system
- A response system

The first decision is the most basic—what are you monitoring?

Check and Check

Effectively monitoring your server requires checks on both the status of the hardware/software that your physical server depends on, and the network connections between your server and the Internet. This section introduces the concepts and tools necessary to do both.

Your Server

When monitoring your server, there are three areas of potential problems: the Mac itself, the server software, or other ancillary programs, such as CGIs. Because problems with the Macintosh are likely to be reflected in the server's capability to respond correctly to requests, you should concentrate on keeping track of the server software itself and its CGIs.

The only way to ensure that your server is operating correctly is to complete a real HTTP transaction with it, retrieve the response, and examine the response's HTML data. Essentially, you use Netscape or other client software to retrieve a URL from your server and examine the page returned for errors.

Some local network (AppleTalk, Ethernet, and so on) administration tools determine whether particular applications are running, and will alert you if there is a problem. The trouble with this approach is that your server software might very well be running, yet have other problems that prevent it from responding correctly to client requests.

Also, because the TCP/IP portions of the MacOS operate at a level different from that for normal applications, it is not uncommon for browsers to report successfully connecting and a "waiting for response" message from crashed Web servers even though a response from the server will never arrive, because the higher-level application functions of the Mac are frozen.

You might want to use LAN-management software to provide information about the performance of your local network and to monitor devices such as routers and printers for problems, but this approach is insufficient for a Web server because your applications could be producing errors only apparent to Web clients. LAN-management applications should complement, rather than compose your server monitoring system.

Checking CGIs

The same model used to check your server software can be used to check your CGIs—simply request a URL that is processed by the

CGI and examine the response for errors. This model requires that the CGI be capable of processing a request without causing other problems.

A form-to-email CGI, for example, like Flexmail (see Chapter 7, "CGI Applications and Usage," or go directly to http://www.netdreams. com/net.dreams/software/ for more information about Flexmail) will send email every time a check is performed, which could be problematic if you are performing checks every five minutes. One solution is to send a malformed request to the CGI, which should then generate an error message. Examining the returned error's HTML data for a keyword (most site monitoring software allows this) will enable you to check that the CGI is functioning, because a different error (minus the indicated keyword) would be returned if the CGI had crashed or was otherwise not working.

If your CGI does not handle errors correctly (Flexmail, for example, will send an email message anyway), you will need to either contact the author and inform them of your situation (because such behavior should be considered a bug in the software), find a different CGI application that performs the same function yet handles errors correctly, or simply cope with the existing CGI by, for example, sending your "test" email with a subject you can automatically delete using the email filtering functions in email clients like Eudora (http://www.qualcomm.com/) or Claris' Emailer (http://www.claris.com/).

Rebooting Servers

The response to these types of errors normally is to reboot your server. If you implement automated rebooting, you need to test your system extensively before allowing it to run unattended, because an unexpected situation could cause your server to be repeatedly and unnecessarily rebooted. You'll look at different ways to restart crashed servers later in this chapter.

Rebooting a server is hard on your Macintosh, especially the disk drives. It is essentially the same operation you perform manually when you are sitting in front of the machine when it crashes. Automated rebooting shouldn't cause any new problems in itself. You will want to be extra careful, however, that your monitoring system knows when to stop rebooting if a problem is not solved by the restart. You also should be careful to set up your system so that only the server itself is rebooted—you shouldn't need to cycle the power on your monitor and external drives every time the server restarts.

The Internet

The second half of your monitoring system performs checks on your Internet connection through your ISP. After all, there's little point in keeping your server active if nobody can reach it! You can do this in either of two ways—from another site on the Internet, or from another machine on your server's local network to a site across the Internet.

Ideally, your server checking and connection checking can occur with one URL retrieval. This, however, will require the checks to originate from elsewhere on the Internet—see Figure 13.1.

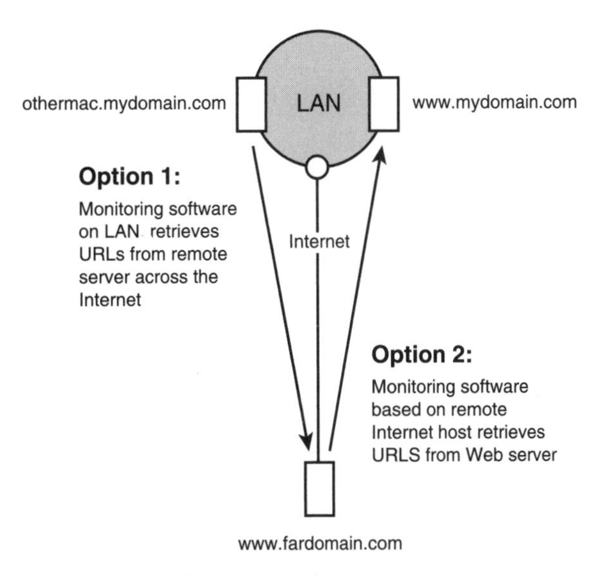

Figure 13.1 *Two methods of checking Internet connections.*

If you use one of the remote site-checking services (see the next section), it might have trouble differentiating between a server crash and trouble with your ISP. It would be unwise to have your server set to automatically reboot when one of these services reports an error, because you could end up restarting unnecessarily every time your ISP's connection hiccups.

Monitoring Services

Now that you know what to check, how do you actually do it? I've made a list of the current options that I can recommend. You can also check the **HTML** folder on the accompanying CD for more URLs and information on other possibilities.

PageSentry

The most recent addition to the monitoring field is a cool little application from Maxum Development (the company that produced NetCloak and NetForms) called *PageSentry* (http://www.maxum.com/PageSentry/) that does all the basics. If you have a Macintosh available from which to run your own monitoring, I highly recommend PageSentry as the option of choice—see Figure 13.2.

Figure 13.2 *A typical PageSentry configuration window.*

PageSentry takes a list of URLs and performs complete HTTP page retrievals at specified configurable intervals. It then evaluates the response from the server to see whether a keyword (which you can define) appears in the response's HTML code. If the phrase is missing, or if the server is down or responding with error messages, PageSentry sends an AppleEvent and/or an email message to notify you or triggers another script or application to execute.

You can use PageSentry with personal paging software (see the next section for more information on paging) or as an email-to-pager gateway service to notify you of problems. Because you can specify AppleScripts to launch in response to error messages, you can also control a modem or scriptable restarting system (see the section on restarting that follows) to get your server back on its feet.

If you don't have access to a separate machine to perform your monitoring checks, you have two options: either buy an older, inexpensive Mac like an SE/30 or IIsi to perform your checks, or subscribe to an Internet-based remote monitoring service. I've listed the two services that seem most robust in the next sections.

LinkAlert

LinkAlert (http://www.interpage.net/) is the only remote monitoring service I know of that is offered by a paging service company, which makes for a nice combination of expertise (see Figure 13.3). They check Web URLs (any URL beginning with http://) and notify you in the event of a prolonged outage via email, pager, fax, cellular phone, or essentially any other form of notification short of actually tapping you on the shoulder when your server stops responding to their queries. The sophistication of their checks is limited, but I am including them here because of the wide range of notification options and their experience with reliable paging.

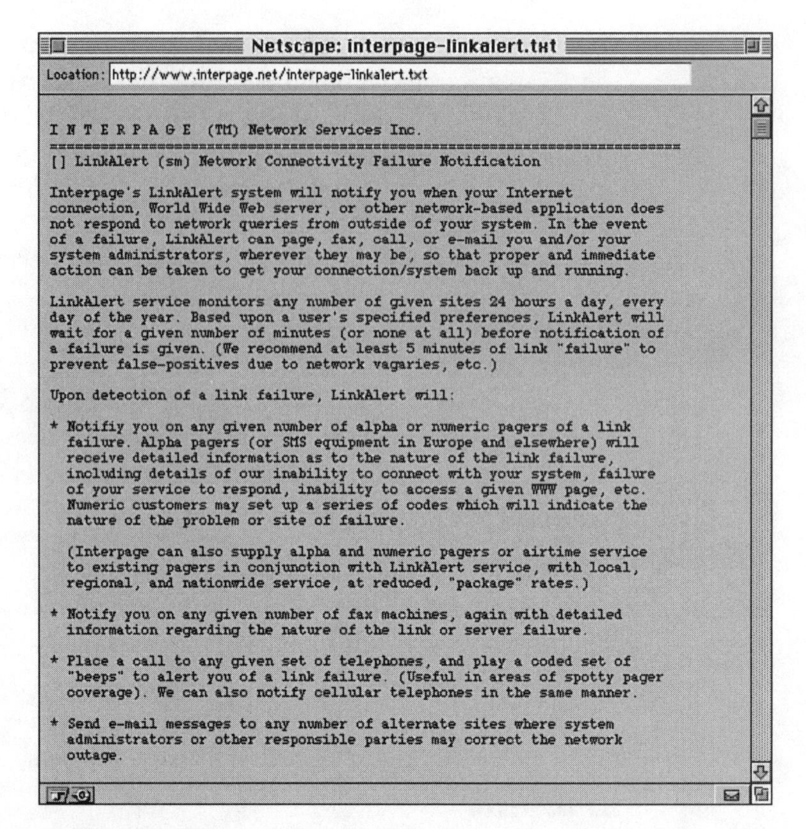

Netscape: interpage-linkalert.txt

Location: http://www.interpage.net/interpage-linkalert.txt

I N T E R P A G E (TM) Network Services Inc.

[] LinkAlert (sm) Network Connectivity Failure Notification

Interpage's LinkAlert system will notify you when your Internet connection, World Wide Web server, or other network-based application does not respond to network queries from outside of your system. In the event of a failure, LinkAlert can page, fax, call, or e-mail you and/or your system administrators, wherever they may be, so that proper and immediate action can be taken to get your connection/system back up and running.

LinkAlert service monitors any number of given sites 24 hours a day, every day of the year. Based upon a user's specified preferences, LinkAlert will wait for a given number of minutes (or none at all) before notification of a failure is given. (We recommend at least 5 minutes of link "failure" to prevent false-positives due to network vagaries, etc.)

Upon detection of a link failure, LinkAlert will:

* Notifiy you on any given number of alpha or numeric pagers of a link failure. Alpha pagers (or SMS equipment in Europe and elsewhere) will receive detailed information as to the nature of the link failure, including details of our inability to connect with your system, failure of your service to respond, inability to access a given WWW page, etc. Numeric customers may set up a series of codes which will indicate the nature of the problem or site of failure.

  (Interpage can also supply alpha and numeric pagers or airtime service to existing pagers in conjunction with LinkAlert service, with local, regional, and nationwide service, at reduced, "package" rates.)

* Notify you on any given number of fax machines, again with detailed information regarding the nature of the link or server failure.

* Place a call to any given set of telephones, and play a coded set of "beeps" to alert you of a link failure. (Useful in areas of spotty pager coverage). We can also notify cellular telephones in the same manner.

* Send e-mail messages to any number of alternate sites where system administrators or other responsible parties may correct the network outage.

Figure 13.3 *The LinkAlert home page.*

RedAlert

Red Alert! (http://www.helpline.com/networthy/) is another remote monitoring service that differentiates between different kinds of server errors, and can even check your DNS service along with your Web server's status. It also performs HTML validation and can report errors via email or pager—see Figure 13.4.

I should note that I was personally involved in the development of the Red Alert service, so you can evaluate its presentation here with that fact in mind.

To find more services like those mentioned here, check the HTML pages in this chapter's folder on the CD. A few new shareware solutions were released while this chapter was being written and, although I haven't been able to evaluate them fully myself, I have provided links to their Web pages so you can make your own judgements.

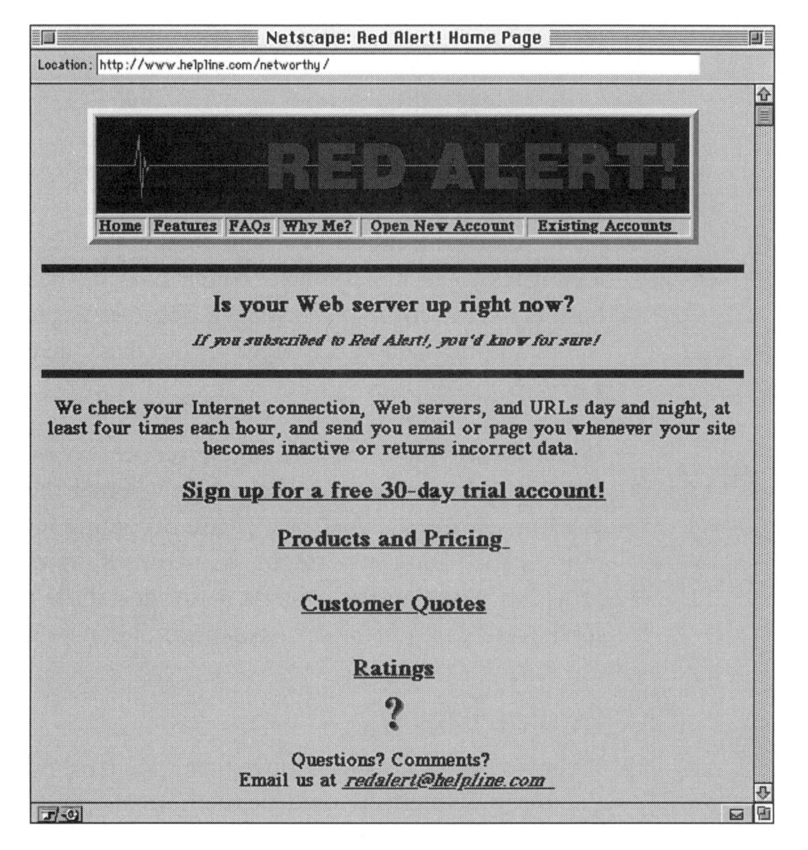

Figure 13.4 *The Red Alert! home page.*

Alerting

Any monitoring system needs to let you know when there's a problem, so that you can respond to it, and so that you can detect patterns that will help you track down and fix problems. Notifications usually occur via email, pager, or both. Here's an overview of what's available.

Email

The simplest form of remote notification is email. For notification of problems that don't require an immediate response, emailed reports create a record of events that can be useful in tracking down problems. They also provide ammunition when arguing with your ISP about its reliability. Email is not suitable, however, for time-critical problems like a server crash, because you might not receive your messages until well after the fact.

Email-to-Pager Gateway Services

The next step in notification is to subscribe to an email-to-pager gateway service. These services provide an email address to which your monitoring system can send email messages and have them forwarded to an alphanumeric pager. Unlike email, you have to budget for the costs of your pager, pager service, and (if the gateway is not included in the pager service fees) the email-to-pager gateway.

If you already subscribe to a paging service, you should certainly check with the service provider to see whether they have an email gateway service available, as they are becoming increasingly common. If they don't, you might want to consider changing service providers. You'll probably get a better deal if the pager gateway service and paging service come through one company.

Personal Paging

If you've been following along so far, you have noticed that all of the previous solutions are dependent on at least one other site's Internet connection being active—it's rather difficult to use an email-to-pager gateway service or even email if the Internet itself is having problems. Your monitoring system needs a way to contact you in an emergency via methods that avoid the Internet entirely.

The usual method is to use a modem and a telephone line to either call a number and beep over the line until you get the hint, or to dial a local number and send a page. This offers the twin advantages of dependability (barring major catastrophe or unpaid phone bills) and multi-functionality—you can use a phone line to call a numeric pager number, control other devices anywhere in the world, or even to call yourself on a normal phone.

If you're uncomfortable with writing AppleScripts to control a modem directly, you might consider using scriptable pager software that handles the communication details.

Ex Machina (http://www.exmachina.com/macprods.html) offers a large product line for single-machine or network-based paging. Ex Machina also offers email-to-pager gateways for internal email systems like QuickMail and cc:Mail.

The other major Macintosh paging package is *PageNow*. It is a similar package produced by Mark/Space Softworks (ftp:/ftp.netcom.com/pub/ms/mspace/).

Both applications are fully scriptable and work by dialing your pager service company's offices and sending you a numeric or alphanumeric page.

An excellent resource for paging information, by the way, is located at http://www.airnote.net/ww/paging.html. See Figure 13.5.

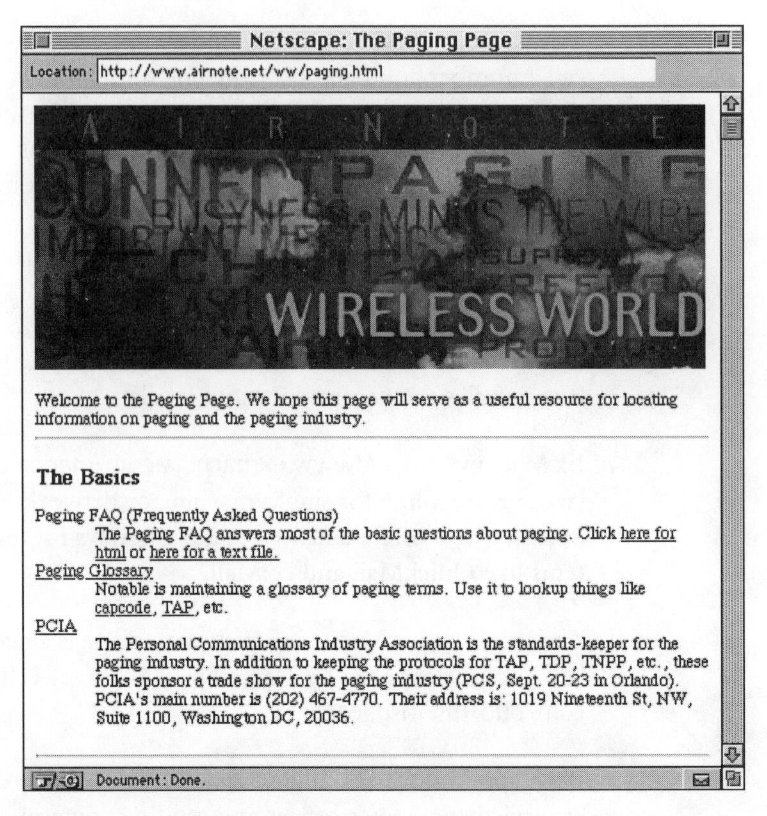

Figure 13.5 *Airnote's paging resources page.*

Restarting

Most recent Macs have an *auto-on* capability—simply rotate the power button on the CPU until the line across its front is vertical, and then push it as though you were turning on the power. The Mac will automatically turn on whenever power is applied, enabling you to reboot the CPU by switching the power on and off at the surge suppressor (you do use a surge suppressor, right?).

This feature enables you to use any of a number of devices designed to cycle the power to your server via remote control. Three products in particular are commonly used to add restart capabilities.

PowerKey Pro

PowerKey Pro (http://www.sophisticated.com/) looks like a fat surge suppressor, and in fact can act as a surge suppressor for your server and peripherals—see Figure 13.6. It enables you to control different outlets on the suppressor, either via a telephone call or AppleEvents. The primary disadvantage of the PowerKey system is that you need a different unit and telephone line for each group of devices you want to control. For a single server, it is ideal, but for an entire LAN, the X-10 system (described in the next section) offers more flexibility.

Figure 13.6 *PowerKey Pro's home page.*

X-10 SmartHome System

The *X-10* system (http://www.techmall.com/smarthome/x10map.html) was designed to control home appliances through the existing electrical wiring in a home, and was pressed into service by Web site administrators only when other options weren't available. It consists of a controller module that plugs into the wall and phone line, and remote modules for each power line (computer, modem, surge arrestor) you want to control—up to 256 individual power outlets on one electrical circuit.

Access to the remote unit is via a telephone call and a numeric password typed on the phone keypad after the controller module answers the call. You can then control each remote unit individually, which enables entire networks of computers and other devices to be managed with one incoming phone line.

An X-10 system, however, is not scriptable. Also, it is difficult to use with surge suppressors, because you need to place the remote modules between the suppressor and your server to avoid cycling power on all your peripherals when restarting. Figure 13.7 shows some options for controlling it.

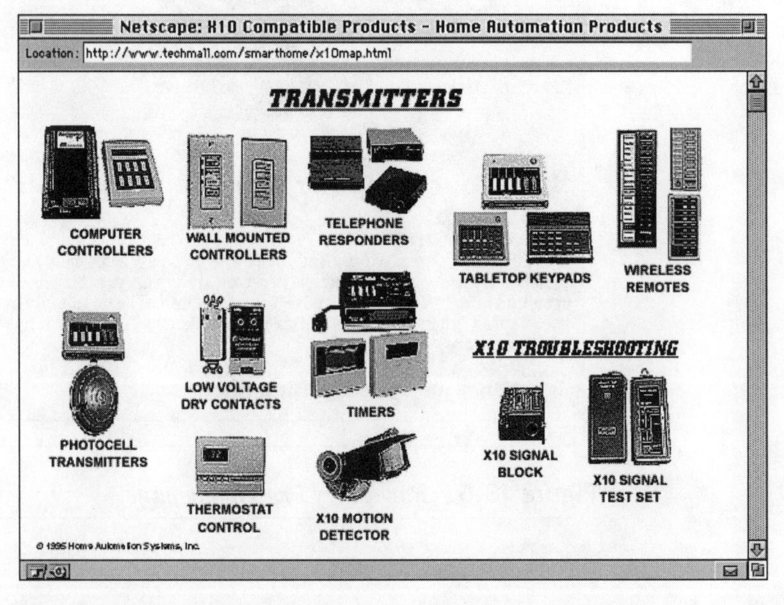

Figure 13.7 *Some options for controlling the X-10 system.*

RoBoot

The simplest restart solution is a relatively new product called *RoBoot* (http://www.webwrks.com/webworks/roboot/roboot.html), which is a device from Holland that attaches to an unused serial port on your Macintosh. A small background application runs on your server and sends a bit of data through the serial port every 20 to 30 seconds—if the RoBoot device does not receive its signal, it reboots the server by cycling the power. Figure 13.8 shows RoBoot's home page.

RoBoot isn't remotely controllable like the PowerKey system, but it offers a simplicity and a lack of dependence on phone lines and networks that can come in handy when disaster strikes.

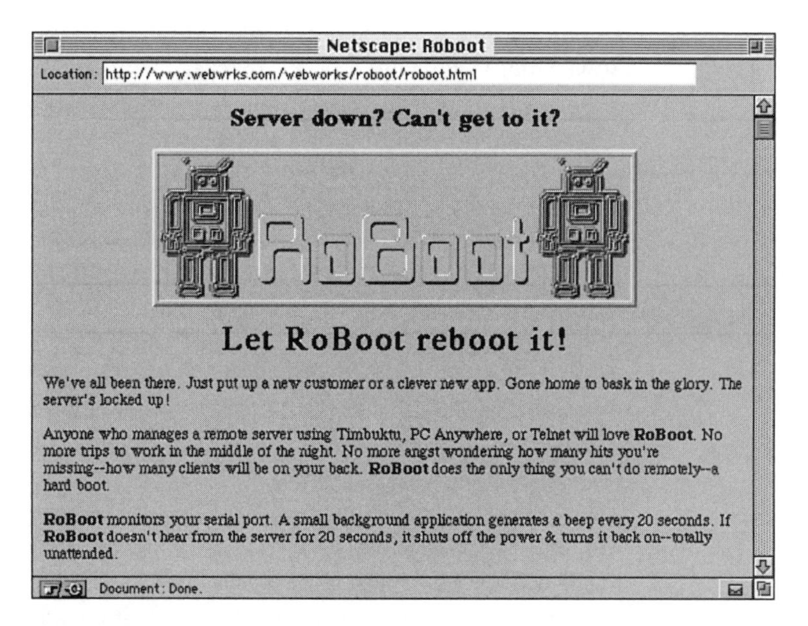

Figure 13.8 *The RoBoot home page.*

WARNING

If you are using a *UPS (Uninterruptable Power Supply)* to protect your server from power outages, you need to install your rebooting devices between the UPS and your server. Otherwise, the UPS will consider your attempts to restart the server to be unwanted power outages and will prevent the restarts from occurring.

Server Monitoring Examples

The following are brief discussions of some common monitoring setups and comments on their pleasures and pitfalls.

Simple Rebooting

The simplest rebooting method available is the RoBoot unit—if the server as a whole suffers a system crash, it will immediately reboot it and get you going again.

RoBoot cannot, however, detect when your Web server software or Internet connection experiences problems that don't actually freeze the main system functions of your Mac, so it's most appropriate for a small budget server that can tolerate rare periods of extended downtime. If your operation, however, demands that the Web server be available with no more than a few minutes of occasional downtime, you should look at some of the other systems described next.

Working with Remote Monitoring Services

Any of the Internet monitoring services I mentioned previously will notify you via email or pager when a problem exists. If you install remotely controlled rebooting systems like the PowerKey or X-10 controllers, a pager can alert you to the problem, and you can reboot the server with a phone call.

My own experience has been that my pager is often unavailable, misplaced, or otherwise temporarily unable to keep me informed of problems. The solution is to use an automatic system that accepts an email message and then executes an AppleScript or other automated response when a problem alert is received (see the ListStar section in this chapter for an application that can launch AppleScripts in response to pre-defined email types).

If your machine receiving the alert messages is not on the same LAN as your Web server, you'll also need a modem and phone line available on the monitoring machine to enable automated calls to your power cycler. A useful application in this kind of setup is *Acid*

Jazz (http://www.claris.com/Team/KJ/KJ.HTML), which provides scriptable control of your modem.

NOTE

All automated response systems beg the question of how you monitor the monitoring machine—your monitoring/rebooting machine might lose its own Internet connectivity or crash, leaving your server defenseless. Using a pager with an automated responder provides a measure of protection, as does adding a backup rebooter like RoBoot to either the Web server or monitoring Macs.

Remote services also suffer from the disadvantage that two different ISPs are required to be operational for your monitoring to be active. If your server experiences a problem while the remote service is inaccessible to the Internet (and it happens to the best of ISPs on occasion), your monitoring system will fail. You need to compare the potential for this problem to occur (rarely) with the benefits of using a remote service to perform your monitoring (no administration of monitoring system, best way to simulate accessibility to actual clients).

Working on a LAN

If you have access to other Macs on the same local network as your Web server, you can run monitoring software like PageSentry on another Mac and use its built-in Applescript and email connections to send pages (via your own paging software), email, or control a scriptable power cycler like PowerKey Pro. See Figure 13.9.

This approach will notify you of Internet connection problems. You can perform checks from the PageSentry application on the major site URLs across the Internet that you expect to be available more-or-less constantly. Potential problems with the monitoring Mac can still affect your system, but a LAN-based monitor offers more direct control over your responses to different problems, because you can use AppleTalk services to control other devices and software on your network.

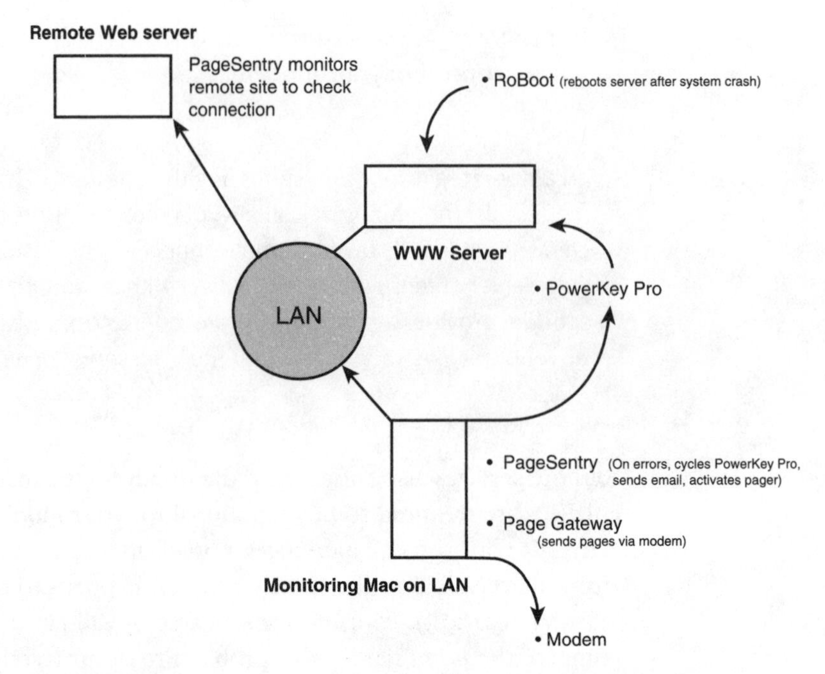

Figure 13.9 *The ultimate site monitoring system.*

The effort you devote to building a robust monitoring system for your server can range from simple emailed alerts from remote Web services, manual restart capabilities, to complex custom installations that focus redundant checks on your server to keep it running and keep you informed of its status at all times. My advice is to start small. Begin with a telephone-controlled restart module and one of the Internet-based monitoring services or PageSentry, and gain experience with the type of errors your server and ISP have before settling on a permanent configuration.

Remote Administration

Setting up your server for remote administration opens a wealth of possibilities for you as an administrator. Remotely controlled servers can be placed anywhere on the Internet and still be as accessible as though they were in the same room. In this section, you'll look at some tools and techniques for remote administration and contemplate the joys of telecommuting.

Timbuktu Pro

"It's the next best thing to being there..."

Timbuktu Pro from Farallon Technologies (http:/www.farallon.com/) is an absolutely essential tool for remote administration of Web servers. It enables you to conduct file transfers, without FTP, over a TCP/IP connection (from anywhere on the Internet), and is the only source I know of for screen sharing technology—see Figure 13.10.

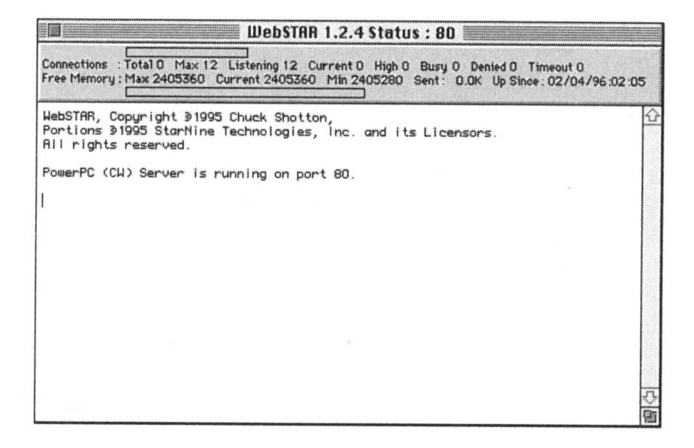

Figure 13.10 *A Timbuktu Pro screen-sharing session.*

Screen sharing refers to the capability to open a window on your desktop that displays everything visible on another computer's monitor. It's like having a monitor within your monitor!

Not only does screen sharing enable you to view a remote screen, it enables you to control the remote computer with your keyboard and mouse just as though you were seated in front of it! No longer do you need a monitor, keyboard, or mouse for your server—just buy the CPU itself and Timbuktu and you're done. (You should have a monitor, keyboard, and mouse available when first setting up your server, but they can be removed once you have stabilized the system.)

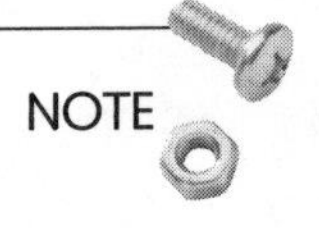

If you are running System 7.5 or higher on your server (as you should), you need to purchase a short *VGA converter cable* to plug into the monitor port on the back of the server. This cable is normally used to connect a Mac to a PC-type VGA monitor, but you'll use it to fool the server into thinking a monitor is attached to it. This is necessary to cause the MacOS to build up the monitor "picture" internally and enable screen sharing to occur on a monitorless (*headless*) machine.

Timbuktu can also transfer files from one Mac to another over the Internet (without installing an FTP server) via a folder browser interface or by dragging icons between your desktop and the screen-sharing view of a remote desktop. Timbuktu operates between Macs or between a Windows-based and MacOS machine. Timbuktu is available with a built-in Apple Remote Access client software, which permits you to mount disks and use other AppleTalk-based services over the Internet.

Just to make sure this doesn't sound too much like a Farallon press release, a word of caution—be aware that the control Timbuktu offers can also be a major security problem if not configured correctly. You can restrict access to a Timbuktu-equipped server by defining usernames and passwords, but a misconfigured or mismanaged Timbuktu installation can open your server up to every conceivable form of unauthorized access.

For more information on Timbuktu, including current pricing, stop by http://www.farallon.com/, and be sure to check out the demo version on the CD in the **Software, Miscellaneous** folder.

ARA

Apple Remote Access (ARA) is another way to gain control of your server remotely. It is not a replacement for Timbuktu, but it will enable you to mount the server's disks for file transfers and to use AppleTalk network-dependent software over a dialup connection. To enable ARA, you either need a Mac on your local network that is connected to a modem, or a network communications server, which is a hardware device that manages dial-in connections for a LAN. You also need a copy of both the ARA server and client software (the client comes with some Powerbook bundles) and, if you want to enable TCP/IP as well as AppleTalk services over the dial-up connection, you'll need Apple's IP Gateway software as well.

It might seem like a lot to put together, but ARA offers a fairly inexpensive way to gain unrestricted access to your local network without having to depend on another ISP for your dial-up connection. With ARA, you won't need PPP or SLIP for TCP/IP networking, and the full suite of AppleTalk-dependent network software and services is available while you're connected.

For more information on ARA, stop by http://www.apple.com/.

ListStar

Another option for remotely controlling a server is *ListStar*, the mailbot software from StarNine, the makers of WebSTAR. Although a bit on the pricey side (street prices were running around $500.00 when this chapter was written), ListStar has an unequaled capability to connect email to Applescripts, so that you can send email to a Mac running ListStar and cause different Applescripts to execute.

ListSTAR functions by providing the capability to process incoming email messages according to series of sophisticated rules that you can define, using the subject lines, message contents, or sender's email address of incoming messages to control responses to email. These rules can connect email to AppleScripts (or other launchable applications) by simply providing a rule that establishes the conditions under which the script should be activated. See Figure 13.11.

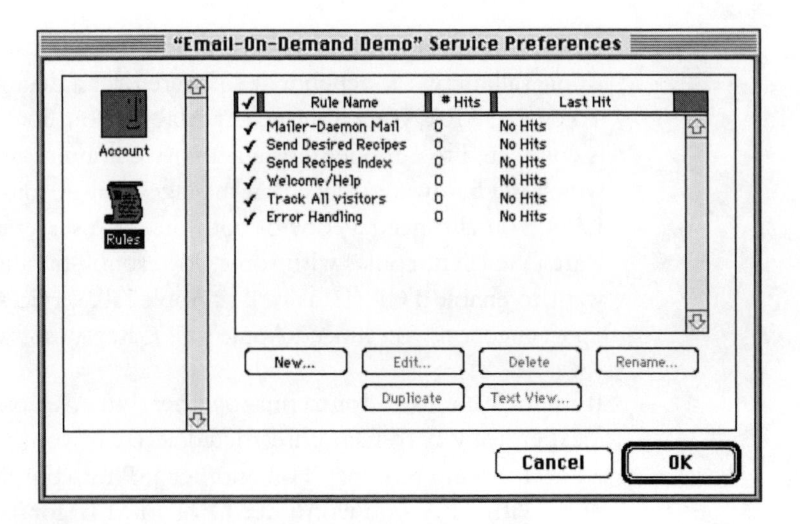

Figure 13.11 *ListSTAR summary of rules for a sample mailbot service.*

Considering that the price of two copies of Timbuktu are about the same or even less than a single ListStar installation, using ListStar solely for remote administration isn't recommended. But if you'd like to control your server with email (probably the most ubiquitous form of Internet access), and don't mind writing a few Applescripts, ListStar can be a nice addition to your server administration toolbox. Of course, you can always use it for its main purpose—maintenance of mailing lists, automated email responses (mailbots), and other types of email-based automation.

For current information on ListStar, visit StarNine at http://www.starnine.com/software/.

Editing/Adding Content

There are two methods of maintaining content remotely without your intervention—one is allowing others access to areas of the server that they control, such as clients renting space on your server to update their pages themselves, and the other is producing the impression that you are constantly updating your own pages without actually doing so.

Because the latter is more dear to the heart of most server administrators, I'll take a look at that method first.

Automatic Updates

This is where a CGI such as *NetCloak* really shines (see Chapter 7, "CGI Applications and Usage," for more information on NetCloak and other CGIs, or go directly to the home page at http://www.maxum.com/NetCloak/). NetCloak enables you to add HTML tags to your pages that send different parts of the page depending on the date, time, or other criteria such as the type of browser used by the client. It's a simple matter to use those tags to set up a week's worth of changing content in advance—perhaps a "Cool Site of the Day" or a feature article—and then return to the server only occasionally to update the content for the next period. The advantage of this approach is that all of your HTML for the week is contained in a single file that you can edit and replace periodically to keep the server current.

I think that's appropriate for Chapter 7, but not here where I'm talking more about usage than about the application.

If your changing content is more complex than can be contained within a single page, you can set up folders for each day's or week's content and then use NetCloak tags to change the appropriate reference URL to "Today's Feature" on your home page.

If you cannot run NetCloak on your site, you could also create a system of automatically changing pages with any sort of custom CGI platform such as Tango, 4D, or Frontier.

Letting Others Do the Work

If you are hosting on your server pages for multiple clients or allowing other individuals to take responsibility for maintaining portions of your server's content, you'll soon find that you need a method to enable people to add and replace documents on your server. You also need a way to control their access so that they are only able to change the areas under their purview and cannot, even accidentally, interfere with the normal operation of your server or disrupt the rest of your pages.

The traditional method has been to use AppleShare's Users and Groups Control Panel to enable client access to particular folders or disks over an AppleTalk network. Often, however, you'll find that you need to offer the same services via TCP/IP. This requires an Internet server such as NetPresenz that permits Internet-based clients to upload documents to your server. Because NetPresenz uses the same Users and Groups permissions as AppleShare to control access, you can use the same security provisions for both AppleTalk and TCP/IP clients.

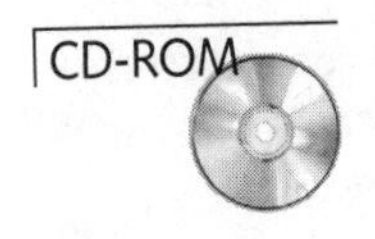

Running an additional Internet service like FTP on your Web server, however, can cause a performance drop that you might find intolerable. A superior solution is to allow clients to upload documents, with their own Web browsers, directly through your Web server. This method is being developed for use with Netscape clients and WebSTAR servers, so be sure to check for updates to this chapter in the **HTML** folder on the CD.

Finally, take careful note of the trust issue when allowing uploads to your server. Simple HTML documents are normally not a problem, but none of the methods mentioned prevent users from uploading an AppleScript or other CGI that they could execute via your server to cause all kinds of mischief. To prevent this, you need to set aside an area inaccessible to your Web server for uploads and review every document before making it available on the Web. You could also use a CGI that screens all incoming URLs and prevents other, unauthorized CGIs from being executed.

Summary

Your talents as a site administrator should be focused on creating new content and features for your site, not constantly checking on your server to see whether it's still running. A reliable monitoring system combined with good remote administration tools will release you from most of the daily grunt work of maintaining a server, and free up more of your time to concentrate on the more creative and enjoyable aspects of managing a Web site.

Now that your server is happily monitored, controlled, and updated with a minimum of fuss, it's time to take a look at how to maximize its performance.

CHAPTER 14

My Other Ferrari Is a Mac: Maximizing Performance

Your server is up, you're connected to the Internet, and all your CGIs are humming along nicely. You've even finalized all your HTML pages and images and enjoyed that full night of sleep you've been fantasizing about for the last six months. So now what do you do?

Shift into high gear, that's what. Anyone can put up a Web server, but it's a small and dedicated group of Webmasters that can take the time to explore all the ways to squeeze out the last drop of performance from their servers.

The busier your site is, the more important small efficiencies become.

This chapter includes a listing of recommendations and advice for tuning up your server to peak levels of speed and reliability. The following main areas are covered:

- ☐ Server options
- ☐ Tweaking the MacOS
- ☐ Limits of the Macintosh file system
- ☐ Using and misusing CGIs
- ☐ Strategies for designing content

Some recommendations are obvious, and some are subtle. Some may strike you as silly, whereas others send you running to your server to make adjustments. Hopefully, they'll all give you reason to think more deeply about what is going on behind the scenes with your Web site and discover new ways to "tweak" its reliability and responsiveness.

Every server exists in a different context, and every Webmaster has a slightly different set of priorities, so the reasoning behind each recommendation is included to help guide you in choosing which to implement. This chapter contains an underlying assumption that your Web server is used exclusively for serving—that is, you don't let your neighbor's kids play CD-ROM games on it, and you may not even switch on the monitor unless you're doing site maintenance. If you do use your server for other tasks, look through the recommendations carefully, consider the rationale behind them, and decide for yourself which are appropriate and worthwhile for you.

A Little Goes a Long Way

Even though most of the tips in this chapter may individually have only minimal effects on your server's perceived performance, they are likely to create noticeably faster page loading for your clients when combined. Keep in mind as well that reducing the time required for a single client's request to be handled increases the performance of your site for other clients as well, because the first client stops using your system's resources a bit sooner, leaving that much more time for your server to devote to other clients.

For example, suppose your site receives 5,000 requests per day, averaging about 12 seconds per connection. If you can reduce the average time to 10 seconds, you just saved almost three hours of processor time on your server that can be used to handle more connections!

This effect becomes more noticeable as the traffic at your site increases, because shorter overall connections will reduce the number of connections you need to handle simultaneously. The busier your site is, the more important small efficiencies become.

Server Options

This chapter contains an underlying assumption that your Web server is used exclusively for serving.

Most servers have their own idiosyncratic settings that can affect performance. Because these settings change with every new version of the server software, I have chosen not to cover specific server issues here and concentrated instead on the more generic issues that affect the performance of all servers. Be sure to read the relevant sections of your server software's user manual and any updates to it, because they will no doubt be more current than this chapter by the time you read these words.

Timeouts

The timeout value is the number of seconds that your server allows clients to pause without communicating with the server as well as the maximum time allotted to CGIs to begin returning data to the server software (and therefore to the client) after the client request has been passed to them.

If you are running a server that is used by clients on a private high-speed network (like a company Ethernet) as well as the general public, you may want to lower the timeout value to prevent clients using very slow connections from delaying your responses to your internal, high-speed clients. This will kick very slow clients off your server during peak traffic times, but that situation is often preferable to not being able to handle any new connections because a few clients are taking more than their share of your system resources.

Generally, your timeout settings should be somewhere between 30 and 60 seconds to keep performance levels high.

Remember that for WebSTAR, the same value you set for the client timeouts will be used for determining whether a CGI has waited too long to return data. Your timeout settings should at least equal the maximum expected time for your slowest CGI to complete its task and begin returning data to the client or server software.

To test the effects of various settings, start with the default provided by your server software. Use the techniques provided for stress testing your server (see Chapter 12, "Not Another Audit!") with an emphasis on long searches or other requests that are likely to be the most time-consuming on your server. Watch your log output for the maximum time required by your slowest connection, and set your timeout to meet or exceed that number.

NOTE

The rule of thumb when setting the server's timeout value is to use the lowest acceptable timeout setting.

Number of Connections

I don't know anyone who maintains a Web server who feels good about turning away clients requesting connections. Receiving a "Busy" message from a Web server can be frustrating for both client and Webmaster. Unfortunately, it can be just as frustrating to realize that all your pages are being served painfully slowly because your server can't keep up with the load of requests coming at it. To avoid this situation, you'll sometimes need to make a choice between maintaining an acceptable level of response speed and increasing the maximum number of connections your server will allow.

To detect the problem, use the stress-testing techniques again from Chapter 12, "Not Another Audit!," to increase your current connection levels to near their maximum settings. Then attempt to connect to your server using a standard browser application. If the time required to load the page is tolerable to you, you're fine at your current settings, otherwise you should reduce the maximum connection levels a few at a time and repeat the same test until you're satisfied with the performance at maximum load.

No matter how fast your connection to the Internet is or how powerful your Mac may be, setting connection levels above 30 to 35 is almost never beneficial. Levels beyond that are much more likely to slow down your server's responses than to provide any benefit to your site.

DNS Lookups

If you're anything like me, you probably spent the first few hours or even days of your site's operation watching the log window scroll by with requests from around the world. It's certainly more interesting to see the actual names of your clients on the screen than a slew of cryptic IP addresses, and it's tempting to leave this setting on.

To display those names, however, your server must go through the process of translating the IP addresses it actually receives into the domain names you're enjoying for every request that comes in to your server. This is perhaps the single most time-consuming server activity you have the ability to turn off.

Every log analysis program available can convert the IP addresses in your log file into the original client's domain name. By turning off DNS lookups in your server and viewing the log results later, you aren't losing the capability to know who is accessing your site—you're just delaying your gratification a bit.

The only caveat here is that if you want to use domain name security (to deny all connections from computers with a microsoft.com address), you'll need to keep DNS lookups on.

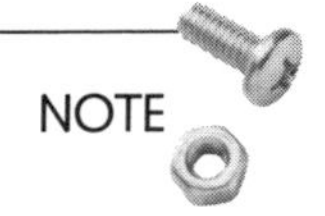

For the single most helpful action you can take to improve server performance: Turn DNS lookups off.

The Operating System

The Macintosh Operating System (MacOS) is undoubtedly the most wonderful and most confusing operating system ever created. It offers enormous power and potential, but contains just enough "gotchas" to cause otherwise stoic system administrators to weep in frustration. As a Webmaster, your job is to minimize the effects of these idiosyncrasies on your site. Your first task is to put away your disks.

Put Away Your Disks

One of the biggest drains on your system resources is file sharing. File sharing is the MacOS way of making disks attached to one Mac available for use by other Macs on the same AppleTalk network. Unfortunately, simply turning this feature on can slow your overall server down by up to 20 percent, depending on how busy your local network is and how the disk is being used.

The effects of file sharing are reduced when the server mounts other disks from the network, but allowing other Macs to mount the server's hard disk can cause major problems.

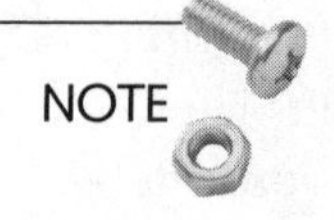

NOTE

Unless you absolutely must have your server's disk available to other users all the time, turn off file sharing on your server's hard disks.

If you need to keep a server disk available to others, at least use a disk partitioning tool to make as small a partition as possible and turn off file sharing on all disks and partitions except that one. The amount of slowdown you experience is directly related to the size and number of disks or partitions being shared, as well as the number of files and folders on the shared disk.

To turn off file sharing on your Macintosh, open the Control Panel "Sharing Setup" and click the button in the "File Sharing" box so that it says "Start." To turn sharing on, click the same button again—when file sharing has been reactivated, the button will contain the text "Stop."

To turn off file sharing on individual hard drives, first click the drive's icon in the Finder, and then choose the "Sharing..." menu item from the "File" menu. Uncheck the box in the upper-left and close the window. Repeat and recheck the box to reinstate sharing on that disk.

Put Away Your Toys

I'll confess—I have a love-hate relationship with system extensions and control panels. There have been times when three or even four rows of icons would light up across my screen while the system was loading. I was willing to put up with the occasional system crashes and pauses because I enjoyed the additional functionality the extensions gave me. Nevertheless, most of those extensions now live on floppy disks because the costs of running them on a serious Web server were simply too great. A high-performance Web server should be devoted to one mission alone, and anything that detracts from that mission unnecessarily should be thrown out.

At some point in the process of developing your server, you must take the time to remove any extension or control panel that is not absolutely essential for your server's operation. Appendix A, "Internet Troubleshooting," lists common extensions that should be removed from most Web servers.

For maximum performance, keep your use of system extensions to the absolute minimum.

Go to the Front of the Class

A Macintosh always has one application in front of all the others, called the "foreground" application. This is the application whose icon appears in the top right of your menu bar. The rest are considered to be "background" applications. Most Macintosh applications can carry on activities when they are in the background and your server software is no exception, nor are most CGI applications.

Nevertheless, if you run your main server application in the background, the overall response speed will drop precipitously whenever another application is running in the foreground.

> If you want your server running at its peak, always keep your server application in the foreground.

The Macintosh File System

Unlike most UNIX systems, the MacOS was not designed around the idea of moving many small files around very quickly, which is the primary task of most Web servers. To make the best use of the existing structure, you need to be aware of how your site interacts with the file system as well as any potential pitfalls.

Macintosh File System Limits

The Macintosh filing system (also called HFS, or Hierarchical File System) is organized in a structure called a b-tree, so that files are found by tracing a virtual tree from its trunk (the top level of your hard drive) out to the individual leaves (the actual files).

The b-tree system, although normally very efficient, can begin to bog down when you overwhelm it with files and folders. An excessive number of files or folders at one level of the tree, or an unusually long path to a file that is nested within many folders, will slow down your server's attempts to locate the files your clients have requested.

> For maximum file system speed, limit the number of files and subfolders within a single folder to 50 or fewer and limit the number of subfolders above a file to four or fewer.

The greatest delay in the file system for those using PPC-based Macintoshes comes from the non-native implementation of the file management system software in System 7.5. Currently, every access to disk causes the translation of the 680x0 instructions found in non-native software into PowerPC instructions, which is a huge drag on a PowerMac's speed. More advanced data caching schemes will help to alleviate this problem—as can hardware technologies like the PCI bus on some new Macs and high-throughput SCSI technologies—but the core problem won't be eliminated until Apple releases the upcoming Copland/System 8 software, which is not expected until late 1996 at the earliest.

The Mac file system also represents a good argument for using a database or CGI application to serve your pages to the Web. Not only can the pages themselves be kept in RAM so that the disk never needs to be accessed, but it also reduces the number of files that must be maintained, because most databases can keep all your HTML pages in one large data file.

Keep in mind, however, that disk access is only very rarely a limiting factor in your server's performance (assuming your drive is not badly fragmented). It is the HFS system and its needs that should be your primary concern.

Aliases

Aliases can help your server work more efficiently with your file organization, provide for multiple URLs pointing to the same page or image on your server, and improve your efficiency when updating your files. They can also slow down your server and occasionally fail completely, making the files and folders they point to inaccessible to your clients.

Every alias you use slows down your server to a small degree. In order to return data from an aliased URL, your Macintosh needs to find the file or folder the alias points to, update the alias information if the target file has moved, and correct the path to the file in the server's memory before beginning to read the file from your disk.

If you use aliases that point to target files on other disks from elsewhere on your local network, additional time is exacted by the process of accessing and moving data across that network. These delays are very small, but they occur during the period when Macintoshes exhibit the most sensitivity to delays when compared to other servers—the time between the initial request for a page and the time when data begins flowing to the client.

Also, if you happen to have set a folder containing frequently accessed pages as an alias, the majority of your clients will cause the alias-processing procedure to be invoked and thus amplify the problem.

On rare, unpredictable occasions, aliases have been known to suddenly lose track of their target and no longer contain accurate or even interpretable information. This happens very rarely, but can cause a tremendous degree of havoc on a site that depends on aliases. If you are having trouble accessing files that use aliases in their URLs, try creating a new alias as your first step toward solving the problem.

Aliases are powerful tools and one of the great blessings of the MacOS, but you must be careful to avoid overusing them, and you should always be aware that they can, on rare occasions, become invalid.

Use aliases sparingly and with caution. Avoid using aliases for frequently accessed folders.

CGIs

Boon and bane, CGIs can give a site its character or sap its strength. Overloading sites with many CGIs is never recommended, but as long as you are planning to use them, you should research the advantages and disadvantages of all your options. Some guidelines follow, but you should always do your own research and ask others for their experiences before committing to a particular CGI.

Oh No, AppleScript!

AppleScript, as described in Chapter 7, "CGI Applications and Usage," is Apple's attempt to provide a relatively efficient and simple-to-use method to control the Finder and other applications so that users without heavy-duty programming skills can automate tasks and manipulate applications. In the early days of Macintosh Web serving, AppleScript was seized upon by eager CGI writers as a rapid way to create CGIs to perform a variety of tasks. Since its introduction, AppleScript has also been extended by small compiled applications called OSAX (Open Scripting Architecture eXtension), available both through Apple and from third parties, to enhance its speed and feature set. In fact, it is now theoretically possible to write an entire WWW server in AppleScript!

However, as CGIs on the Macintosh have become more extensively used and the demands placed on them increased, it has rapidly become clear that AppleScript is no longer an adequate development environment for serious CGI programmers, primarily due to insufficient speed and loss of data integrity protection. A more complete discussion of the problems with AppleScript CGIs can be found in the AppleScript section of Chapter 7.

AppleScript is, however, still great for writing automated maintenance tasks like copying and moving files around a disk, turning applications on and off, and so on. AppleScripts can even be set up to send you email notifications of important events, such as an online sale or a server reboot. Be aware that AppleScripts will cause a drain on your system resources while running. Limit AppleScripts' use to periodic tasks, and you'll be making the best possible use of the AppleScript technology.

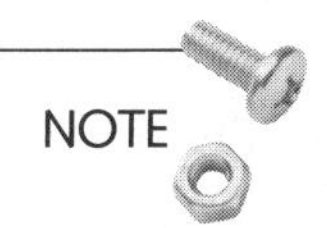

NOTE

If you begin writing or using CGIs and want to maximize the responsiveness of your server, avoid AppleScript whenever possible.

Subcontracting CGIs

As more people begin to connect their Web servers to databases, image processors, and other CPU-intensive applications, the competition for CPU time between the server and the CGIs can adversely impact all your response times. Because of this, many people are starting to "subcontract" their CGI activities to other machines and use only small intermediary CGIs on their servers.

The simplest way out is to put your CGI on another machine. Unfortunately, most server applications can interact only with CGIs running on the same machine as the server software. The solution to this dilemma is to run a small, fast, intermediary application on the Web server that accepts the CGI requests from the server software and passes them to applications running elsewhere on the network. This is the approach utilized by the Butler SQL database, which normally runs on a separate, dedicated Macintosh while a small application called Tango runs on the Web server, handing off requests and results to their appropriate destinations. You can find more information about subcontracting, or chaining together, CGIs in Chapter 7, "CGI Applications and Usage."

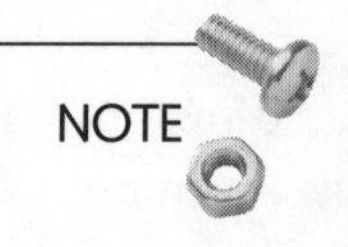

NOTE

If you plan to run disk or CPU-intensive CGIs, you should also plan to move CGI tasks to other machines when appropriate.

Consolidating CGIs

Because the MacOS allows multiple applications to run simultaneously by giving each one control of the CPU in turn, running multiple applications can have a deleterious effect on your server's performance overall. If you have five applications running at once (not unusual for a server with CGIs), the Web serving application must wait.

The solution is to either use a Web server like Web Server 4D or InterServer Publisher that includes many CGI functions in one application, or to use a multifunctional CGI that replaces many individual CGIs. Frontier is particularly useful in this regard, as are database CGIs that can be customized to perform a variety of functions. Your goal should be to settle on a single environment (Frontier, 4D, Tango, and so on) that you can adapt to your needs as your site evolves. This prevents you from having to find and run individual applications for every minor CGI function you want to add to your site.

NOTE

Consolidate CGI functions into fewer applications whenever possible.

Other CGI Issues

Most servers are now using part of the MacOS called the "Thread Manager" which makes it possible for server software to handle multiple clients' requests simultaneously. This "multithreading" produces a three-fold to four-fold increase in server performance when multiple clients are requesting data simultaneously. Unfortunately, many of the older CGI applications (such as those written in AppleScript) were designed to handle one connection at a time and can't keep up with the new and improved server capabilities.

The chief problem arises from the situation occurring when your server passes one request off to a CGI, and then another and another before the CGI has finished with the first client. The second and third clients' requests must "wait their turn" for the CGI to finish with everybody else before handling their request.

In this scenario, the first client received a fairly speedy response, the second had to wait almost twice as long as the first, and the third almost three times as long. For CGIs that are used only rarely, this may not be a significant concern, but for commonly used CGIs, always use multithreaded CGI applications.

NOTE

For frequently accessed CGIs, always use multithreaded CGI applications.

Scripting with Frontier

If you would like to develop your own CGI applications but don't have the time or desire to learn a traditional programming language like C, there is another option besides AppleScript.

Frontier (also called Aretha, but more commonly Frontier) is a full-featured scripting language that offers all the functionality of AppleScript plus a built-in database system, multithreading, the capability to compile all your CGIs for the fastest possible speed, native PowerPC versions, and a whole lot more (see http://www.hotwired.com/staff/userland/aretha/ for more information). Best of all, it is a formerly commercial (and pricey) product that has been released into the public domain by its author, Dave Winer. In other words, it's completely free, and I've written about it in detail in Chapters 7 and 8.

Frontier's scripting language is definitely harder to learn than AppleScript (although some have argued differently), and is vaguely C-like in its syntax. But if you plan to write your own CGIs and would like a way to do so without becoming a full-fledged computer programmer or suffering the limitations of AppleScript, try Frontier as a scripting system.

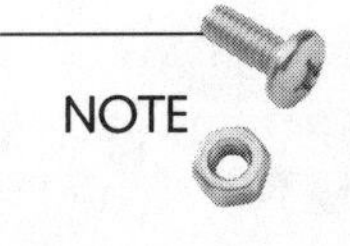

NOTE

To maximize speed and efficiency, use Frontier (Aretha) as a scripting system.

Content

Content is the heart of every site. It is the look and feel of your site, and it is the medium through which you communicate with the world. When designing content, you should continue to be informed of the effects that different design decisions will have on your site's performance. This section should get you headed in the right direction.

Big and Little

Loading a single large page is always more efficient than loading many small pages of the same total size as the large one. Even so, you should also consider that slow clients accessing large files will exert their stifling effects on your server for a longer period of time, thereby affecting your overall performance. Ideally, small pages (less than 5K) with a few images (less than 10 1–5K images) used repeatedly throughout your site offer the most efficient structuring of most publicly accessible sites.

NOTE

> Some of your pages may end up unavoidably large, but if your site is used by many dialup users, you will need to find a balance between large and small HTML pages.

Inlined to Death

Inlined images are the graphics you place into your HTML pages using URLs that point to the actual image files on your own or others' servers. It's important to think of these images not just as files of a particular size, but also as individual connections to your site. If you have 10 images on your home page, every client that visits that page will need to open 11 different HTTP connections to view it. Because the time required to open a new connection is normally about a second for dialup users, your images have added 10 seconds to the time required to download and view your page, simply by virtue of their existence.

Once you also add in the performance hit on both your server and the client that comes from having to handle all these connections at once, your home page of a mere 30K in size, including the graphics, now takes as long to load as a single page or image many times larger because of the overhead of all those extra connections. One simple way to reduce the connection overhead is to combine images together to form single, larger images, or to repeat images (like bullets in a list) as much as possible.

The same concerns raised about page sizes in the previous section also apply to inlined images, with the additional factor of multiple connections conspiring to drag down your performance even more. A good rule of thumb is that your page should never take more than 20 seconds for a typical 28.8Kbps modem user to download.

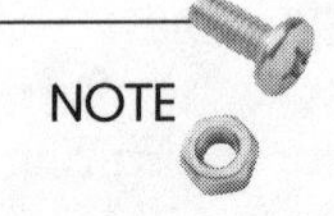

NOTE

If your design constraints allow it, you should always attempt to minimize the number of individual inlined images on a page.

Sharing the Joy

One of the great qualities of the WWW is that every server in the world is technically a "peer" with every other server. Whether your images are on the same server as your HTML documents, a server down the hall, or a server on the other side of the world, the client's browser must still open a new connection to request each and every image in your pages.

In practical terms, a server in Australia is normally not equivalent to a server in Massachusetts to a client living in California. The distance and often limited bandwidth across unpopulated areas can slow down connections and data transfer rates dramatically. The principle, however, of distributing your images can be applied effectively on a local basis.

For the best possible performance, every inlined image on a page would be on a different server—this is clearly impractical, but for busy sites, assigning popular graphics to a second local server can dramatically improve the client-perceived loading rate of pages with inlined images.

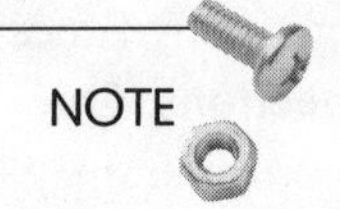

NOTE

Consider placing inlined images on a second WWW server.

Summary

I've listed a summary of all the recommendations for your reference—but please don't treat this as a simple checklist. Read the context in which each recommendation was given before applying it to your specific situation.

Summary of performance recommendations:

- ☐ Use the lowest acceptable timeout setting.
- ☐ Don't overload your server with excessive connections.
- ☐ Turn DNS lookups off.
- ☐ Turn file sharing off on your server's hard disks.
- ☐ Limit your use of system extensions to the absolute minimum.
- ☐ Keep your server application in the foreground.
- ☐ Limit the number of files and subfolders within a single folder to 50 or fewer.
- ☐ Limit the number of subfolders above a file to four or fewer.
- ☐ Use aliases sparingly and with caution.
- ☐ Avoid using aliases for frequently accessed folders.
- ☐ Avoid AppleScript whenever possible.
- ☐ Move CGI tasks to other machines when appropriate.
- ☐ Consolidate CGI functions into fewer applications whenever possible.
- ☐ Use multithreaded CGI applications.
- ☐ Use Frontier (Aretha) as a scripting system.
- ☐ Find a balance between large and small HTML pages.

- ☐ Minimize the number of individual inlined images on a page.
- ☐ Place inlined images on a second WWW server.

Now that you've optimized your server for maximum performance, you can take a look in the next chapter at ways to advertise your site and attract the clients you want to serve.

CHAPTER 15

To Market You Go: Promoting Your Site

"If you build it, they will come."

—Field of Dreams

"...as if!"

—Clueless

You can spend gobs of money developing content, investing in equipment, and leasing a blazingly fast Internet connection, but if you do not spend the time and energy to promote and build traffic on your site, you'll just be throwing your time and money away.

It's easy to forget, in the headlong rush of building a new Web site, that simple word of mouth is unlikely to attract many clients. The Web, like television, is a passive media that depends on its users/viewers to decide what they want to see and make the effort to go there. The Web, however, adds a unique element to the problem of publicity—people need to know how to find what they're looking for, and that makes the problem of attracting clients much more difficult.

Unless you're developing a private Web site, a primary goal of every site administrator is to attract as many people as possible to visit—and return to—their pages. This chapter explains many of the primary methods of attracting and keeping clients on your site.

The end of the chapter includes a list of URLs I've found useful for Web marketing—use the URLs as springboards for your own investigations of what's current on the Web. The list of URLs will provide you with many ideas to increase your traffic and success. They also will help avoid those uncomfortable conversations with clients or bosses who demand to know why only 1,500 of the millions of folks on the Internet stopped by their site this week.... You can also find these URLs on the CD for quick access to the site.

Getting the Word Out

The first step in marketing your site is attracting first-time visitors. People can come by out of interest in the subject of your site or out of a more general desire to visit someplace new. Your job is to put your URL in front of as many people as possible, as efficiently as possible. In this section, you'll find a variety of ways to attract first-time clients to your pages.

Announcements and Guides

What's new? What's cool? Where should I click today?

Announcement services answer these questions for people and can be a terrific site-publicizing mechanism. Some services take the form of Web pages, some are mailing lists, and some offer commentary, depending on the service. Figure 15.1 shows Yahoo's site.

What they all share is the capability, to a greater or lesser degree depending on the audience for that particular service, to create a sudden spike in your site's visitor count. These spikes can be short-lived. It is your responsibility to design a site that turns one-time visitors into regular clients, but the first step is to simply expose your pages to the eyes of as many people as possible.

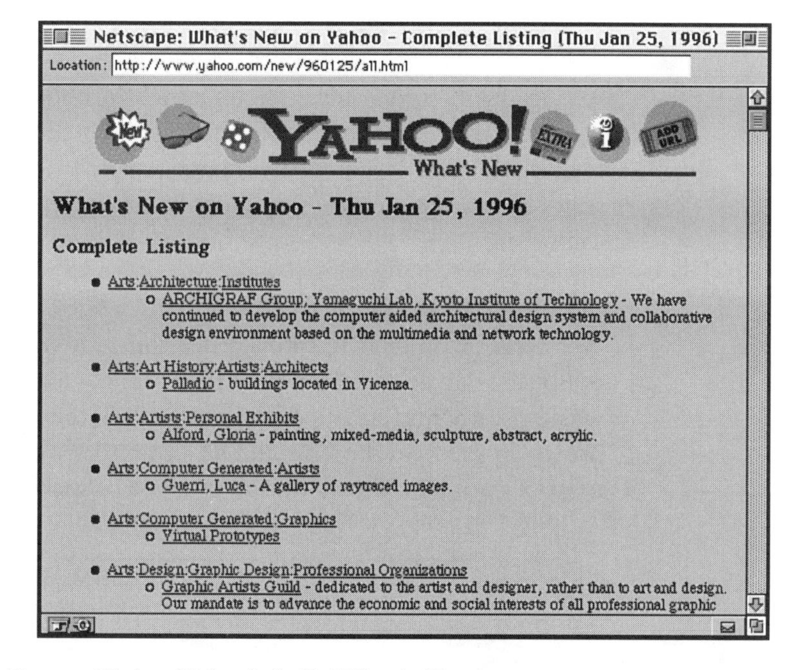

Figure 15.1 *Yahoo's daily What's New page.*

It is your responsibility to design a site that turns one-time visitors into regular clients.

As the Web expands and the capacity of the average person to investigate even a reasonable number of new sites diminishes, services that act as intelligent agents or editors will become increasingly important as directors of the public's use of the Internet. Some of these agents will be software added onto existing Web indexing systems, whereas other agents will be built from entirely new technologies. There will always be a need for human editors and reviewers as well, but automated methods are increasing in both usage and effectiveness.

Most importantly, don't hesitate to resubmit your site for consideration to these services whenever you make a substantial change to the look or the content of your site. The criteria and standards for inclusion in these listings can vary from day to day, so don't take exclusion as a final decision.

Guestbooks and Registration

Asking clients to register is always a tricky proposition—you want people to provide as much information about themselves as possible, yet you don't want to discourage people from visiting your pages by forcing them to stop and fill out various forms before they can proceed.

One nice compromise is to provide a guestbook (using a CGI or a Web server with built-in forms processing) for visitors that they can optionally decide to fill out with their name, email address, and whatever other information you want to ask them. For this approach to succeed, there should be a reward for completing the form. Figure 15.2 shows a good example of such a guestbook.

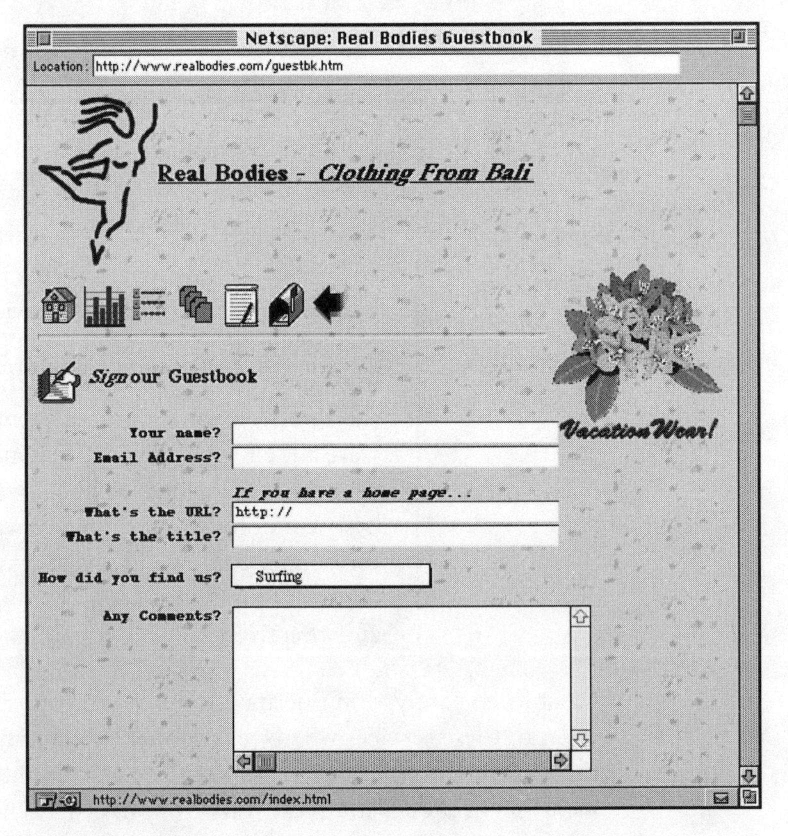

Figure 15.2 *An inviting guestbook form.*

The reward can be emailed announcements of new site contents or other information of interest to the client, or it could be access to an expanded or different section of your site (provided there is enough content available in the public portions of your site to pique people's interest in the hidden pages).

Getting people to join a private mailing list is also a nice way to keep your name and URL in their minds. Just be sure that there's a reason for every mailing, so that the client feels that each one has some value beyond a simple reminder to visit your site once again.

You Link My Page, I'll Link Yours

Reciprocal linking is the term used to describe arrangements where you add a link to your pages that sends clients to another site, the Webmaster of which then also agrees to list your URL in their own pages.

Before entering into such an agreement, ask yourself if the potential of increased traffic is worth the commitment of cross-listing URLs. If clients click off to the other site, is there a good reason for them to return to yours? Does the reciprocal link make sense in the context of your own pages, or does it look out of place? How prominent does the link need to be? (A single page linked to your home page with links to *recommended* sites can be an unobtrusive way to add off-site links to your pages.) Do the types of people likely to visit the other site mesh well with the target audience of your own site?

Think carefully before committing to any reciprocal linking arrangement, and try not to add links unless they make sense in the context of your site's overall goals.

Hurl That URL

Your URL should be displayed anywhere your name or your organization's name already appears. If you are building a central corporate Web site at a company whose employees use email or newsgroups on the corporate network, ask everyone to include your site's URL in their email signatures. If your organization already purchases advertising in traditional media, talk to the people responsible for those ads about including your URL in their material.

Too often, a large organization's Web site is considered an autonomous unit and is not integrated into the activities of other groups in the organization. You may not be able to replace the company stationery overnight, but you should certainly ensure that the next batch ordered contains your site information.

Here's a brief list of places where your URL could appear:

- ☐ Email signatures
- ☐ Press releases
- ☐ Invoices
- ☐ Checks
- ☐ Business cards
- ☐ Letterheads
- ☐ Return addresses on letters
- ☐ Promotional material
- ☐ Automated telephone systems
- ☐ Manuals

Remember, this is about promoting your site as the online presence for your organization. It's a cost-effective method of communicating with the public, and part of your duties is to integrate your Web presence with whatever forms of marketing and communication you or your organization already use.

Search Engines/Indexers

The most basic step to Web advertising, of course, is to list your site in the standard Web search engines and directories so that people looking for sites with your type of content can find your URL. There are services that claim to provide one-stop registration of your site with a variety of directories, but they all suffer from some degree of ineffectiveness. The problem is that each directory has a unique method of submitting URLs and site descriptions, and one method may not take advantage of the opportunities for adding keywords or other information another site offers. I highly recommend that you register your site individually with each service. Figure 15.3 shows the Submit It! site submission form.

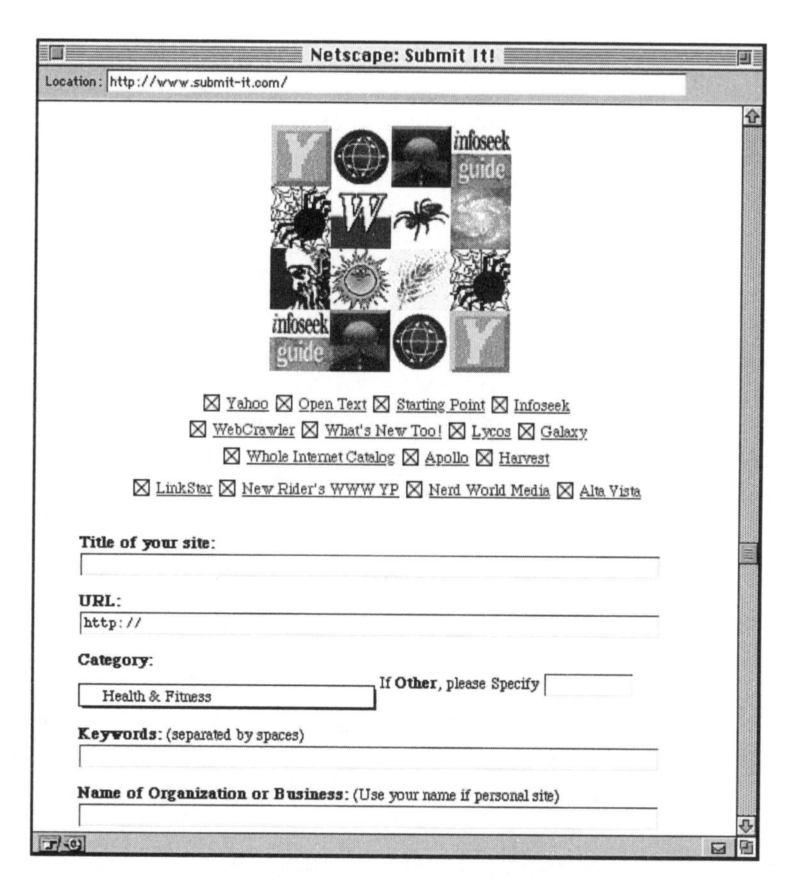

Figure 15.3 *The beginning of the Submit It! site submission form.*

Here are some tips on effectively submitting your site's URLs:

- ☐ Make your site's title as long and descriptive as possible when adding it to submission forms and when writing HTML. Also, beginning titles with numbers or letters appearing early in the alphabet can get your site's entry to the top of some listings, just like in your Yellow Pages.
- ☐ Make a list of keywords for your site and include as many as you can in every description and title you enter.
- ☐ Include as many important keywords as possible near the top of your pages, because the first bit of text is often displayed by search engines when returning results.
- ☐ Follow up with the sites you submit your URLs to and make sure that your listings are in their catalogs.
- ☐ List multiple URLs in different submissions if your site can be divided into areas with different, specific subjects.

Search engines such as Lycos probably will find your site eventually regardless of whether you submit it for registration, but submitting your site starts the process sooner and, depending on the service, increases the effectiveness of directing people to your site in the future.

Sponsorship (Nonprofits)

Here's another cool way to get your URL out to the people—sponsor a couple of pages on your Web site for nonprofit or public service organizations. Many of these groups struggle with a very limited budget and would appreciate the opportunity to place even one or two HTML pages on the Web. Because you can add a link back to your own URLs from the group's pages, you've gained a positive image and a link back to your site with minimal effort.

If you are already set up for commercial activities on your Web site, you could offer to collect donations via credit cards or First Virtual accounts for the nonprofit group.

Paid Advertising

Most of the Web sites offering popular free content like search engines, indexes, or other services support themselves by selling space on their pages to advertisers, who pay for the right to insert their logos and links on the pages of the service's site. It's unclear how effective these ads are, but in general you can assume that the more narrowly directed they are, the more effective the advertising will be at inducing people to take an interest in your site. Figure 15.4 shows Walt Disney World's attempt at Yahoo's Recreation page.

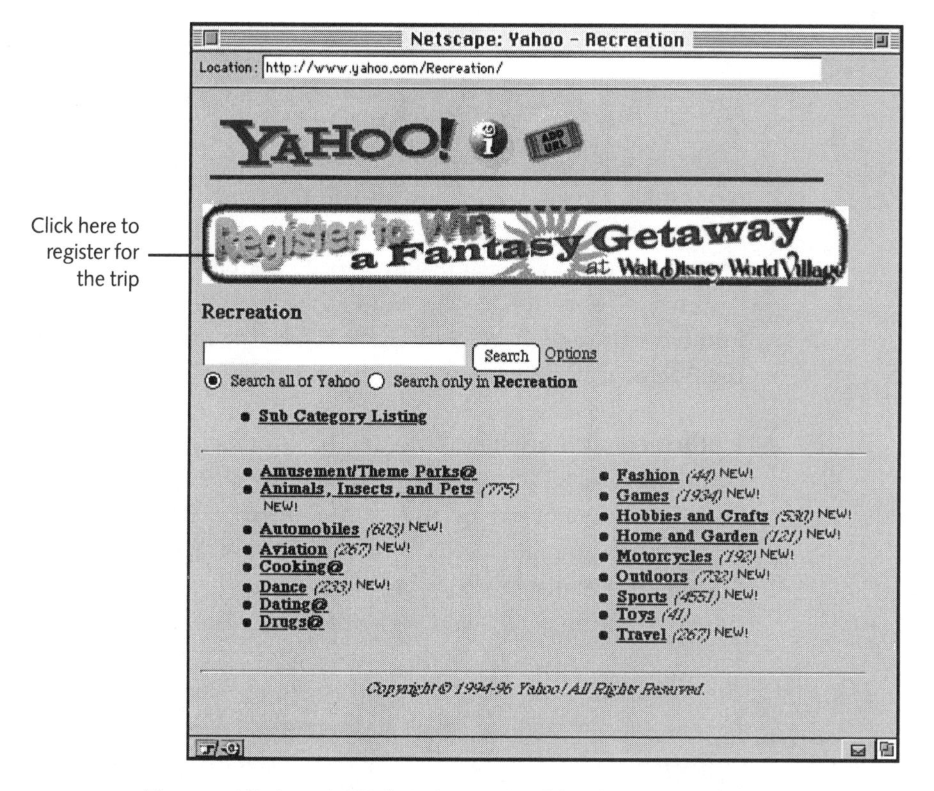

Figure 15.4 *A Walt Disney World ad at Yahoo!.*

I'd Like to Buy a Vowel, Please

The Web has already inspired at least one unique way of selling advertising space—advertisers purchase sponsorship of particular keywords or combinations of keywords in Web indexes like Lycos and Alta Vista. If your site is aimed at windsurfers, for example, you could pay Lycos to put your ad image (with a link to your site) above the search results whenever someone uses the word *windsurf* in a query. The methods of selling this kind of sponsorship are still being worked out—searches using more than one keyword, for example, can have conflicting sponsors.

The same principle can be applied to Web directories such as Yahoo!, which sell sponsorship of their index categories. This is an excellent way of directing your marketing budget at a self-selected category of clients. Notice that Disney purchased an ad specifically in the Recreation section of Yahoo!, as shown in Figure 15.4.

Measuring Effectiveness

In the beginning, there was the *hit*—an instance of a single client requesting a given URL. The hit was the basic measure of how many times a page or image had been seen by a client, and it was simple and compelling. Hits are usually the basis for the page counters on some pages that tell you how many people have requested that same page since noon today, the previous Friday, or the Age of Enlightenment.

Unfortunately, pure hit counts can be extremely misleading as they count every access equally, regardless of whether the client had visited the page before or, in the case of pages with graphics, whether the graphics were downloaded along with the HTML. See Chapter 9, "Statistics and Usage," for more information on methods of counting clients and how reliable (or unreliable) they can be.

An honest site will quote statistics or set advertising rates on the basis of unique client accesses to a particular URL. They should be able to give you numbers for any given page that indicate the number of unique clients (defined as IP addresses) who that have accessed the page as well as each image on the page, if any.

A really sophisticated site can even quote demographic statistics that they have been able to collect from visitors, using questionnaires and registrations, so that you don't waste your marketing budget buying ads for your twenty-something Web site on pages visited primarily by forty-somethings.

Ideally, you should pay only for the hits to your site that were referred via the ad. You can and should ask for your payments to be based, at least in part, on this kind of measure if the ad space seller collects the information. Ask about this kind of rate before signing a contract.

Rates

Ad rates on the Web vary a great deal from place to place and method to method. Although the industry is certainly selling ads at a brisk clip, there really isn't a consensus yet as to how much a client's visit is worth to advertisers. You'll need to make inquiries before even guessing what the rates are at any given site. If there isn't a page with ad information already available at a site in which you're interested, try sending email to the Webmaster.

Online Services

When planning your online marketing, don't neglect the online services such as AOL, CompuServe, and Prodigy. Millions of people are browsing the Internet from these services, and are exposed regularly to the service's private site listings and other resources unavailable to the rest of the Internet.

A side benefit of joining CompuServe or AOL is that you can use the service's Web access to audit your site and look for potential incompatibilities or other problems between the browsers they supply to their subscribers and your site.

These services are organized into subject areas, or forums, that are frequented by clients looking for information. The moderators of these forums are constantly on the lookout for new information that will add value to their listings and keep their members satisfied. If your site addresses a particular subject area, look into joining at least the more popular services and contributing to their online content via postings to discussion groups or by providing files, culled from your Web site, for their libraries. Include an invitation to visit your Web site for more detailed information.

If your site is more general or doesn't mesh well with the forum subjects of a particular service, you can also seek out the Internet-related portions of the service and list your URL in their internal directories of sites. Either way, the goal is to take advantage of these online services to publicize your URL efficiently.

A side benefit of joining CompuServe or AOL is that you can use the service's Web access to audit your site and look for potential incompatibilities or other problems between the browsers they supply to their subscribers and your site.

Offline

It's easy to forget that there's a world outside the Web that can still effectively reach potential clients. Despite the fact that the audience for traditional media is less Internet-savvy in general than the audience you reach online, the numbers of people you can reach via traditional means are much larger. Also, the presentation of your URL offline offers encouragement to people who are not currently online to get that PPP account now!

In this section, we'll take a look at some of the ways to reach a mass audience via traditional media and put your URL in the public eye as affordably as possible.

Affinity Groups

Affinity groups are organizations whose focus is in some way related to the focus of your Web site. You can often expose your URL and site description to a highly specialized group of potential clients by inserting material into the regular mailings these groups send out periodically. If the group has a newsletter or other material that addresses the interests of its readers, you can write an article on using online resources or even about the resources on your own site! Most small publications that address specialized groups are always looking for more material, and if you can do a bit of writing this can be a win-win situation for you, the group, and its members.

For example, my local American Automobile Association's newsletter recently carried an article about researching hotels via the Web—not coincidentally, the author included the URL to a site of his own that provides that very service to visitors.

Some good sources for affinity groups are professional associations, unions, nonprofit organizations, or newsletter subscribers. In fact, you can often get started in this area by offering to speak at a local chapter meeting about how the Internet can serve their members. If you have any expertise in the group's area, you can usually offer a more focused argument for integrating the Internet with their other activities than the more general, "ain't the Net neat?" approach members might already have seen.

Magazines and Newspapers

Most people still read more than they surf, and reaching a broader audience often involves publicizing your URL via traditional media. You can always buy a small ad in a newspaper or magazine, but a more cost-effective method is to reach the short "What's New?" columns or blurbs that are part of most publications, and tell them about your site and the value it offers their readers. A short write-up (even just a couple of sentences) in a magazine can do wonders for your traffic.

Putting your URL in print has another advantage—longevity. A magazine can be passed from person to person and be reread for some time after publication. Internet-based publicizing tends to have a much shorter lifespan, as any given announcement is quickly displaced by another.

Direct Mail, Really

Huh? Junk mail for Web advertising? Not exactly. Direct mail is only cost-effective for advertising Web sites if you can target very small groups of people who are either potential customers or people who influence others' usage of the Web.

You can, for example, collect the names and addresses of television and radio shows in your area (or national programs) that address Internet or Web-related subjects and send them postcards with a picture of your home page on the front and a blurb about the site on the back. Or, if you offer a specialty site, buy mailing lists from relevant magazines and target their subscribers with the same postcards.

Most small sites can't afford this kind of marketing, but if you are establishing a commercial operation or adding an online presence for your company, it can be a distinctive and effective way to boost your visibility.

Change Your Tune

To inspire clients to return to your site, you either need content that is repeatedly requested (such as that from a search engine or a phone directory) or you need new content that is updated as often as possible. This activity (along with more general marketing efforts) is often the most under-budgeted item when planning a Web site. Unless the nature of your site's content is sufficiently compelling and rich that people will return of their own accord, it is difficult to inspire people to return after their first few visits.

Please refrain from adding lines such as, "This page last updated:" and a date to your pages unless you can maintain the effort of changing or adding to your site on at least a weekly basis. Few things are so glaringly unprofessional as a "last updated" date of three months ago...

I have two words that will force you to update your content regularly: automated agents. They are already built into the Netscape browser. I can count half a dozen available for Macintosh users, and there are at least twice as many more available as free services over the Web. Their numbers are growing, and they will force you to make regular and substantial changes to the content of your sites.

What are they? *Automated agents*, in this context, are programs or functions that periodically check a list of URLs to see whether any have changed since the last check. So, rather than clients searching a list of bookmarks in search of new content, the agents report when a page has changed and alert the client to visit the page.

As the Web grows beyond the capability of any single person to keep current in even a few areas of interest, automated agents will be the prime vehicle for cueing people to visit a particular site. Clients are alerted when automated agents detect changes in a site's HTML. Any of your URLs that a client might bookmark should be changed regularly and substantially.

Note that when I say "substantially," I don't mean that most of the text must change, but rather that there should be at least one substantial new or changed item on your page that will reward the client for returning to your URL. Changing the "today's date" line won't bring your clients back—adding a new page, however, will.

This Site Requires Netscape 45.23/beta9 Download Now!

Browsers, browsers everywhere, yet not a standard in sight.

One of the most difficult decisions to make when designing a site is deciding which browsers you will support. Do you use tables? Font control tags? Server-push mechanisms? What about images? Are images necessary to navigate and absorb your site, or are you willing to accommodate those people who don't download images at the expense of a little graphic razzle-dazzle?

There are several options available to maximize the number of clients that can enjoy your site without compromising the quality of your graphics and HTML formatting.

Parallel Web Sites

The first is to simply provide two versions of your critical pages—one high-graphic, Netscape-only or otherwise limited, and another for text-only viewers who might not be using the most current browser version. Sun Microsystems, Inc., (http://www.sun.com/) provides a nice example of this approach. The key is to provide essential information in a basic, accessible format that parallels your main site's pages, as shown in Figure 15.5.

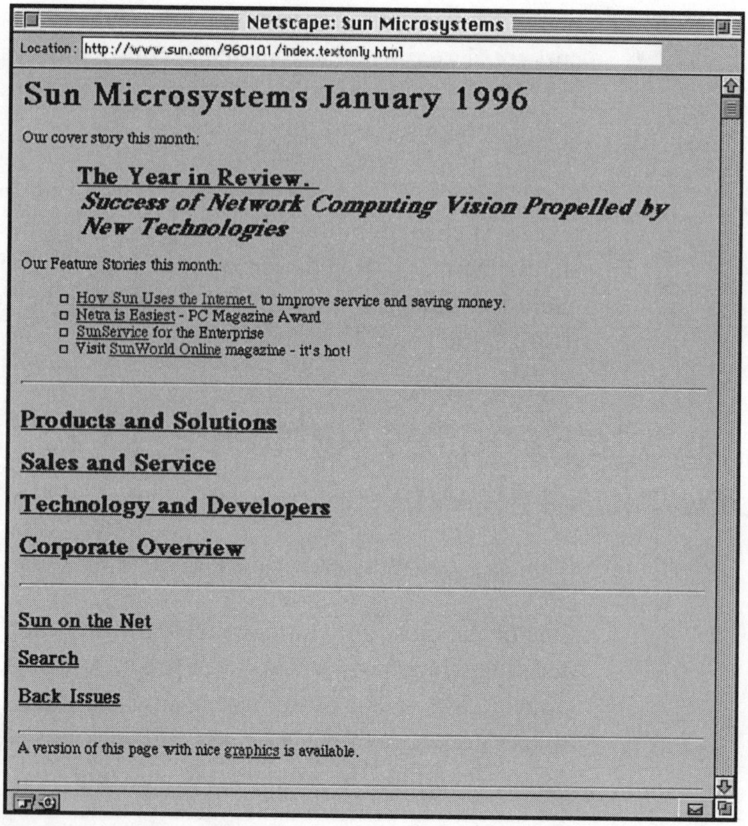

Netscape: Sun Microsystems

Location: http://www.sun.com/960101/index.textonly.html

Sun Microsystems January 1996

Our cover story this month:

The Year in Review.
Success of Network Computing Vision Propelled by New Technologies

Our Feature Stories this month:

- How Sun Uses the Internet, to improve service and saving money.
- Netra is Easiest - PC Magazine Award
- SunService for the Enterprise
- Visit SunWorld Online magazine - it's hot!

Products and Solutions

Sales and Service

Technology and Developers

Corporate Overview

Sun on the Net

Search

Back Issues

A version of this page with nice graphics is available.

Figure 15.5 *The Sun Microsystems text-only home page.*

Use <ALT> Tags

Most browsers can interpret <ALT> tags in image URLs and display text next to the icon of an image that wasn't loaded. If the image links to another URL, the <ALT> text will enable the client to follow the URL without downloading the graphic. If your clients are browsing the Web with image loading off (as do many modem users), a page filled with nothing but image icons isn't very enticing or usable. <ALT> tags can fill this gap by providing clues to the functions of different images and enable people to navigate your site quickly and effectively.

You can add <ALT> text to an image URL very easily: simply include the word <ALT> in the image tag with the text you would like displayed in double quotes, as follows:

```
<IMAGE HREF="/mylogo.gif" ALT="Company Logo">
```

One problem with <ALT> tags is that they aren't very helpful with imagemaps, because the text-based link can only lead to a single URL. A solution to this dilemma is a text menu, in small type just below the imagemap, that duplicates the URLs linked by the map. This enables text-based browsing without significantly intruding on the look of your pages for those clients who do download the imagemap graphic.

Because automated site indexers can't interpret URLs reachable via imagemaps, it also provides a way to allow such robots to find and index the rest of your site. See Figure 15.6.

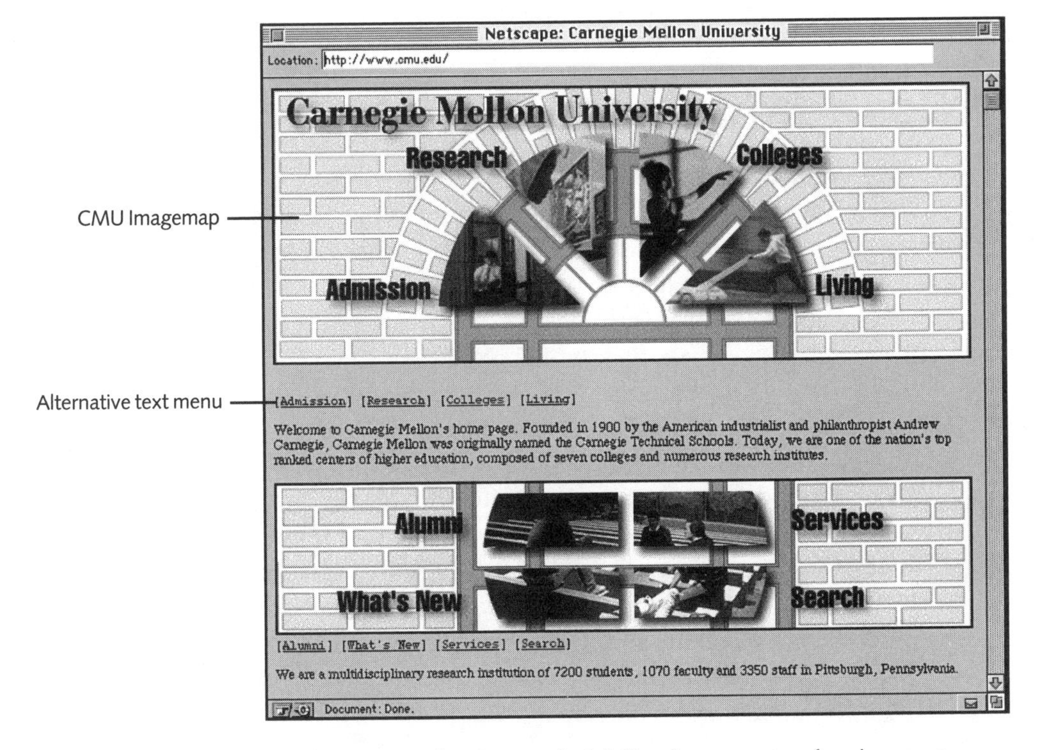

Figure 15.6 *The Carnegie Mellon home page, showing text menu alternatives.*

Name That Browser

A more sophisticated approach to meeting your clients' needs is to use a CGI to present different versions of your HTML to different clients, depending on their browser type. You can find out more information about this approach in Chapter 7, "CGI Applications and Usage."

Another approach is to add a page that uses tables, and ask clients to choose different links depending on whether the table was displayed correctly. This enables you to separate your tables-capable from incapable clients without keeping track of which versions of which browsers support tables.

Finally, you should at least provide a link to a location for clients to download the browser you would prefer them to use—Netscape will even provide an icon for you to put on your pages for doing this (http://home.netscape.com/comprod/mirror/netscape_now_program.html).

Welcome to My Web Site—Now Go Away!

Think about the URLs that you revisit most frequently, and you might be surprised. For myself, it turns out to be the pages with local weather information and movie listings. I stop by daily (and sometimes even more often) to get a small bit of information and then move on. If an advertiser wanted to target me, those would be the pages where they should place their ads.

The audience for those pages isn't nearly as large as most Web sites aim for, but the point is that some of the most valuable pages are those that move the users off the Web. I might not have the time or inclination to sit and browse the Web for hours every day, so the sites I visit most are going to be those that offer me a "quick fix" of something that adds value to the rest of my life. The connections between real life and the Web are often hard to distinguish, yet it is exactly these connections that add value to your clients' lives and, by extension, to your site.

Take as an example a shopping site that offers items from a catalog. The Web is not quite at the point where browsing an online catalog is as effective as flipping pages in a magazine. Most people shopping on the Web, therefore, are looking for something fairly specific. They want to find it, order it, and move on. The site that completes this operation as quickly as possible will leave the client with a better impression than a catalog that forces them to click through five or ten pages before they can finish the transaction.

You can extend this idea to almost any site by providing an incentive for people to stop by often and briefly. It can take the form of a daily announcement, news item, or even an editorial essay, as long as it is both compelling and short, as is done at http://www.interbiznet.com/ibn/nomad.html.

Resources for Web Marketing

Table 15.1 lists some sites I've found valuable in marketing new Web sites. I've tried to include links that provide their own listings of marketing sites so the listings found here provide current resources for promoting your site.

You can also find this list on the CD in the **HTML** folder so that you can simply click on the links while on the Web for quick access.

Table 15.1 *General Web Marketing Resources*

URL	Description
http://www.interbiznet.com/ibn/nomad.html	"Updated Nearly Daily," an excellent resource for all kinds of online marketing information. It's my default home page.
http://www.wilsonweb.com/rfwilson/webmarket/	Web marketing for small businesses.
http://arganet.tenagra.com/Tenagra/books.html	Index to Web marketing publications.

continues

Table 15.1 *Continued*

URL	Description
http://www.interbiznet.com/ibn/promophop.htm	General Web site promotion topics.
http://www.netcreations.com/ipa/adindex/	Index of Web advertising rates.
http://www.orst.edu/aw/stygui/propag.htm	Tutorials on promoting Web pages.
Submitting and Announcing URLs	
http://www.netcreations.com/postmaster/	One-stop URL submission/announcement site.
http://www.submit-it.com/	Same as above.
http://www.sme.com/webpost/	Same as above.
http://www.cam.org/~psarena/promote-it.html	Same as above, but organized by type of site.
http://www.vir.com/~wyatt/index.html	Index of site announcement services—great resource for manual submissions.
http://www.euro.net/5thworld/metapick/	Subjective listing and criticism of announcement services, also nicely organized.
Indexes and Directories	
http://www.lycos.com/	Lycos
http://www.infoseek.com/	Infoseek
http://www.yahoo.com/	Yahoo!
http://www.altavista.digital.com/	Alta Vista
http://www.excite.com/	Excite

Summary

Promoting your site, as you may have gathered from what you've read so far, is not a one-shot job. You don't need a degree in marketing (although it wouldn't hurt), but you do need to plan and budget for your site's promotion as much as you need to plan your site's design and your content.

Marketing can be an even more creative activity than designing HTML layouts, and I encourage you to be innovative in your approach. There's a lot of room for new approaches, and, as the Web continues to grow, the need to stand out from the crowd becomes even more acute.

This chapter is the last of the book about Web serving—congratulations on getting this far! The next chapter includes some background information about the Web and the Internet, some information about the future of the Macintosh, and discusses how changes in these areas will affect your role as a site administrator.

CHAPTER 16

Coming Attractions

There have always been valid reasons not to choose a Macintosh for critical applications—the operating system is prone to crash and burn, other platforms seem to have software and updates written for them first, and MacTCP has been prone to strange and unsolvable fits from time to time. But all that is changing, some of it by the time you read this, others within the next few months or years. The future of the Macintosh platform (by which I mean PowerPC-based machines capable of running the MacOS) is an exciting one, and it promises to offer more real power and options for Web site administrators than any other option.

Here are a few of the reasons why:

Open Transport

By the time you read this, Open Transport should be available for all PowerPC and 68040-based Macintoshes. Open Transport is the new networking system software that is supposed to greatly simplify and improve connecting to and using different network services on Macs, whether the services are based on AppleTalk, TCP/IP, or Novell's IPX networking technology, which allows Macs and Windows-based machines to share a common TCP/IP network infrastructure.

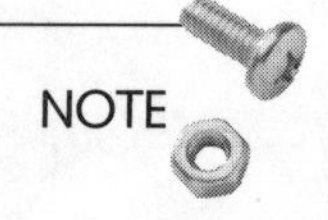
NOTE

Apple's documentation on Open Transport includes an HTML-ized version at `http://pilot.njin.net/~msproul/macintosh/OpenTpt_QA.html` and the original at `ftp://seeding.apple.com/ess/public/opentransport/OT_gen_info/WORD/OT%20QA%20Update.hqx`.

There are three major areas in which Open Transport will affect Macintosh-based Web servers, all discussed in the following sections:

- Speed
- Connections
- Reliability

Speed

Open Transport will run completely native on PowerPCs. This single improvement could create speed increases for handling TCP/IP-based connections of a quarter or more for applications that take advantage of Open Transport's new structure.

Additionally, much of the system software that handles AppleTalk networking, such as the services Appleshare depends on, should exhibit performance increases under Open Transport. When combined with the fast new data buses and SCSI interfaces available on the PowerPC 603- and 604-based Macs, Open Transport should represent as big a boost to server performance as moving from a Quadra to a PowerPC did once PowerPC-native applications became available.

Connections

MacTCP is limited, on all Macintoshes, to handling a maximum of 64 connections at a time. If you wanted your server to handle 65, you would need another Mac to handle the single extra connection. Open Transport, however, allows your Mac to open hundreds of connections at once. Assuming your server's CPU can keep up with the load (no small assumption by any means), this knocks down one of the most glaring deficiencies of the Mac platform when compared to UNIX or Windows NT servers. You will, of course, still have the option of adding more machines to handle part of your site's load, but the reason this time around will be purely performance rather than working around MacTCP's limitations.

Note that although serving a hundred different files at once is probably not something a single Mac could accomplish very well, the simple capability to keep many connections open at once provides important flexibility for sites that offer multiple Internet services (email, FTP, Web) and opens the door to more exotic applications such as TCP/IP "broadcasting" of information in real-time to dozens of clients. This is feasible because without the limits on total connection numbers imposed by MacTCP, TCP/IP connections can be kept open indefinitely without limiting the capability of other services, such as a Web server, to handle new requests.

Reliability

MacTCP has been subject to some strange problems throughout its life, as any long-time Mac Web site administrator can attest. Chief among these have been problems in coping with slow networks that drop IP packets in transit and occasional odd behavior when performing DNS lookups. Open Transport, rewritten from the bottom up to provide a robust networking environment, is expected to solve most of these problems and provide a simpler and more efficient means of administrating TCP/IP services on the Mac.

Overall, Open Transport is expected to vastly increase the reliability and power of Macintosh servers that provide Internet or other network services.

OpenDoc

OpenDoc is an Apple technology developed to write applications and system software as a collection of components or "parts" that can be combined ad hoc to create new combinations of functionality. For example, the spell checker of your word processor could, as an OpenDoc part, be added to a spreadsheet application or email program with its full functionality intact. Users will be able to add buttons, menu items, or other interface elements to existing programs that support the OpenDoc architecture to "customize" applications for their specific needs.

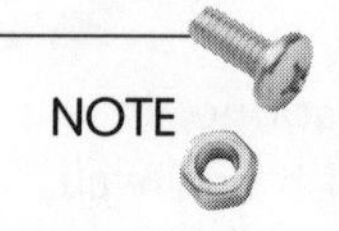

NOTE

Check out Apple's OpenDoc home page at `http://www.opendoc.apple.com`.

So what does this mean for you as a Web server? Your control over how applications meet your administrative needs will be greatly expanded and enhanced, as you become increasingly able to construct applications and interfaces in intuitive, "drag and drop" style by assembling parts in the manner that is most effective for meeting your particular needs. Even your server software, if it is written to conform to OpenDoc standards, may change dramatically, opening new methods of customization and an even tighter coupling to CGIs. It also means that the capability of clients to construct new ways of interacting with your site will be expanded as well, and it may become difficult to predict how your site will actually appear to a user.

Finally, OpenDoc is being officially supported by companies outside Apple such as IBM and Oracle, with OpenDoc support planned for both the Windows and OS/2 operating systems. Should you want to migrate CGIs or other portions of your site to another platform, OpenDoc and its kin may greatly ease the process of doing so. This industry support will add value to your server as more cross-platform parts are released, thereby making the range of tools at your disposal wider than ever before.

The general OpenDoc release occurred in November 1995, although some time may need to pass before applications that take advantage of the new architecture are widely available. The success of OpenDoc is still a bit hazy, as developers struggle with new concepts of marketing and selling OpenDoc "parts" rather than applications and everyone waits to see if the promised cross-platform support becomes a reality. Nevertheless, OpenDoc seems poised to become an important part of the MacOS, just as Apple Events have become, and it has the potential to transform the way we manage and use software on the Mac.

The New OS—Copland/System 8

Copland is the code name given to the MacOS version 8.0, due to replace version 7.x sometime in 1996 or early 1997. Copland and its successor, Gershwin, will represent a dramatic change in the way Macintoshes work and behave.

NOTE

Check out Apple's Copland Web site at `http://www.info.apple.com/macos/rels/coplandsumm.html`.

The most important improvement will come from an entirely PowerPC native operating system—all parts of the system software will be written for the PowerPC processor, thereby accelerating every activity from disk access to AppleEvents on PPC-based Macs. Copland has, for example, been reported to process AppleEvents at the phenomenal rate of 1,500 events per second.

But raw speed is only part of the story—it is the integration of new versions of all the parts of the MacOS that will lead to important improvements in reliability for the Mac. System 7 and its descendants have become a bewildering and crash-prone stew of updaters, enablers, and extensions that regularly fail to interact successfully. OpenDoc and Open Transport, for example, are available now as interim upgrades to the MacOS but they will, along with other technologies, be built into Copland and therefore become even more reliable and efficient.

Finally, while PC-Windows technology continues to build ever more complex and frustrating variations of DOS and the CISC-type processors used in Windows desktop machines, Apple has committed itself to the next generation of microprocessors, the PowerPC RISC architecture. Copland is designed entirely around PowerPC technology, and will be written to the specifications of the Common Hardware Reference Platform, which will enable Copland to run on any CHRP-standard PowerPC machine, including advanced workstations from IBM and other manufacturers.

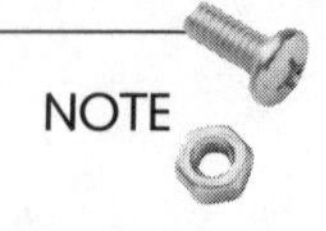

Like most advances in the MacOS, the new technologies in Copland will depend on support from software developers for you to realize their benefits. Even after Copland is released, there will be a period of transition as applications are rewritten to take advantage of the Copland OS, and as the release of Copland draws closer, you should begin to pay attention to "Copland-ready" claims of competing applications to ensure that your servers are able to make full use of Copland's advanced functionality.

The two most significant changes Copland and Gershwin will bring are multitasking and protected memory, discussed next.

Multitasking

Another common criticism of Macs is their lack of true multitasking, which refers to the capability of applications to share the CPU cooperatively. It's true that you can run multiple applications at the same time on the Mac, but if you've ever watched the screen in frustration while a print job completed, you already know about some of the limits of the current system.

With Copland, waiting for printing to complete or experiencing a "freeze" while one application works in the background will be but a distantly unpleasant memory. No longer will applications run at different speeds in the foreground and the background, and the likelihood of one program causing your entire system to crash will be greatly reduced.

Protected Memory

The MacOS has always been known as being "brittle," meaning that it is quite common for a small problem with one application to cause a system error and force rebooting of the entire machine. For a server that needs to operate as reliably as possible, this can be a real problem.

Protected memory is part of a larger system design that will limit the damage a single out-of-control application can create. Under Copland, if one of your CGIs experiences a serious error, it will still quit on its own, but your main system and other applications will continue on as usual. Other changes in memory management will reduce RAM requirements across the board and allow applications to share RAM more efficiently.

Copland will bring many more advances to the Macintosh desktop, such as searching a disk for words within files as easily as searching for filenames.

All that, and your System 7 applications will still run!

Summary

The "Macintosh advantage" has always been associated with ease of use issues and the savings in time and cost derived from its superior interface and seamless integration of advanced technology for networking and graphics. The "Macintosh disadvantage" has always been a higher initial cost, more than its share of system crashes, and a smaller installed base than other platforms.

All that is changing. Already, prices on Macintoshes are comparable to Windows machines, and the performance of the PowerPC processor has been repeatedly shown to exceed what can be wrung out of the Intel Pentium-based machines. With the changes in system software mentioned previously, the Macintosh advantage will extend into the areas of networking performance, reliability, and cross-platform interoperability. For Web servers, I believe the Mac is evolving into the most powerful and cost-effective platform available, bar none.

Closure

Whether you plan to start serving just a few HTML pages to the world over a dialup connection or create a sophisticated, interactive site that breaks new ground on the Web with innovative design or services, I've tried to include the information, both on these pages and on the CD, that you will need to succeed. As your experience grows and you face new challenges in managing your server, this book should continue to provide the guidance and resources you'll need to help you realize your vision for your site and reach the level of expertise that allows you to take the title of "Webmaster" for your own.

NOTE

If you find this book helpful in setting up your own Web server, please let me know so that I can visit your site! You can reach me at the email address `stewart@prowillen.com`. I'd love to hear from you.

Go forth and serve! The Web is waiting…

Part IV

Appendixes

APPENDIX

Internet Troubleshooting

Eventually, you'll need to examine the inner workings of the Internet more closely, either to diagnose problems or gather information that helps you increase the performance of your Web site. This appendix introduces you to the basic tools for examining TCP/IP networks across the Internet and provides examples of their uses.

NOTE

You should have already read Chapter 3 before going through the tutorials in this appendix; they depend heavily upon your understanding the terminology and concepts described there.

MacTCP Ping

MacTCP Ping is a small shareware application from Apple Computer that provides basic "ping" functionality for Macs. You will need to have an active TCP/IP connection before launching it. (You should be able to use programs like Netscape Navigator or Eudora.) You can get the MacTCP Ping at http://sir-univ-rennes1.fr/pub/mac/reseau/Mactcp/MacTCP_PING.hqx.

What Is a "Ping"?

A "ping" is the network term for a minimal exchange of information between two hosts on the Internet (or other TCP/IP network) that verifies that the host the ping is sent to is actually on the Internet at the IP address indicated, and that valid TCP/IP software is running on the remote machine.

Just like sonar on a submarine, pinging another machine on the Internet involves sending a signal and waiting for a response to arrive back at the sender. The difference is that a computer's ping is directed at a single, specific host.

MacTCP Ping is useful for:

- ☐ Verifying that a remote host is connected to the Internet.
- ☐ Identifying problems with TCP/IP network efficiency.

Let's look at how to accomplish both these tasks next.

Verifying Remote Hosts

MacTCP Ping (as well as just about every other TCP/IP utility for the Mac) may not run successfully with Open Transport. If you are using Open Transport and have trouble with MacTCP Ping, you need to either switch back to MacTCP temporarily (see `http://www.starnine.com/support/gettingstarted/ot-mactcp.html` for instructions) or check this book's Web page at `http://www.mcp.com/hayden/webserver/` for alternatives that may have become available since publication.

To verify that a remote machine is connected to the Internet, follow these steps:

1. Make sure that the Mac you're running MacTCP Ping on is already connected to the Internet. If you can use a Web browser or other Internet client application successfully, you are already connected.

2. Launch MacTCP Ping and enter either the domain name or the IP address of the machine you want to test in the box labeled "Ping Host Address" (in Figure A.1, www.mcp.com is the example).

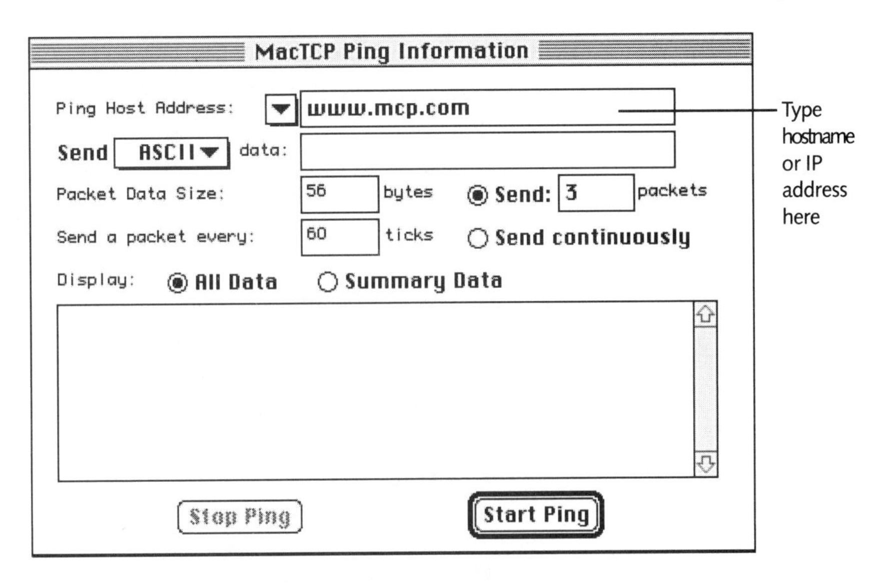

Figure A.1 *Identifying the machine to ping.*

3. Click the "Start Ping" button or press Return. The display box shown in Figure A.2 will show the results of the test.

MacTCP Ping Information

Ping Host Address: www.mcp.com

Send ASCII data:

Packet Data Size: 56 bytes ◉ Send: 3 packets

Send a packet every: 60 ticks ○ Send continuously

Display: ◉ All Data ○ Summary Data

```
Source: [128.2.191.38] --> Destination: www.mcp.com
[198.70.148.1]
RESULT      PKT#      TIME      LENGTH
success       1         3         56
success       2        14         56
success       3         3         56
Packets out/in/bad/%loss = 3/3/0/0
Round Trip Time (Ticks) min/avg/max = 3/6/14
```

Stop Ping Start Ping

Ping results are displayed here

Figure A.2 *Ping results for* www.mcp.com.

The first and second lines show the IP addresses of the machine you are sending the ping from as well as the IP address of the destination.

The three lines with "success" listed in the RESULT column represent the results of each of the three individual pings that were performed. If a ping was not successfully returned, the RESULT column will display the word "timeout," meaning that the ping was not answered in the time allowed (usually several seconds). The TIME column reports the number of "ticks" (1/60 of a second) that passed between the time the ping was sent and the time the answer was received. You'll read more about how to interpret time-outs in the next sections.

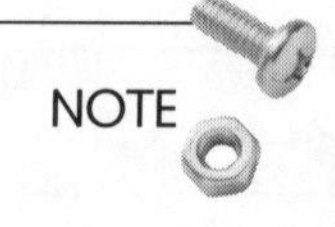

NOTE

The "Send" radio button has an entry box next to it that allows you to set the number of ping attempts you want MacTCP Ping to perform at a time. You can set the number of pings to any number you want, although I recommend using a number between 5 and 20.

You can also select the "Send Continuously" radio button before starting to ping to force MacTCP Ping to keep making attempts until you press the "Stop Ping" button to view the summary statistics discussed previously.

You can ignore the LENGTH column, as it is not significant in this context.

The summary statistics at the bottom of the output window are the next area to examine. Because many factors can interfere with a single ping's results, you should always look at the averages before evaluating the results.

The average round trip time (the last line in the ping results area) in particular acts as a summary of the efficiency of the connection between your machine and the remote host. Typical values range from 0 (for machines on the same local network) to about 15–20 for pings performed over dialup modem lines. Anything above 20 is cause for concern because the connection is fairly slow, and anything above 35 definitely indicates a serious problem. An average below 10 is very good, and usually means both machines are on high-speed connections to the Internet.

You should always compare the round trip times for the host you are interested in with the times reported for other Internet hosts that you consider to be both reliable and speedy (large commercial or university sites are often good bets). Doing so establishes a baseline performance number for the machine you are pinging from that you can compare with the times reported for your target machine to determine whether the target machine is having problems as opposed to your own local network being slow.

Packet Loss

So what does it mean that a packet is lost, or timed out? There are three possibilities:

- The remote host is not answering the ping properly, either because it has crashed, been disconnected from the Internet, or was too busy to answer within the timeout period for the packet.
- An intervening network or router is busy or otherwise too slow to successfully pass the packet within the packet's timeout period.
- An intervening network or router is misconfigured and is routing IP packets improperly or inconsistently.

If all the pings you send time out, that usually means the target machine is disconnected or crashed. Be sure and check the IP address or domain name you are using to ensure that it is correct, and also check to see whether you can ping other hosts on the Internet successfully.

If both checks are OK, the problem is specific to the machine you are pinging or in the internal networks of the ISP that provides the target machine's Internet connection.

If only a few of the pings time out, it's most likely a case of an intervening network being especially slow or busy. Identifying where on the Internet the problem may be is the subject of the next section.

Traceroute

Traceroute is a program available on most UNIX machines that reports the IP addresses and domain names, where available, of all of the routers and machines that IP packets travel through from one point on the Internet to another. It is an immensely valuable tool for tracking down the source of network outages or slowdowns between your server and other points on the Internet.

Traceroute services work by taking an IP address or domain name and attempting to list every host or node on the Internet that IP packets travel through between the machine performing the traceroute and the target machine.

Traceroute also reports the round trip times between the traceroute machine and each node (usually three times per node so you can calculate averages) in milliseconds. This allows you to identify not only what parts of the Internet are slow, but also where IP packets are timing out (see the previous section on ping timeouts) so that you can detect where network problems are located.

Traceroute Services on the Web

Unfortunately, there is no decent traceroute program currently available for the MacOS. However, there are a number of Web sites around the world that provide a Web form interface to traceroute programs running on other platforms, so as long as you have a connection to the Internet, you can use traceroute successfully from your Mac.

Because using traceroute services on the Web means that the route being reported is between the traceroute site and the target machine, rather than between your Web browser and the target machine, it's important (and informative!) to perform multiple traceroutes from different points around the world to make sure that reported problems are not isolated to a particular service. Table A.1 shows a few sites I use regularly.

Table A.1 *Finding Traceroute Services on the Web*

Traceroute Web Site	Location
http://www.net.cmu.edu/bin/traceroute	Pittsburgh, PA, USA
http://www.brownell.edu/cgi-bin/traceroute.bt	Omaha, NE, USA
http://hookomo.aloha.net/hol/docs/trace.html	Hawaii, USA
http://www.lublin.pl/cgi-bin/trace/traceroute	Poland
http://hplyot.obspm.fr/cgi-bin/nph-traceroute	France

Using Traceroute

For this example, I use the traceroute program provided by Carnegie Mellon University (http://www.net.cmu.edu/bin/traceroute) for illustrations, but the displays are almost exactly the same for any of the services listed in Table A.1.

After connecting to the Internet, go to the traceroute URL and fill in either the domain name or IP address of the host you want to run a trace to and press Return, as shown in Figure A.3.

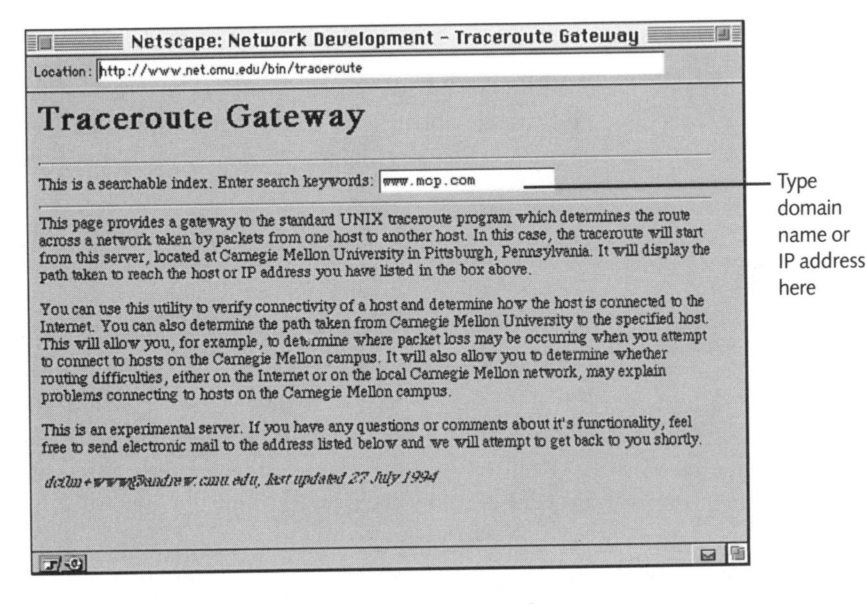

Figure A.3 *The CMU Traceroute gateway form.*

The results should look similar to Figure A.4.

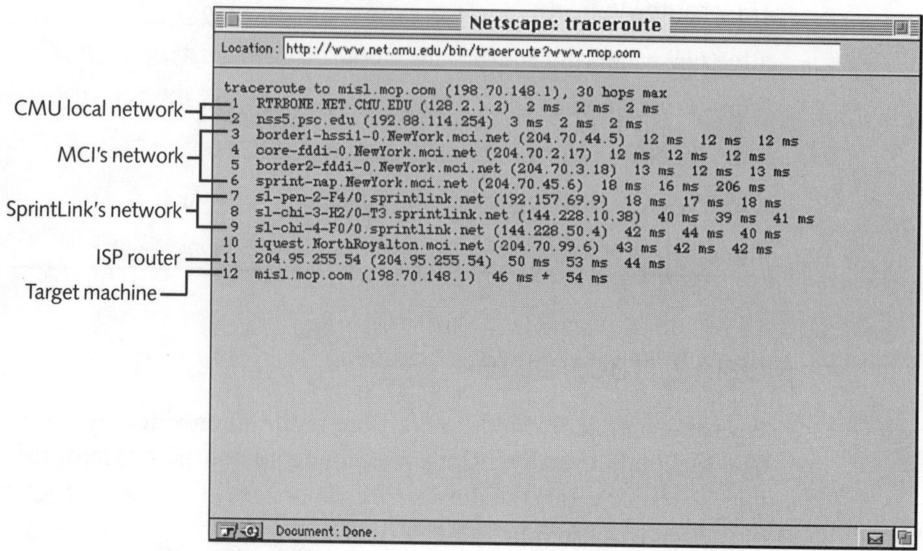

Figure A.4 *Traceroute results from CMU to* www.mcp.com.

Let's examine this report line by line:

```
traceroute to misl.mcp.com (198.70.148.1), 30 hops max
```

This line indicates the name and IP address of the target machine and the maximum number of Internet nodes (hops) the program reports before timing out. Thirty hops is a standard number.

```
1  RTRBONE.NET.CMU.EDU (128.2.1.2)  2 ms  2 ms  2 ms
2  nss5.psc.edu (192.88.114.254)  3 ms  2 ms  2 ms
```

These lines report nodes within CMU's internal local network. The times for each line indicate the total round trip time IP packets took to travel between the traceroute machine and the indicated IP address (up to three packets per node). You can tell when two nodes share a high-speed connection because the times reported are very close to each other, typically just a few milliseconds between lines.

```
3 border1-hssi1-0.NewYork.mci.net (204.70.44.5) 12 ms
  12 ms 12 ms
4 core-fddi-0.NewYork.mci.net (204.70.2.17)  12 ms
  12 ms 12 ms
5 border2-fddi-0.NewYork.mci.net (204.70.3.18) 13 ms
  12 ms 13 ms
6 sprint-nap.NewYork.mci.net (204.70.45.6) 18 ms
  16 ms 206 ms
```

These lines tell you two things:

- First, that CMU uses MCI to provide its Internet connectivity (notice that all the domain names end in mci.net).
- Second, that the slowest portion of the route traced before is the connection between the nodes at line 2 and 3—notice how the round trip times jump by almost 10 milliseconds at that point.

```
7 sl-pen-2-F4/0.sprintlink.net (192.157.69.9) 18 ms
  17 ms 18 ms
8 sl-chi-3-H2/0-T3.sprintlink.net (144.228.10.38)
  40 ms 39 ms 41 ms
9 sl-chi-4-F0/0.sprintlink.net (144.228.50.4) 42 ms
  44 ms 40 ms
```

These lines show that the packets then traveled through Sprint's backbone network, and that the connection between the seventh and eighth nodes is either very slow (unlikely) or too busy to route packets efficiently.

The round trip times almost double at this point, and are indicative of trouble in Sprint's system—not serious trouble, but certainly an overburdened connection. This type of result can help you make informed decisions about choosing an ISP for your site. If you notice that your ISP's network access provider (such as SprintLink or MCI) is regularly being overwhelmed with traffic, you may be better off with a different provider whose network access is more reliable.

```
10 iquest.NorthRoyalton.mci.net (204.70.99.6) 43 ms
  42 ms 42 ms
11 204.95.255.54 (204.95.255.54)  50 ms  53 ms  44 ms
12 misl.mcp.com (198.70.148.1)  46 ms *  54 ms
```

These last three lines show that our target machine has a fairly efficient connection to the Internet (the round trip times don't change much, if at all), which is of course what you want to see if you are tracing the route to your Web server. A big jump in round trip times anywhere in the last two or three lines before the end of the traceroute is a warning flag that the ISP has either an overburdened or slow connection to the Internet.

Note that line 11 has no domain name listed—this is typical for ISP routers, which don't need a domain name because they don't run server software.

The last line also has an asterisk—this indicates that a packet timed out, in exactly the same way as described for the ping results you examined previously. If a node is completely unresponsive, the appropriate line contains three asterisks in a row, like so:

```
12 * * *
```

If you see this result, it means that the node involved is disconnected from the Internet or unable to answer traceroute requests (see the next section on limitations of traceroute).

If you do detect problems in your network connection, your first call should be to your ISP to tell it what you've seen and ask its advice for coping with the problem. Normally, it will either correct malfunctions on its network or contact its access provider to determine the cause of the outage or slowdown.

NOTE

You can find more information about traceroute and how to utilize its reports fully at `http://www.cis.ohio-state.edu/htbin/rfc/rfc1739.html`, which discusses traceroute along with other Internet tools.

Limitations of Traceroute

The primary limitation of traceroute is that Macintoshes normally do not respond to traceroute requests, meaning that they usually show up in the traceroute results as a series of asterisks. If, as is typical, you are performing traceroutes to your Web server, just be aware that the last entries on the traceroute results are always blank, and use MacTCP Ping to verify that your server is available.

Traceroute can be a useful tool for comparing the performance of different servers and getting a quick look at the "guts" of the Internet, but its primary value to you is in identifying network problems as they occur so that you can act to either have your ISP correct them or to move your server to another location.

APPENDIX B

Glossary

A

Alias A Macintosh document that holds the location of another document or application within it. Aliases can often be treated as though they were the original file itself, but may become invalid if copied.

Apple Events The data structures used by the MacOS to enable inter-application communications. Applications may send and receive Apple Events to enable information sharing. Apple Events are used by Web servers to enable CGIs to communicate with Web servers.

AppleScript Apple's free (with System 7.5) scripting system for the Macintosh. Offers a relatively convenient way to use Apple Events to automate tasks and actions on a Mac. Currently being supplanted as a CGI development environment by Frontier.

AppleTalk Apple's Mac-only networking protocol. AppleTalk is the protocol that common Mac network services like File Sharing depend upon.

Applet The term for an application written with the Java programming language.

Asynchronous CGIs CGIs that can accept a CGI request and enable the Web server to continue processing other requests until the CGI is ready to return an HTTP response.

Authentication The process of requesting, receiving, and validating a username and password before serving protected information to a Web client.

B

Backbone Very high-speed networks maintained by NAPs that form the network "core" of the Internet and over which most Internet and Web traffic is routed. When a backbone network has problems, large portions of the Internet may be affected.

Bandwidth The amount of data in bits that can pass across a given point in one second. Usually quoted to describe Internet connection speeds in terms of kilobits per second (1 Kbps = 1,024 bits per second).

Binhex The process of converting a binary file such as an application or image into a text file, which can be transferred via email or FTP to another computer and "de-binhexed" into its original form. Binhexing is often used to combine the resource and data forks of Mac files into a form suitable for transferring across the Internet.

Browser Software used on the Internet to send requests to your Web server and display or interpret the server's response.

C

Caching The computer term for holding local, temporary copies of information either in RAM or as disk files that can be used more rapidly or efficiently than original copies.

Caching Proxy Servers Proxy servers that store copies of HTTP responses locally, so that new requests for the same information can be answered by returning the copy rather than retrieving the information from the original Web server.

CGI (Common Gateway Interface) Common term for applications that use the CGI protocol to process HTTP requests when called upon to do so by the Web server.

CGI Protocol A protocol that defines how Web servers can call upon other applications to process HTTP requests.

Client The person or program that sends an HTTP request to your Web server.

Client-Side Imagemaps HTML tags that enable imagemap definitions to be stored in Web pages, thereby giving Web browsers the capability to use imagemaps without having to communicate with the Web server.

Colocation The practice of physically placing your Web server at a remote site, typically with the purpose of obtaining a high bandwidth Internet connection at a discounted cost.

Cookies A Netscape Navigator feature that enables Web servers to force browsers to store information sent to the client by your server or CGI and to return that information whenever certain URLs are requested from the same server. Also implemented by the Microsoft Internet Explorer Web browser.

Copland The Apple code name for System 8.0. Copland and its successor, Gershwin, will represent a dramatic change in the way Macintoshes work and behave.

CSU/DSU (Channel Service Unit/Data Service Unit) An interface between the telephone line and your local network that acts as a bridge between your LAN and the telephone company.

D

Datagrams A more technical (and proper) term for IP packets.

Dialup Connection Internet connections implemented via 28.8Kbps or slower modems. Usually used for temporary connections without fixed IP addresses. Most clients of public Web servers are accessing the Internet via dialup connections.

DNS (Domain Name System) The protocol that defines the methods of translating domain and hostnames (such as www.mydomain.com) into the numeric IP addresses that the IP protocol needs to route packets correctly across the Internet.

Domain Name The alphanumeric name, such as www.mydomain.com, that identifies either an Internet domain or a specific machine within a domain. Also see *IP Address.*

E-F

Encryption Any of many methods to convert meaningful information, such as a credit card number, into characters that are meaningless to anyone but the intended recipient, who can then decrypt the data into its original form.

Firewall A type of router that watches the IP messages being passed through it and controls which messages are allowed through.

Frame-Relay An Internet connection that gives you a private line between your site and the telephone company, but enables multiple sites to share a line from the telephone company to an ISP. Frame-relay is normally less expensive than the alternative leased-line service, but is not often used for connections with more than 56Kbps of bandwidth. Also see *Leased Line.*

Frontier An alternative scripting system to AppleScript, Frontier is a PowerPC native development environment that can be used to create custom CGIs as well as customizing the Mac interface and automating tasks.

FTP (File Transfer Protocol) The Internet protocol most often used for transferring files across the Internet.

G-H

GIF (Graphic Interchange Format) File format for images, used to compress image information for transfer over a network or storage on a disk. The most common graphic file format for Web pages.

Guestbook A Web server function (often implemented by CGIs) that enables clients to leave messages or comments at a site via HTML forms.

Hit A single HTTP transaction. The event occurring when a client requests a URL from a Web server.

HTML (HyperText Markup Language) The combination of markup tags and definitions for those tags that enables Web pages to be formatted and displayed for clients properly. HTML is a subset of the more general markup language, SGML.

HTTP (HyperText Transfer Protocol) The defining protocol of the World Wide Web. Defines the standards and practices for communication between a Web client and a Web server. Also see *Request, Response,* and *Transaction.*

I

Imagemaps Graphics that enable clients to click portions of an image to go to different URLs on or off your own site. They are often used in navigation bars, home pages, or wherever a graphic interface (as opposed to text-based anchors) is desirable. Also see *Client-Side Imagemaps.*

Inline Image An image that appears within an HTML document by referencing the image's URL in the original HTML.

Interlaced A method of saving GIF images so that a rough image of the complete graphic is displayed and filled in gradually, rather than simply being drawn line by line from top to bottom. Interlaced images enable clients to preview images before they are completely downloaded.

Intermediary CGIs A CGI that translates messages from the Web server into Apple Events understandable by another application.

Internet The complete and dynamic collection of interconnected TCP/IP networks that agree to pass TCP/IP traffic amongst themselves. Also used to encompass online culture and the people who use Internet services.

Intranets A growing proportion of Web sites are being placed on TCP/IP networks that have either no or very limited access to the general Internet. These networks, often confined to a single company or institution, act as mini-Internets that use the same technology as the global Internet, yet are invisible to people outside their private area.

IP (Internet Protocol) Defines the format that data packets use for carrying information and the methods of routing packets from their source node to their destination node across the Internet. Also see *Datagrams.*

IP Address The unique numeric identifier of a node on the Internet (or any other TCP/IP network), such as 192.0.1.2.

ISDN (Integrated Services Digital Network) A protocol for sending digital information over normal telephone lines. ISDN connections are commonly set at a maximum of 128Kbps of bandwidth, and can be used for standard voice communications as well as data transfers simultaneously.

ISP (Internet Service Provider) An organization with a high-speed Internet connection that sells access to its connection to dialup users.

J-L

Java A programming language developed by Sun Microsystems that offers the capability to write small, secure, cross-platform applications that can be integrated into Web pages.

JPEG Common graphic file format that is more efficient than GIF at compressing images but loses some detail when uncompressed.

LAN (Local Area Network) Consists of a group of nodes that can send data to each other without passing that data through another node. Your LAN consists of every computer or device you can reach solely by following the cabling or wire used by your network. The Internet consists of many LANs linked by routers into one gigantic network that can move information from any given node to any other given node.

Leased Line Internet connections that reserve (lease) switches in the telephone company's offices to route calls between two specific points, typically your LAN and your ISP's LAN. Leased lines are used for high-speed Internet connections (56Kbps or greater) and are the most expensive type of connection that Web sites normally use.

Link Checker Software that verifies that URLs referenced on your Web pages will return valid responses when requested.

M-O

MacTCP The pre-Open Transport Control panel that enables TCP/IP network communications on the Macintosh.

Mailbots Systems that automatically reply to requests for information from clients.

MIME (Multipurpose Internet Mail Extension) Types Codes used to identify the type of information attached to an email message or HTTP transaction. Client software uses MIME types to determine how to display or process HTTP responses.

Multithreaded Processing When multiple independent scripts or instances of a single script can run simultaneously; supported by Frontier.

NAP (Network Access Provider) A provider of the high-speed Internet backbone networks that carry most traffic over the Web. Most ISPs buy Internet connections from NAPs.

Network A wire or set of wires over which data is transferred.

NNTP (Network News Transfer Protocol) The Internet protocol used for transferring Usenet newsgroup information across the Internet.

Node A computer or other data processor connected to a network. On the Internet, each node is uniquely defined by an IP address.

OpenDoc An Apple technology developed to write applications and system software as a collection of components or "parts" that can be combined ad hoc to create new combinations of functionality. For example, the spell checker of your word processor could, as an OpenDoc part, be added to a spreadsheet application or email program with its full functionality intact.

Open Transport A new PowerPC-native rewrite of the Macintosh networking software, expected to increase efficiency and reliability for both AppleTalk and TCP/IP networks.

P

Packets The smallest amount of information that can be carried as an individual entity across a network. It is useful to think of packets as envelopes, with an address on the outside and some kind of data inside.

Packet Sniffers A computer that is listening or watching messages that are not addressed specifically to that machine.

Path Either a description of the position of a file on a disk, such as HardDisk:System Folder:Extensions:QuickTime, or the portion of a URL immediately following the hostname. For example, /home.html is the path portion of the URL http://www.mydomain.com/home.html.

Ping A single IP packet sent from one Internet node to another and acknowledged by the target machine. Used to determine the time for packets to travel between two nodes and to detect when an Internet node is crashed or otherwise disconnected from the Internet.

Plug-In A recent feature of the WebSTAR Web server application that enables developers to add new functions directly to the WebSTAR server, eliminating the need for separate CGI applications to add functionality.

Port Part of the URL that refers to a particular Internet service on the host you are attempting to connect to. Ports are indicated in URLs by appending the number to a colon after the hostname. A site can run multiple Internet servers on one machine by assigning the server software different ports.

PPP (Point-to-Point Protocol) Standard protocol used to implement Internet protocols over dialup connections.

Protocols Definitions of methods and assumptions for communication across a network. Also see *HTTP, FTP,* and *NNTP.*

Proxy Server A "gateway" Web server that acts as a conduit for URL requests from the clients it serves. A client using a proxy server sends all URL requests to the proxy, which then sends the request to your server, retrieves the response, and forwards a copy back to the original client. Also see *Caching Proxy Servers.*

R

Realm A character string that defines a protected set of files, for example, any file or folder whose name includes the realm string requires a username and password from a client for that file or the folder's contents to be served by a Web server.

Reciprocal Linking Describes arrangements where you add a link to your pages that sends clients to another site, and that site then agrees to list your URL in its pages as well.

Request The message sent from a Web client to a Web server, consisting of the path portion of a URL plus any data or other arguments, such as information from an HTML form.

Response The information a Web server sends to a client in response to an HTTP request. Consists of informational headers and data, if appropriate. HTTP responses may contain any sort of data the server wants to make available, such as HTML pages, images, or applications, but can only contain one type of data in each response.

RFC (Request For Comments) A constantly evolving series of Internet protocols and definitions that refers to quasi-official statements of how standards on the Internet are to be implemented.

Robot An application or script designed to pose as a client and perform HTTP transactions without user intervention. Commonly used in reference to the programs that collect Web pages for indexing by Web cataloging services.

Router A computer or dedicated hardware device responsible for managing the flow of IP packets among networks.

Routing The process of transferring IP packets across and between local networks as the packets travel between their source and destination nodes.

S

Server An application that waits for clients to request information and is responsible for returning responses to the clients, sometimes with the assistance of other applications such as CGIs.

Sessions A common technique to group a client's actions together to trace that individual's progress through your site and to discover what links visitors are most likely to choose after viewing your home page for the first time. Also called *clickstreams*, and are often used to construct sites that serve different pages to different clients depending on their identity or history.

Shells Sample CGIs that you can modify for your own purposes.

SSL (Secure Sockets Layer) A protocol developed by Netscape and others that encrypts the data being sent between a client and a server using a TCP/IP connection. Because it is actually encrypting all the data in each packet, it can theoretically be used to provide secure communications for any protocol that uses TCP/IP communications, from HTTP to email to FTP.

Suffix Mapping The process of examining the suffix of a file to determine what type of file it is according to a reference table, and then assigning it the appropriate MIME type.

Synchronous CGIs CGI processing in which the server sends an event to the CGI and waits, suspending all other activities, until the CGI responds or the Apple Event times out. Synchronous processing is very rarely used any more, because it completely locks up your server for the duration of the CGI's activities.

T

Tag An element of HTML enclosed between angle brackets used to control the layout and display of HTML documents. For example, the HTML tag <BR> indicates that a line break should be inserted into the displayed document.

TCP (Transmission Control Protocol) The second most ubiquitous protocol on the Internet after IP. TCP is responsible for three aspects of Internet communications: guaranteeing that data sent arrives at its destination correctly, combining the data from IP packets together in their original order as sent, and maintaining multiple channels of communication that can operate simultaneously.

Threading The capability of an application to perform multiple tasks simultaneously; used by Web servers and CGIs to efficiently process many requests at once.

Tick A ubiquitous Macintosh timing mechanism, equivalent to 1/60 of one second.

Tokens Character strings inserted into URLs to control the content of pages delivered to clients and to record a visitor's actions during a single session on your Web site. They change the URLs of your document's links to include a code that is specific to one client.

Traceroute A program for tracking the progress of IP packets as they travel across the Internet.

Traffic General term for data being transferred over a network.

Transaction The complete cycle of HTTP request and response actions.

U-W

UDP (Universal Datagram Protocol) IP packet transmissions without the protection (or overhead) of TCP error correction. Often used for real-time communications (such as audio) that can tolerate small bits of missing data.

URL (Uniform Resource Locater) Also known as a URI, Uniform Resource Identifier, a magical incantation that identifies a unique resource on the Internet. Includes the protocol (HTTP, FTP, and so on), server identity (hostname), TCP port, path, and data arguments.

Virtual Domains The capability to make a single Web server application respond differently to different hostnames, producing the illusion that multiple machines are running separate Web server applications.

Virtual Pages HTML pages constructed by a procedure or CGI application at the time the client requests the page's URL, as opposed to simply sending preconstructed pages from a disk to a client.

World Wide Web The protocols, servers, clients, and networks that implement HTTP transactions on the Internet (also Web or WWW).

INDEX

Symbols

A

G

H

I-K

T

U-V

W-Z

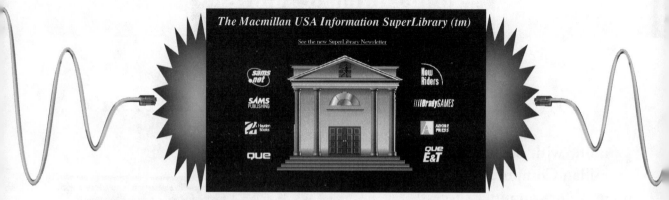

REGISTRATION CARD

Web Server Construction Kit for the Macintosh

Name ______________________________ Title ______________

Company ______________________________ Type of business ______________

Address ______________________________

City/State/ZIP ______________________________

Have you used these types of books before? ☐ yes ☐ no

If yes, which ones? ______________________________

____

How many computer books do you purchase each year? ☐ 1–5 ☐ 6 or more

How did you learn about this book? ______________________________

- ☐ recommended by a friend
- ☐ recommended by store personnel
- ☐ saw in catalog
- ☐ received ad in mail
- ☐ read book review
- ☐ saw on bookshelf

Where did you purchase this book? ______________________________

Which applications do you currently use? ______________________________

Which computer magazines do you subscribe to? ______________________________

What trade shows do you attend? ______________________________

Please number the top three factors which most influenced your decision for this book purchase.

- ☐ cover
- ☐ approach to content
- ☐ logo
- ☐ layout/design
- ☐ price
- ☐ author's reputation
- ☐ publisher's reputation
- ☐ other ______________

Would you like to be placed on our preferred mailing list? ☐ yes ☐ no e-mail address ______________

☐ **I would like to see my name in print!** You may use my name and quote me in future Hayden products and promotions. My daytime phone number is: ______________________________

Comments ______________________________

____

____

Hayden Books Attn: Product Marketing ◆ 201 West 103rd Street ◆ Indianapolis, Indiana 46290 USA

Fax to **317-581-3576** Visit out Web Page **http://WWW.MCP.com/hayden/**

Fold Here

NO POSTAGE
NECESSARY
IF MAILED
IN THE
UNITED STATES

POSTAGE WILL BE PAID BY THE ADDRESSEE

HAYDEN BOOKS
Attn: Product Marketing
201 W 103RD ST
INDIANAPOLIS IN 46290-9058

What's on the CD

The CD is organized by topic so that you can find resources easily as you read the appropriate portions of the book.

To begin navigating the contents of the CD, open the "home.html" file with your Web browser and simply follow the links from that page to the chapter-specific pages. All the HTML links work regardless of whether the **HTML** folder is located on the CD or on another disk. You also can just go to the appropriate folder, depending on what you are looking for. The full contents of the top level of the CD are summarized here:

- **Servers**—This folder contains copies of all the software and installers you need to try out the different Web server applications and demos mentioned in the book (includes InterServer Publisher, NetPresenz, httpd4Mac, Web Server 4D, NetWings, and WebSTAR). If you want to start installing servers immediately, simply copy this folder to your hard drive and read through Chapter 5 for installation instructions.

- **Software**—This folder contains all the freeware, shareware, and demo applications, scripts, and examples provided on the CD. This includes HTML utilities, programming shells, CGIs, graphics-manipulation programs, and more.

- **HTML**—This folder contains copies of all the HTML pages on the CD gathered together in one place. This folder is provided so that you can copy all the individual chapters' HTML files to your hard disk at once for editing or updating without having to make room for all the software that appears in the individual chapter folders.

When trying out the software provided on the CD, copy an application's folder to your hard drive first—many applications and scripts need to write information to disk when they first launch, and launching from the CD can cause unexpected problems or even crashes for some shareware applications. See the Introduction for information on ReadMe files and on Shareware fees and licenses.